"What I learned from this book: (1) That 'grammar' has meant mastery of all arts and letters (to the Greeks) and power, magic, and enchantment (to the Scots). Wow. (2) That for the artful writer, no decision is too small, including whether to use 'a' or 'the.' Awesome. (3) That there are 'right-branching,' 'left-branching,' and 'middle-branching' sentences. How cool! (4) That Roy Peter Clark, a modern-day Pied Piper of grammar, makes good writing both approachable and doable. Phew!"
— Constance Hale, author of *Sin and Syntax*

"Who, other than a word lover like Roy Peter Clark, would dare link 'glamour' with (ugh) 'grammar'? Here it is—a book of enchantment about words and how words work and what they mean and how to spell them, where even lowly semicolons get appreciated as 'swinging gates' in a sentence. Who'd a thunk a book on grammar could be fun? And humorous. Check out 'cleave' and 'cleaveage.'" —Sister Helen Prejean, author of *Dead Man Walking*

"Roy Peter Clark, the Jedi Master of writing coaches, has delivered another indispensable classic for every author, young and old. *The Glamour of Grammar* crackles with wit and wisdom and with page after page of rock-solid strategies to guide writers toward prose that sings with vivid clarity. Somehow, Clark makes grammar seem both playful and understandable, even for those who have trouble telling the difference between a dangling participle and a wandering antecedent." — Thomas French, author of *Zoo Story*

"An indispensable book in this Twitter world, where so few words must push your story forward. Roy Peter Clark shows you a fun way to say exactly what you mean." — Bob Dotson, NBC News national correspondent for the *Today* show's "American Story with Bob Dotson"

"If there is indeed a glamour to grammar, I should have known Roy Peter Clark would be the one to spot it. In his latest book, Clark is a trusty guide for anyone wanting to avoid the (many) pitfalls and scale the (hard-won) peaks of perpetrating prose. To his great credit, he generally avoids the somewhat limited and limiting issue of right or wrong, instead focusing on the essential question for every serious writer: how do I make my words stronger, richer, fresher? And his frame of reference is as wide as the horizon in Big Sky country. Anybody who can (knowledgeably) discuss Frank Sinatra's 'That's Life' and Gerard Manley Hopkins's 'The Windhover' on the same page is okay by me." — Ben Yagoda, author of *Memoir: A History* and *The Sound on the Page: Style and Voice in Writing*

"If grammar is medicine, then Roy Clark gives us the spoonful of sugar to help it go down. A wonderful tour through the labyrinth of language." — Anne Hull, Pulitzer Prize–winning reporter, *Washington Post*

"Roy Peter Clark takes the language so seriously, he dares to play with it. What other English professor would seriously write 'A good pun is its own reword'? *The Glamour of Grammar* is required fun, seriously." — Eugene C. Patterson, Pulitzer Prize–winning editor and retired chairman and CEO, *St. Petersburg Times*

# THE GLAMOUR

## *of*

# GRAMMAR

A GUIDE TO THE MAGIC AND MYSTERY
OF PRACTICAL ENGLISH

ROY PETER CLARK

LITTLE, BROWN AND COMPANY
NEW YORK   BOSTON   LONDON

Little, Brown and Company
Hachette Book Group
237 Park Avenue, New York, NY 10017
www.hachettebookgroup.com

First Edition: August 2010

Little, Brown and Company is a division of Hachette Book Group, Inc. The Little,
Brown name and logo are trademarks of Hachette Book Group, Inc.

Excerpt from "The Word Detective" by Evan Morris, copyright © 2006.
Reprinted by permission of Evan Morris.
Excerpt from "Mendel's Laws" from Liquid Paper: New and Selected Poems by
Peter Meinke, copyright © 1991. Reprinted by permission of the University of
Pittsburgh Press.
Excerpt from "Semicolon" by Maurya Simon, copyright © 1991. Reprinted by
permission of Maurya Simon. First appeared in A Brief History of Punctuation,
published by Sutton Hoo Press.
The letter appearing on page 126 is reprinted by permission of Susan Stanton and family.
Excerpt from "Figs" from The Complete Poems of D. H. Lawrence by D. H. Lawrence,
edited by V. de Sola Pinto and F. W. Roberts, copyright © 1964, 1971 by Angelo Ravagali
and C. M. Weekley, Executors of the Estate of Frieda Lawrence Ravagali. Used by
permission of Viking Penguin, a division of Penguin Group (USA), Inc.

Library of Congress Cataloging-in-Publication Data
Clark, Roy Peter.
    The glamour of grammar : a guide to the magic and mystery of practical English / by
Roy Peter Clark.—1st ed.
        p. cm.
    Includes index.
    ISBN 978-0-316-02791-5
    1. English language—Grammar.    I. Title.
    PE1112.C528 2010
    428.2—dc22                                                                    2009051781

10   9   8   7   6   5   4   3   2   1

RRD-IN

Printed in the United States of America

*To Jane Dystel and Tracy Behar,*

*my glamorous sisters of the word*

# Contents

• • •

...

# Embrace grammar as powerful and purposeful.

My first rock 'n' roll record, a heavy 78 rpm vinyl disk, was "Hound Dog" by Elvis Presley. Most of the adults I knew thought that rock was "the devil's music," the pathway to moral degeneracy and juvenile delinquency. Even worse, they thought it would screw up our grammar. When they heard the King growl "You ain't nothin' but a hound dog," the grown-ups would holler: "There ain't no such word as 'ain't.'" Not to mention that double negative: "Well, if you ain't *nothin'*, then you must be *somethin'*."

Back then, our parents and teachers subscribed to the school of grammar we all learned in, well, grammar school. They framed grammar as a strict set of rules we must master in order to use language "correctly." I did not know it then, but this school of grammar had a name. It was called *prescriptive* because it prescribed proper ways to use the English language.

I was an eighth grader at St. Aidan School in 1961, the year *Webster's Third* included the word *ain't*—without disapproval—for the first time. The conservators of language were outraged, denouncing the dictionary as a glorification of ignorance, and its editors as "permissive." But the *Webster's* team was doing nothing more or less than taking note of the way people actually used the language. These lexicographers were members of the *descriptive* school because they described the language used in spoken and written English.

More than a half century later, the grammar wars rage on, with the prescribers and describers professing antagonistic visions of what constitutes grammar, how it is learned, and how it should be taught. It is in this contentious context that I offer for your consideration *The Glamour of Grammar*.

If you are holding this book in your hands, it means that the English language lives inside you. That is a wonderful gift, one that many of you learned from the cradle, one that will grow with you until you whisper "Rosebud" or whatever your final word happens to be. But you have an even greater power at your fingertips. It comes not when your language lives inside you, but when you begin to live inside your language.

To help you live that life, this book invites you to embrace grammar in a special way, not as a set of rules but as a box of tools, strategies that will assist you in making meaning as a reader, writer, or speaker. Living inside the language requires a grammar of purpose, a grammar of effect, a grammar of intent. This type of grammar puts language into action. It doesn't shout at you, "No, no, no," but gives you a little push and says, "Go, go, go." This type of grammar enables us to practice the three behaviors that mark us as literate human beings: it helps us write with power, read with a critical eye, and talk about how meaning is made.

These reflections lead me to the purpose of this book's fabulous title, *The Glamour of Grammar*. At first glance, the phrase must seem oxymoronic, as paradoxical as a sequined pocket protector. Was there ever in the popular imagination a word less glamorous than *grammar*? But what if I were to tell you that at one time in the history of our language, *grammar* and *glamour* were the same word? Need proof? Let's consult the *Oxford English Dictionary*.

The bridge between the words *glamour* and *grammar* is magic. According to the *OED*, *glamour* evolved from *grammar* through an ancient association between learning and enchantment. There was a time when grammar described not just language knowledge but all forms of learning, which in a less scientific age included things like magic, alchemy, astrology, even witchcraft.

Evan Morris, editor and publisher of "The Word Detective," leads us through the maze:

> "Glamour" and "Grammar" are essentially the same word. In classical Greek and Latin, "grammar" (from the Greek "grammatikos," meaning "of letters") covered the whole of arts and letters, i.e., high knowledge in general. In the Middle Ages, "grammar" was generally used to mean "learning," which at the time included, at least in the popular imagination, a knowledge of magic. The narrowing of "grammar" to mean "the rules of language" was a much later development, first focusing on Latin, and only in the 17th century extended to the study of English and other languages.
>
> Meanwhile, "grammar" had percolated into Scottish English (as "gramarye"), where an "l" was substituted for an "r" and the word eventually became "glamour," used to mean specifically knowledge of magic and spells.

Even though the association between *grammar* and *glamour* is surprising, it's not hard to find a trail of connections leading to modern usage. In popular gothic stories detailing the misadventures of witches and vampires, the word *glamor* (without a *u*)—as both a noun and a verb—describes a magic spell that puts someone in a trance or makes a person forget. When we see a glamorous movie star walking down a red carpet, don't we sometimes hear the words *magical, alluring,* and *enchanting?*

The word *grammar* has taken a bit of a nosedive since the days when some tipsy scholar north of Hadrian's Wall mixed up his *r*'s with his *l*'s. Today *grammar* connotes everything unglamorous: absentminded professors; fussy schoolteachers; British grammazons with binding names like Lynne Truss; nagging perfectionists; pedantic correctionists; high-school students asleep at their desks, stalactites of drool hanging from their lips. Long lost from grammar are associations with power, magic, enchantment, and mystical energy.

I've written *The Glamour of Grammar* so that you can feel that energy and put it to use. You will be guided by the broadest definition of *grammar* possible, used here to include pronunciation, spelling, punctuation, syntax, usage, lexicography, etymology, language history, diction, semantics, rhetoric, literature, and poetics. Words and definitions that now seem strange to you will become familiar and practical.

I've organized the grammar tools into these simple parts, extending from the subatomic level of language to the metaphysical:

**Part One. Words:** These tools deal with the smallest units of meaning: sounds, letters, symbols, words that help turn thought into language. You'll discover that no distinction is too small, that parts of speech can cross-dress, and that language is a source of limitless creativity.

**Part Two. Points:** To work together, words need help. They need connecting words, and they need punctuation. All methods of punctuation point the way for the reader, gathering, linking, separating, and emphasizing what truly matters. These marks are more than squiggles on the page. They are the ligaments of meaning and purpose.

**Part Three. Standards:** To make meaning with clarity and consistency, users of language lean on conventions, sets of informal agreements about what constitutes proper and improper usage. Violations of these are often perceived as errors. But to describe these standards as "rules" is to underestimate their value. As "tools" they offer strategic options for the speaker, reader, and writer.

**Part Four. Meaning:** Most human beings are born with the capacity to create an infinite number of sentences, each with the potential to capture meaning in a powerful way. While the number of sentences may be limitless, their forms are limited enough so that we can master them and influence how meaning is made and how it is experienced in the minds of an audience.

**Part Five. Purpose:** The tools of language, it turns out, are morally neutral, which is to say that good people can use them for good effects, and bad people can use them to lie, exploit, even to enslave. Living inside the language enables you to use grammar with a mission, to embrace ways of reading, writing, and speaking that inspire virtues such as justice, empathy, and courage.

With its practical and purposeful approach, *The Glamour of Grammar* tries to make grammar useful and memorable. Every little lesson in this book points to an immediate application. A feature called "Keepsakes" ends each chapter, reviewing the most important points in ways that can be saved, savored, and remembered, and offering a few fun exercises. Why learn grammar if you're not going to use it with intent? Why spell except to symbolize spoken words and avoid distracting the reader? Why punctuate except to point the reader toward pace, emphasis, and meaning? Why learn to identify subjects and verbs unless you can join them to achieve a specific effect?

I hope that this rhetorical grammar will help you grow in confidence and understanding so that you can master the rules, turn them into tools, and use those tools to break the rules with a purpose. On the inside, language will feel like muscle, not magic. I hope you will come to identify with my enthusiasm (a word that once meant "to have God in you"), just as I identify with lovers of the language such as Bryan A. Garner, author and editor of *A Dictionary of Modern American Usage,* who in my opinion is an apostle of a grammar of intent:

> The reality I care about most is that some people will want to use the language well. They want to write effectively; they want to speak effectively. They want their language to be graceful at

times and powerful at times. They want to understand how to use words well, how to manipulate sentences, and how to move about *in the language* without seeming to flail. They want *good grammar,* but they want more: they want *rhetoric* in the traditional sense. That is, they want to use the language deftly so that it's *fit for their purposes.* [my emphasis]

That paragraph makes the perfect distinction between rules and tools. It helps me understand that my interests in the technical aspects of language extend beyond simple correctness. I want to use these tools for effect, to help the reader learn, laugh, cringe, and turn the page.

For the lover of language, lessons come from everywhere, as British novelist and scholar David Lodge describes: "That is why a novelist...must have a very keen ear for other people's words...and why he cannot afford to cut himself off from low, vulgar, debased language; why nothing linguistic is alien to him, from theological treatises to backs of cornflakes packets, from the language of the barrack room to the language of, say, academic conferences." I got that message, even at age eight, when my teacher was Elvis Presley. By age thirteen, I was buried in hagiography and pornography; treatises on politics and stories about vampires; holy cards and baseball cards; scholarly books and comic books; the highest and the lowest our culture had to offer. I was living inside the English language.

PART ONE

· · ·

# Words

Living inside the language requires a love of words: the sound of words in the air, the sight of words on the page or screen, the feelings and images created by words in our hearts and heads. Words can even stimulate our senses; I can almost smell *pungent,* taste *honeycomb,* touch *sandpaper.*

In the practical world of language, many people want to become more literate. They want to read with insight, write with persuasive power, and speak with some authority. For such a person, words fly in all directions—from head to hands, from page to eyes, from mouth to ear, from ear and eye to head—in a brilliant recursive spiral that defines our humanity and, for believers, our share of divinity.

"In the beginning was the Word," says the Bible. "The word is love," sang the Beatles. Groucho Marx told his quiz-show contestants: "Say the secret word [pronounced "woid"] and win a prize." What's the word? Word up! Word to your mother. The word *word* derives from the Latin *verbum,* which gives us *verb, verbal,* and for the windy among us *verbose.*

Some words, *cathedral,* for example, are large and spectacular, while others, *on* or *off,* are small and functional, barely noticeable in a text. But if you love words, no word is insignificant. No part of a word can be changed without some impact, even if it's just a brief recognition of an alternate spelling.

This section begins with that great storehouse of words, the dictionary. We then turn to letters, how they make smooth sailing possible through spelling, and how, over time, they seem to take on lives of their own, almost independent of the words they form.

Synonyms are stored in a thesaurus, a word that means "treasury." A thesaurus is a resource that can teach us new words and, more important, help us recall ones we already know. We explore the roles words play in order to make meaning, roles commonly called *parts of speech.* But, as you'll see, words can jump from role to role, sometimes in the same sentence.

There is no expression of language too small to spark the curiosity of the literate human being. Words can sound the same or almost the same, and be gathered or invented, the result of creative mistakes. Words can be long or short, English or foreign, amazing products of a history of usage that goes back thousands of years.

# 1

...

# Read dictionaries for fun and learning.

To live inside the language, I need the help of my two favorite dictionaries, which I will cite throughout this book: the *Oxford English Dictionary* (or *OED*) and the *American Heritage Dictionary* (or *AHD*). These two lexicons keep the history of our language at my fingertips, with the *OED* showing me where English has been and the *AHD* where it's headed.

It was from the *OED* that I first learned, to my shock and delight, that the words *grammar* and *glamour* were related. It was 1971 when a professor sent us on a language scavenger hunt so we could get our hands on that twelve-volume "dictionary based upon historical principles." This means that along with spellings, definitions, pronunciations, and parts of speech, the *OED*—thanks to the work of thousands of volunteers over seventy years—provides the word hunter with 1,827,306 examples of how and when the words came to be used in the English language, according to Simon Winchester, author of *The Meaning of Everything*.

So what? So let's say the president of the United States uses the word *crusade* to build support for an American war against fanatics in the Middle East. You hear this or read it and have a gut feeling that it is not a wise word for the president to use, but you are not sure why. You decide to write about it, but first things first. As my mentor Don Fry would command: "Look it up in the *OED!*"

Here's what you would find: The earliest known use of the word *crusade* in English appears in a historical chronicle dated 1577 and refers to the holy wars waged by European Christians in the Middle Ages "to recover the Holy Land from the Mohammedans." Thirty years later, the word expands to define "any war instigated and blessed by the Church." By 1786 the word is being used even more broadly to describe any "aggressive movement or enterprise against some public evil." As luck would have it, the historical citation is expressed by a president of the United States, Thomas Jefferson, who encouraged a correspondent to "Preach, my dear Sir, a crusade against ignorance."

Move forward in history to the forty-third president, George W. Bush, who promises a "crusade" against fanatics who attacked the United States on September 11, 2001. Those terrorists happened to be Islamic extremists waging their own *jihad,* or holy war, against American and European forces they call "the crusaders." With this new knowledge, perhaps you will justify the president's use of *crusade* by citing Jefferson's secular example. Or perhaps you will cite the perils, as I did, of unintentionally evoking a dangerous historical precedent marked with a cross, the symbol of the crusaders.

A quarter hour of such language research lays a foundation on which to build an argument.

From *glamour* to *grammar,* from *crusade* to *crusado,* the *OED* can serve you as a time machine of language, not merely to satisfy nostalgic curiosity or a narrow intellectual interest but to set you down in the history of your language, providing valuable context, to assist you in your contemporary pursuit of meaning.

I confess intolerance for dichotomous thinking. When it comes to red-state versus blue-state politics, I'm a little bit purple. When the phonics reading zealots wage war against the "whole language" hordes, I stand on the fifty-yard line and shake my head. In a country versus rock debate, call me rockabilly. My favorite ice cream? Neapolitan. And when antagonists of descriptive and prescriptive grammar stand nose to nose, I grab the *American Heritage Dictionary* and hug it like a blanket.

The *AHD* offers a pragmatic reconciliation between "you must" and "you can," thanks to a feature called the Usage Panel, a group of two hundred (originally one hundred) professional users of language who are consulted to discover their language opinions, which, of course, change over time. In simple terms, the editors of the *AHD* poll the panel to get a sense of its preferences. Writers can then make informed judgments when choosing one word or phrase over another.

In the beginning (1969), *AHD* editor William Morris explained:

> To furnish the guidance which we believe to be an essential responsibility of a good dictionary, we have frequently employed usage-context indicators such as "slang," "nonstandard," or "regional." But going beyond that, we asked a panel of 100 outstanding speakers and writers a wide range of questions about how the language is used today, especially with regard to dubious or controversial locutions. After careful tabulation and analysis of their replies, we have prepared several hundred usage notes to guide readers to effectiveness in speech and writing. As a consequence, this Dictionary can claim to be more precisely descriptive, in terms of current usage levels, than any heretofore published—especially in offering the reader the lexical opinions of a large group of highly sophisticated fellow citizens.

The popular, self-proclaimed "Grammar Girl" Mignon Fogarty points out in *The Grammar Devotional* that the publisher of the *AHD*, James Parton, created his new dictionary because he so loathed what he considered the permissive changes in *Webster's Third*. "Yes," writes Fogarty, "the *American Heritage Dictionary* and its usage panel exist because of passions over perceived intolerable faults in *Webster's Third*." You can detect a bit of that history in editor Morris's skillful juxtaposition of the word "descriptive" and his characterization of the panel members as "highly sophisticated fellow citizens." In other words: Teachers and parents, fear not. The rabble is not controlling our choices and recommendations.

Let's look at one of the battleground words for describers and prescribers: *hopefully*. No one objects to the word when it is used as a standard adverb modifying a verb: "He marched hopefully across the stage to receive his diploma." The intended meaning is "He marched with hope." But *hopefully* is now more often used as something called a *sentence adverb*. An anxious parent might say, "Hopefully, he marched across the stage...," meaning "I hope he marched across the stage." Given that possibility, the listener may experience an unintended ambiguity. We can't tell whether the student or the parent had the hope. So should you ever use *hopefully* as a sentence adverb? Not according to a majority of the Usage Panel: "It might have been expected...that the initial flurry of objections to *hopefully* would have subsided once the usage became well established. Instead, critics appear to have become more adamant in their opposition. In the 1969 Usage Panel survey, 44 percent of the Panel approved the usage, but this dropped to 27 percent in our 1986 survey." On the other hand, 60 percent of that 1986 panel approved the use of *mercifully* as a sentence adverb in: "Mercifully, the game ended before Notre Dame could add another touchdown to the lopsided score." If I am to be guided by the Usage Panel, I find *mercifully* in play, but *hopefully* out.

I still confuse *different from* and *different than*. The Usage Panel comes to the rescue: "*Different from* and *different than* are both common in British and American English.... Since the 18th century, language critics have singled out *different than* as incorrect, though it is well attested in the works of reputable writers. According to the traditional guidelines, *from* is used when the comparison is between two persons or things: *My book is different from yours. Different than* is more acceptably used...where the object of comparison is expressed by a full clause: *The campus is different than it was 20 years ago.*"

Who knew you could vote on grammar and usage? But that is exactly how the Usage Panel reaches a decision, a liberating process that makes transparent the quirky human path to conventional usage.

## KEEPSAKES

• The *Oxford English Dictionary* tells you where the English language has been; the *American Heritage Dictionary* helps you understand where it is headed.

• The *OED* is based on historical principles, which means that the earliest examples of a word's use are included with the definition.

• The *AHD* is a descriptive lexicon with an escape hatch. It includes nonstandard uses of a word but offers advice on appropriate usage through a panel of language experts.

• In addition to the Usage Panel, the *AHD* includes these features: marginal photos and other pictorial images that help you visualize, learn, and remember a word; most of the obscene and profane words omitted by the *OED*, that most proper and Victorian lexicon; the names of noteworthy people and places, giving it a bit of an encyclopedic feel; explanatory blocks that describe interesting word histories; lists of synonyms, with advice on how to distinguish among shades of meaning.

• For the record, my publisher follows *Merriam-Webster's Collegiate Dictionary.*

# 2

# Avoid speed bumps caused by misspellings.

This chapter will help you remember why good spelling matters, how it can mean the difference between *public* and *pubic*. But first let me sit in wonder at another link between language and enchantment. Just as we learned that the word *glamour* was a corrupted form of *grammar,* connected by the use of prescribed language as a magical charm, so now we must confront the ancient associations between the spelling of a word and the casting of a spell.

The word *spell* has many important meanings in the history of our language, most of them related to the idea of story, tale, or news. We know, for example, that the word *gospel* translates from the Old English to "good news" or "good tidings." All the modern meanings of *spell* derive from those traditional associations.

Consider these definitions of *spell* from the *OED:*

> *as a verb:* "To name or set down in order the letters of (a word or syllable); to enunciate or write letter by letter; to denote by certain letters in a particular order"
> *as a noun:* "A set of words, a formula or verse, supposed to possess occult or magical powers; a charm or incantation; a means of accomplishing enchantment or exorcism"

The word appears in both senses, and others, in a number of William Shakespeare's plays.

Language and magic. Where is the connection? Think about it this way: when we form letters to write words, we create something out of nothing, so that the still air or the empty space on a page fills with meaning, as if a wizard created a blizzard from a clear blue sky.

But if spelling has the power to express, misspellings have the power to distract and confound. We know that the spelling of a word is arbitrary, a social agreement based on precedent and convention. British spellers prefer *programme, centre, cheque,* and *humour* to the conventional American spellings. And how do you spell *butterfly?* Well, if you are Spanish, you spell it *mariposa;* if you are French, you watch a *papillon* flutter by. An English professor once asked a class, "How important can spelling be if the family of Shakespeare, the greatest writer in our culture, spelled his name forty-four different ways?" But, as you are about to see, incorrect spelling—a single missing or misplaced letter—can make all the difference in the world, can turn *art* into an *ars.*

When I was just a little writer—skinny, myopic, prepubescent, growing up in a New York suburb—I began to feel the first tremors of emerging manhood, and I felt them most powerfully in the presence of a local teenage girl whose nickname was Angel Face. She even wore a brown leather jacket with that name embroidered across the back.

Truth be told, she did have the face of a 1950s-style teen cherub: bright blue eyes framed by a pixie hairdo; a button nose; a little bow of a mouth painted bright red. Along with the leather jacket, she wore pedal pushers, those ultratight forerunners of capri pants.

Each day Angel Face would strut down the hill past my house, and I would spot her, like a bird-watcher, through the picture window. One day this reverie vanished with the sudden appearance of my mother, who snuck up behind me and pierced the bubble of my fantasy with this crack:

"Huh. There goes old Angle Face."

"You mean Angel Face," I snapped.

"Take another look, buddy boy, that stupid little juvenile delinquent misspelled her name on her jacket."

And so it was. A-n-g-e-l Face was really A-n-g-l-e Face, and I could never look at her the same way again, even when she wore her *red* pedal pushers or the shortest of her shorts.

But you might be thinking, *If old Angle Face were a teen today, she'd have the advantage of a spell-checker on her computer.* But since *angle* and *angel* are both properly spelled words, a spell-checker would not (and as I typed this did not) highlight a problem. My checker alerted me of a mistake with *ars,* the antique version of *arse,* or *ass,* and a Chaucerian pun making fun of pretentious "art." Instead of *ars,* my spell-checking minions suggest that I use *airs, arts, arks, arcs,* or *arms.*

Why master spelling, except to make meaning as a reader and writer? The magic will not work if you write *allusion* when you mean *illusion,* except to turn you, like Bottom in *A Midsummer Night's Dream,* into a fool wearing donkey ears, an ass and an ars. To avoid that fate, I suggest these specific strategies:

- Rent the movie *Spellbound,* or watch a televised national spelling bee. You'll be inspired by all those nerdy kids who have worked so hard to be so smart. In the third grade I won a school spelling bee by getting *mirror* correct but lost the following year by stumbling on *mention.* I could spell *mirror* in third grade because I had read and reread the story of Snow White ("Mirror, mirror, on the wall…").
- Commit yourself to more reading and to noticing difficult words you bump into along the way.
- Memorize a list of the most commonly misspelled words in public life. Here's a starter kit: *accommodate, camaraderie, definitely, hemorrhage, inoculate, pastime, seize, siege, threshold.* (You'll find a fuller list in Appendix A.)
- And, finally, don't rely on spell-checkers. Use a dictionary. You don't need to be a nerd to learn how to spell a word. It's not magic. Look it up.

The impulse to spell correctly and consistently is a relatively modern development, writes author and dictionary editor Ammon Shea in the *New York Times:*

> For most of the history of the language, English speakers took a lackadaisical approach to spelling; the notion that a word should always be spelled the same way is a much more recent invention than the language itself.... And although it is unclear at exactly what point our spelling became set,...people have complained that the rules of spelling, such as they are, just don't make sense.

It is important to note that even when spelling becomes more stable in a language, pronunciation can continue to change, which may be why so many of our *-ough* words are pronounced so differently, as in *though, through,* and *tough,* a thorny problem for those trying to learn English as a second language.

## KEEPSAKES

• Each writer has some words that never fail to befuddle. One simple solution is to collect words that you misspell in a notebook or a file. You will find that the act of making the list will help you remember and master words that are tough for you to spell. Check out the list of difficult spelling words in Appendix A. Add words that are on your personal list but not included in this book.

• Use your computer's spell-checker, of course, but don't depend on it. It may not capture homophones, words that sound alike but are spelled differently, such as *currant* and *current*. And it may question unusual or new words not in its database.

• Remember the two purposes of accurate spelling: (1) to convey the word you intend; (2) to avoid distracting the reader when you make a spelling mistake.

# 3

...

## Adopt a favorite letter of the alphabet.

My great friend Pegie Stark Adam is a visionary. She sees things that I can't see. A designer and an artist, she sees shapes, perspectives, and especially colors in creative ways. The way Pegie sees colors is something like the way I see words, even letters. To me, individual letters seem to have a secret meaning, as if they could be detached from the words they help form.

The letter *z* works that way for me. Of course it comes last, the omega point in the alphabet—so we associate it with finality. At the beginning of words, *z* can be playful: *zany, zoo, Zorro, zippy, zilch*. But when it's in the middle, I see trouble: *Nazi, lazy, crazy, Uzi*.

That *U* in *Uzi* reminds me of how unusual and distinctive that rarest of vowels looks on the page, especially when there are more than one of them, as in *Ursula* or *usury* or *usufruct* or *undulate* or *ululate*, or my new favorite twenty-one-letter word *humuhumunukunukuapua'a*, the Hawaiian fish that "go swimming by" in the old song "My Little Grass Shack" (which should be sung to the tune of a *ukulele*, a Hawaiian word that means "jumping flea," a metaphor for the musician's finger action on the strings. Don't forget to wear your muumuu). *U* in the title *Ulysses* has the look of a sacred vessel, a Grecian urn, and James Joyce's novel begins with the phrase "Stately, plump Buck Mulligan..." Lots of U-ness there.

The letter *o* suggests an alluring or erotic roundness, orifices waiting to be filled, hence the infamous *Story of O,* but two of them together (OO) look like fake boobs on an exotic dancer, or two fat men fighting for a seat on the bus: *zoot, moot, booze, tattoo, kangaroo.*

Then there is the letter *v,* the favorite of playwright and performance artist Eve Ensler, author of *The Vagina Monologues* and founder of V-Day, a celebration of five thousand performances of her play in 130 countries. When asked by the *New York Times* what the *V* in V-Day stood for, Ensler responded: "For vagina and victory-over-violence and Valentine's Day. A lot of beautiful words begin with V—voluptuous, vulva, volcanic, vulnerability." She easily could have added: *velvet, venery, Venus, vestal virgin,* and *Vesuvius.* (But not *vermin, venom, vicious,* or *Viagra.*)

Which brings us to *x.* We all must bear our crosses, but this letter, which seems carefree as the figurehead of *xylophone* and *X-ray,* casts a dark mark on the meaning of most words it infects: *hex, sex, XXX, X-rated, X-Men, toxin, Ex-Lax, excess,* "All my exes live in Texas," *excrement, extreme, Generation X,* "X marks the spot," X = the unknown.

Isn't it interesting that even the illiterate are able to put their X on a legal document? Couldn't they as easily put an O or a T? Why does X bear the burden of illiteracy? At a recent conference on the tabloid newspaper, one European editor noted that the letter *x* is the tabloid headline writer's best friend: "No Exit for Sex Fiend."

We know that the addition or subtraction of a single letter can dramatically alter meaning and mood. A *moth* can become a *month; a friend* can become a *fiend.* Learn to love the letter. The sound it symbolizes. The look on the page. The words it helps form.

## KEEPSAKES

For those living inside the language, each sound, each letter offers potential delight and meaning.

• Make believe you have a favorite letter. Write the letter on a piece of paper and then randomly list words that begin with that letter. Read the words aloud. Consult the *AHD,* and write down other interesting words that begin with your letter. Now write a hundred-word profile of your favorite letter.

• Imagine you and your spouse will soon welcome a new child, and you have to select a name. Rather than starting with words, imagine your child will go through life with the most interesting initials, say RPC. From those initials derive some possible names.

• The letters *l* and *r* are called *liquid consonants* because they roll off the tongue. You can hear and feel the flow in a phrase like "roll out the barrel," as opposed to the friction and vibration caused by "shuck and jive." Browse through the dictionary under the letters *l* and *r* and make a list of the most "liquid" words you can find.

# 4

...

## Honor the smallest distinctions—even between *a* and *the*.

When you live inside the English language, you will find yourself tinkering with *a* and *the*. The switch from one to the other can bring dramatic changes in meaning, tone, and reader response. What if the title of the classic book and movie had been *Gone with a Wind*?

When Neil Armstrong became the first person to set foot on the moon, his words, now part of history, came across as garbled and confusing. It sounded like he said "That's one small step for man, one giant leap for mankind." For years I scratched my head, uncertain of the difference between "man" and "mankind" until someone suggested that an "a" was missing: "That's one small step for *a* man, one giant leap for mankind." That single letter *a* can mean the world—and in this case the moon.

I remember the day, not long ago, I was preparing to meet with the mayor of my hometown, St. Petersburg, Florida, with the goal of persuading His Honor to proclaim to the world that we lived in "A City of Writers." But the first time I wrote that phrase, it came out "The City of Writers." A friend asked, "Do we want to be 'the city' or 'a city'?" I couldn't decide. I was definitely indefinite. But I knew that the distinction mattered.

Thanks to a favorite book, *Authors at Work,* I can hold in my hands a photo of the original manuscript of "To a Skylark" by nineteenth-century poet Percy Bysshe Shelley. Very clearly, I see where the poet has revised his title. The handwritten original reads "To the Sky-Lark." The same hand has crossed out the "the" and replaced it with "a." What, I wondered, did the poet have in mind?

In the specialized language about language, the words *the* and *a* (and *an*) are called *articles*. And, in a distinction that is not as useful as it sounds, *a* is called an *indefinite* article, while *the* is termed *definite*. *The* denotes definite, specific nouns; *a* and *an* do not.

There are cases where the *the* seems to define the word it modifies, as in publications such as *The New York Times,* or when overzealous Buckeye football fans in Columbus insist that they attend *THE* (pronounced "Thee") Ohio State University, as if it were the only one.

Check out this sentence by Robert Atwan taken from his foreword to *The Best American Essays 2007:*

> But the hardy type of essay that evolved from Montaigne's innovative prose has long been identified as *the* essay, and it has received many labels over the centuries: the informal essay, the periodical essay, the moral essay, the anecdotal essay, the familiar essay, the personal essay, the true essay, and even...the "right" essay.

If you are a counter, you will find eleven definite articles in this single sentence, but one carries in the author's mind more definite weight than the others, so he casts it in italics: *the* essay.

Historian Michael Kazin understood the importance of *the* in his reflection on the status of his famous father, author Alfred Kazin:

> He routinely wrote long pieces for *The New York Times Book Review,* and, on occasion, the identifying caption would read,

"the critic and teacher Alfred Kazin." The authority of that definite article!…Anyone who didn't [know him] was clearly a
newcomer to serious literary conversation and needed a quick, if
subtle, lesson about who deserved a "the" and who did not.
(from *The Chronicle of Higher Education,* December 21, 2007)

One way to feel the difference between the words *a* and *the* is
to take familiar titles and change one article to the other:

> *The Day to Remember*
> *A Godfather*
> A Holy Bible
> *A Great Gatsby*
> *The House Is Not the Home*
> *Land of the Thousand Dances*
> *A Power and a Glory*
> *The Little Night Music*
> *The Man for All Seasons*
> "A Star-Spangled Banner"
> *The Separate Peace*
> *A Catcher in a Rye*
> *A Wizard of Oz*

Not long ago, I encountered this sentence in an e-mail message:
"*The* Internet is *an* internet."

I'd like to object for a moment, on behalf of the word *a,* to
the designation *indefinite.* For while *a* may not give us the defining example, it offers an effect writers crave: the power of particularity ("one small step for *a* man" or "a star rose in the East").
This is why Shelley crosses out "the" and replaces it with "a":
because he does not want you to see or hear the "idea" of the bird
as a surrogate for the poet before experiencing the bird in all its
physical splendor:

> Higher still and higher
>   From the earth thou springest,

Like a cloud of fire;
   The blue deep thou wingest,
And singing still does soar and soaring ever singest.

At the end of the day, I chose "A City of Writers" rather than "The City of Writers" so as not to turn my palm-treed metropolis into an ideal. St. Pete is a real place, not an abstraction, and might become "a" model for others. There is a humility in *a*, not present in *the*, often used to exaggerate the truth for marketing purposes, as in "The one and only!"

Columnist George Will wrote this about the war in Iraq: "Nancy Pelosi says the surge has not 'produced the desired effect.' 'The'? The surge has produced many desired effects, including a pacification that is a prerequisite for the effect—political reconciliation—to which Pelosi refers."

After I wrote a draft of this chapter, I found an opportunity to play with the meaning of *the* to full effect. The occasion was a meeting with country-western legend Roy Clark before a concert. For most of my life, I had to deal with jokes about whether I played the guitar (I do!) or whether I was related to the star of the old television variety series *Hee Haw*. In a feature story I referred to him as "*the* Roy Clark": "For most of my adult life, I've had to answer the question: Are you *the* Roy Clark, sometimes in jest, and sometimes, over the phone, with serious anticipation." I introduced him to my wife, Karen, who said to him, "I'm married to Roy Clark!" "Well, bless your heart," said *the* Roy Clark.

Novelist Joseph Heller in *Catch-22* reveals how little bits of language can mean a lot. His famous protagonist Captain Yossarian is assigned the tedious job of censoring letters written home from the war front by enlisted men:

> To break the monotony he invented games. Death to all modifiers, he declared one day, and out of every letter that passed through his hands went every adverb and every adjective. The next day he made war on articles. He reached a much higher plane of creativity the following day when he blacked out

everything in the letters but *a, an* and *the.* That erected more dynamic intralinear tensions, he felt, and in just about every case left a message far more universal.

Yossarian went on, no doubt, to teach postmodern literary theory at Yale.

Here's the moral of this story: If you are working inside the language, no decision is too small. The subtlest of changes with the smallest words can create the most dramatic effects. Consider the weight of the definite article (used as a noun) at the end of this critique by author Mary McCarthy about the writings of her rival Lillian Hellman: "Every word she writes is a lie, including 'and' and 'the.'"

## ANOTHER DISTINCTION

There are occasions, of course, when *an* substitutes for *a,* a decision influenced by sound. The path to getting this right is simple and governed by your dialect and your ear. If a word begins with a consonant sound, use *a.* A vowel sound requires *an.* The key word in this lesson is *sound,* not *letter.* "A ball" or "an egg" is easy enough. But some initial vowels produce consonant sounds, which is why we'd say "He delivered *a* eulogy the family will remember for years," or "That garage band was *a* one-hit wonder." (The initial *y* or *w* sound governs.) The problem child, historically, has been the letter *h.* Even though *h* is a consonant, it stands silent (especially in England) at the beginning of some words. I'm inclined to write "She's working on *a* historical novel, *an* honorable effort to be sure." Two tips: (1) let your ear influence your choice; (2) check the stylebook that governs your profession.

## KEEPSAKES

• Little things mean a lot in reading and writing, including the distinction between *a* and *the.*

• The words *a, an,* and *the* are called articles. *A* and *an* are indefinite articles, often used before nouns that "denote a single but unspecified person or thing." *The* is the definite article, used before nouns that "denote specified persons or things."

• *A* is used before consonant sounds; *an* before vowel sounds. Local pronunciation influences this choice.

• Writers often cut *a* and *the* to save space in brief online messages. Take care that such omissions do not detract from your meaning or distort your voice.

# 5

...

# Consult a thesaurus to remind yourself of words you already know.

If I use a distinctive word in a story—say, *highfalutin,* meaning "pompous or pretentious"—I want that word to stand out on the page, as in this couplet:

> A Russian monk named Greg Rasputin
> Was murdered by the highfalutin.

I don't expect any poet anywhere to be salutin' me for those lines. My point is that memorable words must be allowed to breathe. So I try to never, ever repeat a distinctive word on a page, unless I have a specific reason to do so. I created a term to describe this effect: *word territory.*

Because the issues here concern repetition and variation, we should pay attention to our old pal Mr. Synonym. I say "old pal" because in 1960 my mother bought me my first thesaurus, a word from the Greek that means "treasury." What a lovely and useful concept: a book that is a treasure chest of words.

I dove in. Before long I was word drunk, incapable of using a short word when a long word would do. In no time I went from word drunk to word inebriated to word besotted. I became a word tippler, bibber, soaker, sponge reveler, drunkard, sot, wino, carouser, dipsomaniac, devotee of Bacchus.

No longer could you find in my little sixth-grade stories words like *chew, drew,* or *screw.* Instead, you'd get *masticate, delineate,* or *fornicate.* (I didn't really write *fornicate* in sixth grade, but I wanted to. I went to Catholic school, after all.) It took me a while to break my show-offy (or exhibitionistic) addiction to the thesaurus. Then one day I figured it out: Don't use the treasure book to look up long fancy new words. Use it to remind yourself of words you already know.

I arrived at that understanding while coaching a young writer who had written a profile of a medical examiner. Long before the *CSI* television mysteries, the doc's autopsies would help police arrest murderers and rapists, so the writer wanted to emphasize the role of medical examiners as biodetectives. At one point he referred to them as "medical Sherlock Holmeses." The writer expressed his dissatisfaction with that phrase. Sherlock Holmes sounded ugly in the plural and created a distracting, clumsy rhythm.

"Can you help me find an alternative?" he asked.

"Let's take a look at the thesaurus," I said.

Under *detective* we found several interesting synonyms: *sleuth, spy, Sherlock, private dick, cop, investigator, gumshoe.* Then our eyes settled on *bloodhound.* A dictionary gave us this definition for an informal usage: "a relentless pursuer," which fit the doctor like a latex glove. More exciting was the discovery of a synonym that contained the word *blood.*

A teacher of mine once argued that there are no true synonyms. That was a useful lesson when we were deciding whether to call something a movie or a film. (One critic joked that you can't call a cinematic work a film if the theater sells gummy bears in the lobby.) But what about *rock* and *stone,* O wise teacher? What about *sofa* and *couch?* I use those last two words interchangeably to describe the same piece of furniture, unless I'm at home watching my high-definition TV for hours, in which case I am never a "sofa potato"; or when I'm at my shrink's office, in which case I am essentially "on the couch." (No psychiatrist is permitted to own a sofa.)

Such reflection leads me back to word territory and an example I recently discovered from English literature. Let's return to one of the most famous poems of the Romantic period, Shelley's "To a Skylark." The first line ("Hail to thee, blithe Spirit!") is so often quoted that it inspired the title of the Noël Coward play *Blithe Spirit.* What follows is a gorgeous comparison of the songbird to the song of the poet. Here is the fourth stanza:

> The pale purple even
>     Melts around thy flight;
> Like a star of heaven,
>     In the broad daylight
> Thou art unseen, but yet I hear thy shrill delight.

In the original manuscript, a copy of which is included in *Authors at Work,* I see that a revision has been made in that last line. Shelley replaced his original "blithe delight" with "shrill delight." The effect is dazzling. Not only does the poet avoid repetition of the key word "blithe" from the poem's first line, but he replaces it with a sound word, a delight that the reader can hear. That is, Shelley gives the distinctive words "blithe" and "shrill" their own space. More important, in his revision he did not choose a synonym at all but an example. *Blithe* means "carefree or lighthearted," an abstraction made real by the shrill sound of the bird.

## KEEPSAKES

• Examine some of your recent work to see if you have unintentionally repeated a distinctive word. Consult a thesaurus to find a gem in the treasure chest.

• The *AHD* offers these synonyms for *blemish: imperfection, fault, defect, flaw,* and then describes the shades of meaning among them. In addition to *blemish,* look up the following words, and study the distinctions of meaning and emphasis among lists of synonyms: *difference, difficulty, encourage, endanger, fear, grand, inactive, incalculable, innate, lethargy.*

• Remember that words that seem to mean the same thing, such as *rock / stone, sofa / couch,* or *naked / nude,* may differ in sense based on context and association.

# 6

...

## Take a class on how to cross-dress the parts of speech.

Good morning, students.

Today's lesson is on the parts of speech. Can anyone name them?

Wally? No, not the teeth, tongue, and lips. They are body parts that help you speak, but they are not the parts of speech.

Hermione? Very good, young lady. Yes, you got them all. Traditionally, there are eight parts of speech: noun, pronoun, verb, adjective, adverb, preposition, conjunction, and—hot dog!—my all-time favorite, the interjection.

Say that with me, class. Yes, with vigor: *IN-TER-JEC-TION!* Brilliant.

Let's begin by shouting out a few examples of each. Ready class? Go!

[Much arm waving and shouting at the teacher.]

*Noun:* dog, Ralph, mistletoe, Oreo, education, taco, Mississippi, peace, music, pizza

*Pronoun:* I, we, he, she, it, they, them, him, her, who, whom, whomever, that, which

*Verb:* tumble, dictate, zigzag, is, are, was, were, enlist, inoculate, stab

*Adverb:* speedily, tumultuously, harshly, dumbly, voraciously, democratically, tremulously, wherever, well, too

*Adjective:* skinny, enthusiastic, dire, rueful, industrious, yellow, distasteful, Cuban, conservative, phat

*Preposition:* off, on, in, out, over, through, to, under, above, about, throughout, with

*Conjunction:* and, but, yet, so, however, neither, nor, either, or

*Interjection:* Yikes! Whatever! Sheesh! Heck! Omigod!
      Awesome!

Let's talk more about adjectives, shall we? An adjective is a word that changes, or [quote fingers] "*modifies,*" a noun. In "red barn," for example, "red" is an adjective because it tells us what kind of barn it is. So "barn" is the noun, and "red" is the adjective.

Yes, Hermione?

You think "red" is a noun because it's the name of a color—and you think "barn" could be an adjective, as in "barn owl," because it modifies "owl." Hmm.

OK, now let's turn to the part of speech that describes a person, place, thing, or condition: the noun. In fact—this is clever—the word *noun* is a noun! It's the name of a part of speech.

Yes, Hermione? My, you are curious today.

That is correct. The word *verb* is also a noun, as are all the names of the other parts of speech.

Yes, it is a little confusing, but you'll catch on.

OK, let's move on to the adverb. This is a word that changes, or—class?—*modifies,* a verb. Good! You can always recognize an adverb because it ends in -*ly.*

What is it, Hermione? No, you are correct, *July* is not an adverb; it's a proper noun. No, you're right; *lovely* isn't one either. It's an adjective, as in "the lovely flowers."

Well, we're almost out of time for this lesson, but I did want to leave you with some of my favorite interjections, which are words that you blurt out to express anger, surprise, or, perhaps, frustration.

OK. Are you ready, class? Here goes:

Tiddlywinks! Ha, ha, ha. I shouted that once after I hit my thumb with a hammer.

What is it *now*, Hermione? Yes, tiddlywinks is the name of a children's game, which means *yes*, it's a noun.

I suppose you have a better example of an interjection, you insufferable little know-it-all.

What did you just say? Yes, that *is* an interjection, missy, and for that you can march yourself right down to the principal's office.

This little classroom drama reveals the flexibility and versatility of our language, the complex and wonderful ways in which words cross-dress as other parts of speech. This theme is highlighted in Ben Yagoda's fine book *When You Catch an Adjective, Kill It.* Yagoda describes the temptation to name the book *Pimp My Ride,* after a cool television show in which nasty old cars are transformed into customized masterpieces:

> Leaving aside the fact that it would have lent a faint aura of hipness to a book otherwise sorely lacking in street cred, *Pimp My Ride* illustrates a deep and wonderful truth about the parts of speech: they change like the dickens. *Pimp*—a noun meaning a procurer of prostitutes—turns into a transitive verb, meaning, roughly, "to make pimp-worthy." And the intransitive word *ride* becomes a noun, meaning "that in which one rides."

Notice how Yagoda himself turns "street" into an adjective modifying "cred," and how the noun and verb "pimp" acts as modifier in "pimp-worthy." The writer uses parts of speech the way a wild child uses Barbie and Ken dolls. You can dress them up, strip them down, or invite them to wear each other's clothing. (Rumor has it that Ken's got no problem with that.)

## KEEPSAKES

• Words are divided into the roles they play, categories called the parts of speech.

• The same word can cross-dress as different parts of speech, its meaning made through the context.

• The traditional parts of speech are noun, pronoun, verb, adjective, adverb, conjunction, preposition, and interjection. Modern linguists have expanded the list into more than a dozen "lexical categories," but the Great Eight retain their power.

• The function of a part of speech, such as the adverb, can be carried out not just by a single word but also by a phrase, a long phrase, even a clause.

# 7

# Enjoy, rather than fear, words that sound alike.

Some words sound the same but are spelled differently and carry different meanings. Other words, among my favorites, are near misses and close calls, words that look or sound a bit alike but are rarely used in proximity or confused: *poetry* and *poultry*. If I were writing a story about bird-watchers riding on German superhighways, I'd be tempted to use *Audubon* and *autobahn* in the same passage. My wife, it turns out, suffers from *idolatry* of the store *Dollar Tree*.

Peter Meinke has written a sonnet sequence titled "Mendel's Laws" in which the narrator marvels at his wife's pregnancy at Christmastime:

> And in the code that Mendel labored on
> our child will be deciphered; there will merge
> in childish shape and spirit, a paragon
> where paradox and paradigm converge.
> Now I can see Eve's children in your eyes:
> completely new, yet linked to paradise.

When I first heard Peter read this poem, I could not believe my ears: that he had managed to use in a single stanza the words "paragon," "paradox," "paradigm," and "paradise," all with precise meaning, yet not forced for effect. I wonder if he was tempted to get *pair of dice* in there too.

Beyond the close call lies a small pile of English words that look the same and sound the same but have opposite meanings. Think of Mr. Homonym and Ms. Antonym hooking up and creating a love child. Let's call the little bastard "Contranym."

Lots of words, through irony and slang, can be converted to their opposites. The word *bad,* for example, has been transformed in American popular culture, so that if I refer to a blues singer as "bad," there's a chance that I mean he's really good. The context almost always makes the meaning clear. The same can be said with *sand,* which can mean to make smooth or to make rough. If I sand a desktop, my goal is to make it smooth. But if I sand an icy driveway, I want to make it rough to give my tires traction. Again, these are rarely confused.

But what about the word *sanction,* as in the book and movie title *The Eiger Sanction*? For reasons I find puzzling, *sanction* can mean to permit or to prohibit. "I cannot sanction the use of cell phones by students in the cafeteria." Principal Hudpucker better be more specific. If she does not want her students on their cellies in the eatery, she should know that she's given the kiddies permission to think otherwise.

Which leads me to *cleave,* a word that can mean to join together or to split apart. A meat cleaver cuts a steak into two pieces. But Ward Cleaver might have once or twice admired June's cleavage. Hmm. Did he ever cleave to his wife's cleavage?

So is this language knowledge a curiosity or a potential tool? I tried to answer that question in a story about the coincidental deaths of President Gerald Ford and King of Soul, James Brown. It began:

> Gerald Ford saved the nation, it is said, by getting us out of a funk.
> James Brown saved it by getting us into one.

The word *funk*, it turns out, can have a downbeat or upbeat meaning, each with a different word history. According to the *AHD*, the word *funk* can mean "a state of severe depression." This use probably derives from the Flemish word *fonck*, meaning "disturbance or agitation." So—back to my story—Gerald Ford helped lift America out of the blues left behind by Watergate and the corruption of Richard Nixon.

But for James Brown, the word *funk* would carry this definition: "an earthy quality appreciated in music such as jazz or soul." In a wonderful bit of word history, *AHD* traces *funky* to 1784, when it was used to describe "musty moldy old cheese" and other strong odors, an earthiness that would one day soar to convey the joyful, syncopated pleasure of playing or listening to music with soul.

Working with words that sound alike requires special care. A colleague of mine once made a mistake when she used the word *carrot* rather than *caret* to describe a copyediting symbol that looks like this ∧. We all know that homonyms and homophones create confusion, error, and misunderstanding. Even those of us who decades ago mastered *there, their,* and *they're,* and *to, two,* and *too,* and the ever-fatal *its* and *it's* will at times confuse them during hasty and automatic typing.

So homonymphobia should extend to experienced writers using sophisticated language. I remember the day I used the word *discrete* (distinct) when I meant *discreet* (prudent). At the time, I did not know they were different words with different spellings, both derived from the same Latin root for "to separate." I felt bad about it until I was on a panel of writing coaches, not one of whom knew the difference. I did not understand any difference between *hone* (sharpen) and *home* (advance toward a target) until I wrote "hone in" in a newspaper column. Readers beat me with a stick, and I felt bad until two minutes ago when I discovered that the *AHD* considers *hone in* an acceptable variant of *home in*. Go figure.

I've had *cataract* surgery but still have to look up the word to make sure—for the umpteenth time—that the optical meaning has the same spelling as the high waterfall of the same name. (The word history here is fascinating: *cataract,* meaning "a great downrush," derives from a Greek word that also means "portcullis," a gate that drops down, which became a metaphor for the cloudy covering of the eye lens.)

So, for the record:

- A *caret* is a copyediting symbol (^) that derives from the Latin verb *carere,* meaning "to lack or be without." (Not to be confused with the "less than" symbol [<], which can become a caret but only if you're reading with your head resting on its left side on the pillow.)
- A *carat* is a unit to measure precious stones, spelled *karat* when measuring gold, derived from an Arabic term meaning "the weight of four grains."
- A *carrot,* of course, is a bunny's favorite food, good for the eyes, and, metaphorically, a reward that, when it comes to correction, is often more effective than the stick.

It is important to compile a personal list of words that confuse you because they sound or look alike. Errors in spelling and usage sometimes derive from the confusion of standard and nonstandard forms of English. In some community dialects, *ask* is pronounced "aks," which, of course, is a homophone for *ax.* I had family members in New York City who would use the second person plural *youse,* as in "youse guys," which is a homophone for *use.* An old joke in Providence, Rhode Island, involved a children's playground in a place called Tot Park. In that part of the world, *tot* sounded like *tart.* So Tart Park could be the place where ladies of the evening strutted their stuff.

## KEEPSAKES

- *Homonyms* are two or more words that sound alike and are spelled alike but have different meanings and may have different word histories. The *AHD* gives *bank* (place to keep money) and *bank* (pile of snow) as an example.

• *Homophones* are words that sound alike but are spelled differently and have different meanings, such as *write, right,* and *wright.*

• *Contranyms* are rare words with identical spellings and sounds that have opposite meanings, such as *sanction* (permit, prohibit) and *cleave* (join together, split apart).

# 8

...

## Learn seven ways to invent words.

With no disrespect to Abraham Lincoln or Grover Cleveland or Dwight Eisenhower, "Barack Obama" is, by acclamation, the most unusual name among the forty-four men elected to the American presidency. And while his name, including his middle name, Hussein, may have been an obstacle to his election, the musical rhythm of "Obama" inspired writers and commentators to coin a new lexicon to describe his historical achievement.

The online magazine *Slate* offered up this collection of *neologisms,* or new words: *Obamaphoria, Obamanation, Obamarama, Obamanos, Obamatopia, Obamalujah, Obamatrons, Obamascope, Obamanator, Obamalicious, Obamaloha, Oh-bama, Bamelot, Obamerika, Barackstar.* I'm sure we'll hear more in the years to come, both positive and negative.

There are many ways to create new words to describe new things (you will find seven strategies in "Keepsakes"), but two of the most important are the coining of a word from a proper noun (the result being an *eponym*) and the blending of two words to create a third. For example, when I play golf with my friend Bill Mitchell, he sometimes tees off with an iron rather than the riskier driver. When he is successful, I call this cautious strategy by a name. I say that Bill "Mitchelled" the ball. That is, I took a name, a proper noun, and turned it into an active transitive verb.

Among the most famous examples of eponyms, you can choose from *lynch* (named after Virginia law-and-order dude Captain William Lynch), *derrick* (named after a sixteenth-century English hangman), and *gerrymander*. This last word is both a blend and an eponym deriving from Elbridge Gerry, whose rigged political district was drawn in the shape of a salamander. The word *mesmerize*, meaning to "enthrall" or "hypnotize," derives from Franz Mesmer, an eighteenth-century physician who is thought to have applied early examples of hypnosis to the art of physical healing. To *bowdlerize*, meaning "to censor by way of editing," can be traced to Thomas Bowdler, who published expurgated editions of Shakespeare early in the nineteenth century. Lynch, Gerry, Mesmer, and Bowdler—let's call them "The Boys from Eponyma."

You can take a name, of course, and blend it with another word to signify something different, as in the cable television series *Californication* and *Pornucopia*. Such blended words have a technical name, *portmanteau*, referring to "a large leather suitcase that opens into two hinged compartments." The popular word *ginormous* is clearly a blend of *gigantic* and *enormous*. So, revisiting a few words in the list above, we see that the name Obama becomes one half of the suitcase, while the other half derives from *euphoria, utopia, hallelujah, terminator, delicious,* and so on.

As writers, we should never be satisfied with the words we inherit, the ones that already appear in our dictionaries. Learning to use them correctly is the license we need to bend them, stretch them, and blend them with others, as context, meaning, and audience allow.

On his cool website, wordspy.com, Paul McFedries offers clever examples of words coined from blends of two existing words: *netois:* the patois of the net; *multidude:* a bunch of surfers; and *slackademic:* someone who won't leave school. He includes *anecdotage,* which stands for boring stories from old people. Not long ago, I coined the word *anecdotty,* for writers who overuse anecdotes.

*Blog* is a blend of *web* and *log.*

Among the words in Alonzo Westbrook's *Hip Hoptionary* (a blend of *hip-hop* and *dictionary*) are several that combine the meanings of existing words:

- *One-mo-gen* is a blend of *once more* and *again.*
- *Hivestock* combines hip-hop magazine *The Hive* with *Woodstock.*
- *Crooklyn* blends *crook* and *Brooklyn.*
- *Crackitute* is someone who sells sex for crack cocaine.
- A *prima dog* is the male equivalent of the prima donna.

These and other neologisms flow easily from any culture that seeks to separate itself from mainstream authority and conventions. Sometimes the words are perceived as "mistakes," such as *trickeration.* According to the Urban Dictionary, *trickeration* was coined for a Cab Calloway song in 1931 but was adopted into the language to denote a creative play in college football.

But we can also see where the portmanteau works on the high end of the culture, such as in the Canadian Broadcasting Company's competition to create new words to describe things or situations for which there is no obvious language. So if you are a terrible cook, can we call you a *gournot?* The noise that a cold engine makes on a winter morning in Toronto is a *cranksinatra.* If you are a person who routinely kills plants—the opposite of a green thumb—we can call you a *bloominator, earth-smother, grass-assin, green reaper, hortician, necrofloriac, veggiscarian,* or the winner: *herbicidal maniac.*

The portmanteau, or blend, teaches us one very important lesson about language and about creativity in general: new things are not created out of nothing but usually grow out of what is already known or understood. What a relief.

# KEEPSAKES

Here is a quick list of some of the ways new words are coined into the English language:

• The *portmanteau* or *blend: Octomom* became a tabloid word to describe the mother of octuplets, while Ian Fleming gave us the mischievous James Bond title *Octopussy*.

• *Eponym:* The word *boycott* is named after Charles C. Boycott. When the British land agent evicted some tenants, he and his family "found themselves isolated—without servants, farmhands, service in stores, or mail delivery," according to the *AHD*.

• The *compound* or *kenning:* This is a kind of metaphor, common in Old English poetry, in which two words are combined to form a third word that may make little or no reference to the two original elements. According to author Simon Winchester's study of the *OED*, there are "50 words in Old English that signify the sea," including such combinations as *whale-way, drowning-flood,* and *waters-strife.* Modern compounds include *firearm, highball,* and *outgoing.* Examples of classic slang are listed in *The Little Hiptionary: the bee's knees, the cat's pajamas, fix his wagon, fly by the seat of your pants, heavens to betsy, peace out, spend a penny* (go to the bathroom in the days of pay toilets), *spill the beans.* Just remember that the *outgoing mail* may be delivered by an *outgoing male.*

• *Front clipping* or *back clipping:* The blend of *taximeter* and *cab* gave us the word *taxicab,* which was then clipped at the front and at the back to give us the shortened versions *cab* and *taxi.* (By metaphorical extension, a *taxi dancer* is a professional dancer hired for a partner dance for a fee, just as taxis are hired to provide short rides.)

• *Brand names* or *trade names:* Many brands work hard to legally protect their trademarks, but the struggle gets more difficult when the word appears without capital letters, a sign that it has evolved from product identification. Words such as

Band-Aid, Jell-O, Laundromat, Kleenex, and Xerox fall into this category.

• *Acronyms:* Many words are formed from the first letters of a phrase. John H. Cover invented the Taser, a "high-voltage stun gun," its name an acronym drawn from one of his favorite boyhood adventure stories: *Tom A. Swift and His Electric Rifle.*

• *Sound words:* Words that imitate sounds are common in English. It may not be obvious that these common words derive from the sounds they describe: for example, "As the old women *cackled* in the corner and the children *buzzed* with excitement, a *murmur* of disgust could be heard from the choir loft."

There are many other ways in which new words enter the language, but there is no better source than a playful writer trying to say something new.

# 9

...

# Become your own lexicographer.

A person who compiles and writes a dictionary is called a *lexicographer*. But I would argue that all avid readers and curious writers are lexicographers, collectors of words that define a group and help break down the doors of a culture or subculture. To get "inside," you need access to the special language of the tribe, which may be expressed in a foreign tongue, dialect, jargon, or slang. Whether the vessel is a legal document or a rap song, language is often chosen to exclude. To use a scholarly phrase, "discourse communities" are often gated, so it's the good writer's job to offer readers a set of keys.

Take, for example, Roald Dahl's description of British citizens living and working in Africa and India during the days of the empire, from his autobiography *Going Solo*:

> They were the craziest bunch of humans I shall ever meet. For one thing, they spoke a language of their own. If they worked in East Africa, their sentences were sprinkled with Swahili words, and if they lived in India then all manner of dialects were intermingled. As well as this, there was a whole vocabulary of much-used words that seemed to be universal among all these people. An evening drink, for example, was always a sundowner. A drink

at any other time was a chota peg. One's wife was the memsa-
hib. To have a look at something was to have a shufti.... Something of poor quality was a shenzi.... The Empire-builders'
jargon could have filled a dictionary.

In her book *The Argument Culture,* language and gender
scholar Deborah Tannen offers examples of societies that use language to bring people together or to align them as adversaries:

> In native Hawaiian culture, for example, there is a word,
> *ho 'oponopono* ("to set things right"), for a ceremony in which
> family members invite an elder ... to oversee the resolution of a
> dispute.... Hierarchical social relations play a major role, as they
> do in another ritual, *ho-opapa,* a verbal contest of wits and in-
> sults that can be played either for fun or in earnest combat, to
> establish superiority between rivals.

This last example sounds like the "yo mama" jokes of African
American culture, sometimes called "playing the dozens."

Writers can use this word-gathering strategy to advance a
narrative, as in this example from Anne Fadiman, who grew up
in a family of famous word lovers:

> The English professor said, "*Mephitic!* That must mean foul-
> smelling. I've seen it in *Paradise Lost,* describing the smell of
> hell." My brother, a mountain guide and natural history teacher
> who lives in Wyoming, said, "*Mephitic,* hmm, yes. The scientific
> name for the striped skunk is *Mephitis mephitis,* which means
> *Stinky stinky.*" (from *Ex Libris: Confessions of a Common Reader*)

And here is a passage from Michael Heim, author of *The
Metaphysics of Virtual Reality*, on how technology has influenced
our language:

> During the 1980s a new vocabulary established the computeriza-
> tion of English. To be initiated, you had to repeat buzzwords like

*access, input,* and *output.* You learned to speak of *files* having no apparent physical dimensions, *menus* offering a selection of nonedibles, and *monitors* providing vigilance over your own words.

Every group, no matter how small, develops its own lingo over time. As a reporter or anthropologist or ethnographer, you can't get very far inside without learning the language. Let me offer, as an exhibit, the amazing Clark family. If you hung around our house long enough, you would hear odd phrases and invented words—neologisms—that help define our values and relationships. Here's a minilexicon:

*poop du jour:* A sign that a family member is a "regular" person.

*fooding hand:* Meaning your "left hand," created by daughter Emily when she was a little girl. She ate, or "fooded," with her left hand.

*no say woo-woo:* When you happen to catch a family member partially clad, you are required to say "woo-woo," but baby daughter Lauren didn't like it, so her retort was "no say woo-woo." It can be used to fend off any objectionable language.

*Mr. Pelican Pants:* Used to ridicule loud and obnoxious clothing, inspired by a gent who used to wear his golf pants to church.

*keysta louista:* Your keys, but only to remind you to grab them. Probably derived from *keister,* meaning "derriere." Like saying "Did you remember your butt?"

*left ovary:* the yucky stuff at the bottom of mayonnaise and jelly jars. In other words, it's the gunk that is "left over," but in a family with three grown daughters we spell it o-v-a-r-y.

*tarantula rains:* Tropical-style Florida thunderstorms, an obvious mishearing of "torrential rains."

*sticky-uppy-outie:* Used almost exclusively to describe your bad hair in the morning. But if it is the result of the dog licking your head to wake you up, it becomes not a hairdo but a fashionable *doggie do.*

Many paths will get the writer into the specialized language of others, among them intensive listening, hanging around, eavesdropping, interviewing with language in mind ("What do you guys call that thing?"), attention to family rituals, documents such as letters and family albums, and memories of grandparents and siblings. It was T. S. Eliot who described the hope that the poet could "purify the dialect of the tribe." All writers can do that by attending to the craft, but there is a task just as important: listening to the language of others and translating it so we can all understand.

## KEEPSAKES

• When reading or writing about a special group—a discourse community—keep a list of the words that are most essential to that community.

• Collect a list of the words and phrases that are special to your own family. Pay attention to made-up words that may be the result of creativity, accident, or mistakes.

• Attend a meeting of a group or a club and listen to the specialized language of its members. Soccer clubs, choirs, gay bars, the teachers lounge—all are small communities with specialized vocabularies. See how many special words you can discover.

• Look through some old high-school and college yearbooks, paying special attention to the signed messages. See if you can identify language that was special to the class but now may be meaningless to outsiders.

# 10

## ...

# Take advantage of the short-word economy of English.

When I was a kid, I read everything, including the backs and sides of cereal boxes. I still try to read everything, even on airplanes, killing time not just with novels and newspapers but also product catalogs and the text on airsickness bags. Since I can read a little Spanish, I also enjoy studying the bilingual safety-information cards.

Now the Spanish equivalent of the phrase "safety information" is "*informacion de seguridad*." It takes three Spanish words to translate two English words, twenty-two letters to translate seventeen. That discovery led me to hypothesize that, in general, it takes more language (more letters, more words) to express oneself in Spanish than in English, and that, in some respects, English is the "shorter" or "tighter" language.

My suspicion was reinforced when Barack Obama's supporters chanted one of his campaign catch phrases: "Yes we can." There's a lot of meaning squeezed in those three words and eight letters. Or how about this for economy: "To be or not to be..."

Of the dozens of sentences on the safety-information card, almost every one maintained this pattern. The greatest disparity I could find came with the Spanish phrase "*y mientras la luz de abrocharse el cinturon esta encendida,*" which in English appears as "and while fasten seatbelt light is on." It takes ten Spanish words and forty-nine letters to convey what we can say in English in seven words and thirty-one letters.

Even if you do not know Spanish, you can recognize cognate words (words with the same root) that exist in English. I often notice that there are at least two English words that substitute for Spanish ones, so that, in some contexts, *encendida* (in which I see *incendiary*) can be translated as "lit" and "illuminated."

But how did English get two such different words, one short and one long, for the same act? If you look them up in the *AHD*, you will discover that *lit* is the past tense of *light* and derives from the Old English word *liht*. *Illuminated,* on the other hand, comes from a Middle English word that derives from the Latin.

We can trace these effects back to 1066 when the Norman invasion of England brought with it longer words of French and Latin origin, words that would be added to the shorter Anglo-Saxon lexicon, so that early in 1919 G. K. Chesterton, that round mound of literary renown, could use the long and the short with great effect: "Coincidences are spiritual puns." (That may be true, G.K., but I believe that a good pun is its own reword.)

A 2009 memo from the *New York Times* offered a list of the fifty words that its online readers were most likely to look up. (I was unfamiliar with five.) More than seventy-five hundred readers looked up the Latin phrase *sui generis,* a legal term meaning "unique," earning it the top spot. Only three words of the fifty are one syllable, and just one of them, *swine,* derives from the Anglo-Saxon. The great majority are multisyllable words of French, Latin, or Greek origin. My favorite on the list earned the number three spot: *louche,* meaning "of questionable taste or morality," derived from the Latin word meaning "blind in one eye."

To show how the mixture of short and long words works, and why it matters, let's examine a passage from Joan Didion's memoir

*The Year of Magical Thinking.* Here, her daughter wakes up in the hospital, only to learn that her father has died of a heart attack:

> Telling her that day had not been the plan....If she woke and saw me she would wonder where her father was....We had decided that only Gerry should be with her when she first began to wake. She could focus on him, on their life together. The question of her father might not come up. I could see her later, maybe days later. I could tell her then. She would be stronger.
>
> As planned, Gerry was with her when she first woke. As not planned, a nurse told her that her mother was outside in the corridor.
>
> Then when is she coming in, she wanted to know.
>
> I went in.
>
> "Where's Dad," she whispered when she saw me.

There are words in this passage drawn from French and Latin, such as "focus," "question," "planned," and "corridor." But what strikes me is how Anglo-Saxon it is, mostly simple short words at the emotional high points: "I could tell her then....when she first woke....I went in."

In the titles of her books, Didion is as comfortable with longer words and phrases (*Slouching Towards Bethlehem*) as she is with short ones (*Play It As It Lays*). In general, the writer will find her way to short words and short sentences to say important and memorable things. When short words are used in short sentences, the effect is like a power-loaded spring.

Short words have a special effect after a litany of longer ones, as this passage from Marshall Frady, the southern biographer, demonstrates. Frady is describing the last gasp of segregationist George Wallace, a victim of an assassination attempt that left him in a wheelchair:

> Over the course of a day, he will range back and forth from the sodden sepulchral inertness of a mummy to abrupt crackling animation—actually change visibly, as if glimmering physically

back and forth between two different creatures. He can, in fact, rally himself now and then to those old angry energies, clangoring apocalyptic helter-skelter incantations like those he would deliver in hotel rooms and the back seats of cars during the Sixties. (from *Wallace*)

Those cascading comma-less polysyllabic abstractions ("clangoring apocalyptic helter-skelter incantations") would seem florid if they did not resolve themselves into the drip-drop-drip simplicity of "hotel rooms and the back seats of cars." Such prose reminds me of an episode of *CSI* in which a beautiful scientist observes that a victim "exsanguinated." At a similar moment in *Law and Order,* a gruff detective notes that the dead guy "bled out." There you have the English language in a nutshell: *exsanguinate* versus *bled out.*

A master of spare language is Bob Dotson, one of the best storytellers in the history of broadcast news. In his book on the craft, *Make It Memorable,* Dotson reveals many of his tested techniques and illustrates them with scripts of his stories. The first describes the aftermath of a terrible crime: the shootings of four schoolchildren in Jonesboro, Arkansas. The script of the three-minute story contains visual cues and transcriptions of soundbites, but I will quote only Dotson's narration:

Sometimes the yearbook of life closes too soon.
We are left with grainy pictures and long-lens grief.
No way to measure a loss.
The four little girls who died in that Jonesboro schoolyard were more than what happened to them. They were small-town kids...a lot like these.
Their friends thought you might like to see where...
Paige Herring perfected her jump shot.
And Natalie Brooks practiced her cheers.
Stephanie Johnson sang her first sweet song right here.
And Britthany Varner gave her a hug. She always had hugs for her friends....

Our children are like library books, with a due date unknown.

These lives stopped at the start of their stories.

But their stories live on…in friends who can tell them.

To describe such terrible grief, Dotson strips down the language beyond spare—almost to bare. Let's do an accounting: of the 123 words in that passage, ninety-six are words of one syllable.

There are lots of lessons to learn here: When a story is powerful, keep the language spare. In English, spare language depends on short words, short sentences, and short paragraphs at the points of highest emotion. If that strategy works for you, give thanks to the Angles and the Saxons for what was preserved under Norman domination.

Critic Camille Paglia grew up in a household of Italian immigrants, all speaking a variety of dialects from the southern provinces of Italy. In her book *Break, Blow, Burn,* Paglia testifies about how that experience led to her love of the English language:

> What fascinated me about English was what I later recognized as its hybrid etymology: blunt Anglo-Saxon concreteness, sleek Norman French urbanity, and polysyllabic Greco-Roman abstraction. The clash of these elements, as competitive as Italian dialects, is invigorating, richly entertaining, and often funny, as it is to Shakespeare, who gets tremendous effects out of their interplay. The dazzling multiplicity of sounds and word choices in English makes it brilliantly suited to be a language of poetry.

## KEEPSAKES

• English has a history, of course, and one of its pivotal moments came in AD 1066 when the Normans conquered England and brought with them from France their language and culture. As a result, we often have two words for the same thing: a short word from an Anglo-Saxon root, and a longer word from a French and Latin root: as in *lively* and *vivacious.*

• In *The Sounds of Poetry,* poet Robert Pinsky argues that

one long word, *hippopotamus,* reads more quickly than a staccato litany of short words: "horse of the sea." If you can pronounce it, *horripilation* flies by more quickly than "that feeling we call 'goose bumps.'"

• Writers can emphasize certain words and influence the reader's pace by making good selections from the stocks of short and long words.

• Examine something you have written, and study it for word length. Can you now think of revisions that will better serve your purpose? Try saying the most important thing using short words in short sentences.

...

# 11

# Learn when and how to enrich your prose with foreign words.

American English never stands still. Without pause it moves and changes. Along the river of time, some words are lost, some words are found, and some may look the same but carry a different, even opposite meaning.

Many forces join to change our language. One of the most powerful is contact with other languages and cultures. Because of our relative affluence, Americans travel round the world, bringing back to our homes artifacts of culture and new names for new experiences. Think of *pizza,* my favorite food, which became more popular in America after soldiers returned from Italy after World War II. Not only do I love the food, but I love the word, the look of it, the sound of it, and those zesty double *z*'s in the middle. (I was about to write that I adore any word with two *z*'s in it, until I looked up *pizza* in the dictionary and found *pizzazz* below it. Origin unknown, but dig those four crazy *z*'s.)

For a long time I subscribed to E. B. White's advice in *The Elements of Style:* "Avoid foreign languages." That headline is harsher and more dogmatic than the paragraph that supports it: "The writer will occasionally find it convenient or necessary to borrow from other languages. Some writers, however, from sheer exuberance or a desire to show off, sprinkle their work liberally with foreign expressions, with no regard for the reader's comfort. It is a bad habit. Write in English."

White wrote that sentence some fifty years ago (circa 1958) when American English and American culture were quite different than they are today. As I write this, America has elected its first African American president. Millions upon millions of Spanish-speaking immigrants—some legal, some not—work in America. A global economy has replaced the one I grew up with during the years of Eisenhower and Elvis. Our splendid diversity has created a backlash, in the form of immigrant bashing and proposals to make English America's official language. But that same diversity has also introduced countless opportunities for cultural enrichment, with the children of immigrants learning American English, and all of us getting to taste, smell, feel, see, touch, sing, and speak the influence of new people and new cultures. The 2009 Oscar for best picture went to the masterpiece *Slumdog Millionaire,* set in Mumbai, India, which had us humming and dancing—Bollywood style—to the best original song, the catchy "Jai Ho."

At some point foreign words introduced into the English language cease to seem foreign, as this simple inventory of adopted words reveals, a tiny selection I've culled from *The Origins and Development of the English Language* by Thomas Pyles. These words were loaned into English *from Latin:* abdomen, area, compensate, composite, data, decorum; *from Greek:* allegory, anemia, aristocracy, barbarous, chaos, comedy; *from Irish Gaelic:* banshee, blarney, brogue, colleen, leprechaun, shamrock; *from Scandinavian languages:* geyser, rune, saga, smorgasbord; *from French:* amateur, ballet, bureau, café, camouflage, champagne; *from Spanish:* guitar, junta, mosquito, silo, tango, tomato, tornado, vanilla; *from Italian:* cameo, carnival, casino, inferno, influenza, lagoon, lava, miniature, motto, piazza; *from German and Dutch:* booze, brake, hop, kindergarten, luck, pickle, Santa Claus, sleigh, spool, waffle; *from Yiddish:* kibitzer, phooey, schlemiel, schmaltz, schmuck; *from Arabic:* amber, orange, saffron, sugar, syrup, zenith; *from Sanskrit:* avatar, mahatma, swastika, yoga; *from Chinese:* chow, ketchup, tea, tong; *from Japanese:* banzai, geisha, judo, kimono, samurai, soy, tycoon.

An essay by British poet Ted Hughes points out that William Shakespeare's written vocabulary contained some twenty-five thousand words, double that of his closest rival. This does not surprise me: best writer, most words. The Bard wrote during a time when many new words were being introduced into the English language from foreign tongues, especially from French and Italian, Greek and Latin. All those new words of the English Renaissance created an environment in which some of our most treasured literary works were produced, from *Hamlet* to the King James Version of the Bible.

Those new words were more likely to be understood by the educated aristocracy enjoying *As You Like It* from the expensive seats in the Globe Theater. But there were commoners sitting in the cheap seats, and Shakespeare wanted their money too. (These folks were called *groundlings* because they sat or stood on the ground in front of the stage.) According to Hughes, the poetry of the Shakespearean theater turns out to be a brilliant mixture of new and old words, of short and long, of Anglo-Saxon as well as Latin and Greek. To form a bridge of language between the two audiences, Shakespeare learned to make the meaning of the new words clear from the action, that is from the context of the dramatic narrative, or to translate them by offering a familiar old-school synonym in the same line of dialogue.

In this case, I choose Shakespeare's model over E. B. White's advice. You *should* write in English. But don't be afraid to use a word or phrase from another culture that captures a distinctive idea in an authentic way and reflects the current influence of other cultures on our language. Here's the catch: the word must be understandable from context or its meaning clear from your translation.

When homemaking maven (a great Yiddish word) Martha Stewart was sent to prison for lying to prosecutors about insider trading, it was said that many Americans, sick of her perfectionism, expressed a form of *schadenfreude* (a German word describing the pleasure that some take in others' pain). We're far from the tipping point when the word will seem—like the German word *kindergarten*—part of our language. But such is its rising influence that it serves as the title of a song in the musical *Avenue Q*. Writers understand audiences. They don't presume everyone will understand the meaning of unusual words. The dialogue in *Avenue Q* offers a definition, then the song provides humorous examples. From Stratford-upon-Avon to Avenue Q, we can follow this wise path: either offer a translation of the new or foreign word, or make sure its meaning is clear from context.

Let's examine how such strategies work in the hands of skilled writer Sonia Nazario, who won a Pulitzer Prize for her work "Enrique's Journey." It begins:

> The boy does not understand.
>
> His mother is not talking to him. She will not even look at him. Enrique has no hint of what she is going to do.
>
> Lourdes knows. She understands, as only a mother can, the terror she is about to inflict, the ache Enrique will feel, and finally the emptiness.
>
> What will become of him? Already he will not let anyone else feed or bathe him. He loves her deeply, as only a son can. With Lourdes, he is openly affectionate. "*Dame pico, mami.* Give me a kiss, Mom," he pleads, over and over, pursing his lips. With Lourdes, he is a chatterbox. "*Mira, mami.* Look, Mom," he says softly, asking her questions about everything he sees. Without her, he is so shy it is crushing.

The author's strategy works to perfection. She keeps the Spanish phrases short, sets them apart in italics, then offers a quick translation.

Here is Nazario again:

Enrique wades chest-deep across a river. He is five feet tall and stoop-shouldered and cannot swim. The logo on his cap boasts hollowly, NO FEAR.

The river, the Rio Suchiate, forms the border. Behind him is Guatemala. Ahead is Mexico, with its southernmost state of Chiapas. *"Ahora nos enfrentamos a la bestia,"* migrants say when they enter Chiapas. "Now we face the beast."

This is not the equivalent of watching a foreign language film with subtitles. Nazario is writing in English, thank you very much, Mr. E. B. White. The Spanish words—the tiniest fraction of the whole text—add the flavor of speech, place, and culture, creating one of narrative's most powerful effects: authenticity.

## KEEPSAKES

- Don't use foreign words or phrases just to show off, but if a foreign word or phrase captures something special, use it.
- The judicious use of foreign words can reflect the growing ethnic diversity of American culture.
- If you do use a foreign word or phrase, make sure you translate it unless its meaning is clear from the context.
- During revision, check with someone who knows the foreign language to make sure you've got it right.
- One great way to live inside your own language is to study a foreign language.

PART TWO

• • •

# Points

It occurred to me one day that the words *punctuation, punctual,* and *puncture* must all come from the same root, probably the Latin word for *point*. A quick trip to the dictionary confirmed my suspicion. A sharp object—a pencil, a stylus, an icepick—makes a mark, a dot, a point. A sharp point makes a sharp point. To be punctual means to arrive "on the dot."

Punctuation is a convention, of course, which means that each culture decides over time the general "rules" that govern it. In Spanish, the question mark (called the "mark of interrogation") not only follows the sentence but precedes it—and upside down—like this: *¿Como esta usted?* "How are you?" In England our period is called a *full stop*. The Brits leave their full stops and commas outside of quotation marks, while we Yanks tuck them inside. Different keystrokes for different folks.

While rules guide formal practice, let's remember that spoken language contains no visible punctuation, unless you count the hand gestures of orators and the "phonetic punctuation" comedy routine of the late Victor Borge. Speech is filled with the punctuation "mistakes" that are apparent on the printed page, everything from misplaced modifiers to run-on sentences to ambiguous language, mistakes that context and tone of voice often overcome.

Transformed from rules to tools, marks of punctuation influence the creation of white space, pace, emphasis, narrative flow, mood, authorial voice, and many other important effects of writing. You'll learn why the Brits call the period a full stop, how the question mark generates narrative energy, how the semicolon and exclamation point are ready to make comebacks.

When we first learn the standards of punctuation, we focus on what is correct and what is an error. It is crucial, though, for every writer to ascend to a higher rhetorical purpose. For example, the capital letter defines the act of naming; quotation marks offer surprisingly different effects; and ellipses have the ability to speed you up or slow you down. And you'll be delighted by a splendid passage in which author Laura Hillenbrand uses many of these marks to her strategic advantage.

# 12

...

## Use the period to determine emphasis and space.

I am the only person I know who suffers at the same time from Anglophilia and Anglophobia. I love Shakespeare and Oxford University and Canterbury Cathedral and Harry Potter. But I rebel against British bullies, from soccer hooligans to tabloid editors to Simon Cowell to that nasty "You are the weakest link" lady to Lynne Truss and all her trussed-up punctuation corrections.

I also generally prefer American punctuation conventions to British ones, with one huge exception: the name we give to the little dot at the end of this sentence. We call it a *period*, but the Brits prefer *full stop*. I too prefer *full stop* because it describes the effect on the reader. The period signals to the reader that the sentence is over, a thought completed, and another about to begin. Stop.

That stop sign is important, but just as important is the word or phrase that comes immediately before the stop. Take, for example, my favorite seven-year-old writer, Maggie Jacobson, who wrote and illustrated a booklet she called "My Seventh Birthday!!" Her energetic prose style demonstrates an understanding of one of my most reliable language tools, strategic use of the full stop:

> On my seventh birthday I had a sleepover. I invited my friends
> Julia and Blaire. I had my birthday with Jessica. It was a blast!

First we have a water balloon fight. Then we get out the hoses.
Second we ate dinner. We had fruit. It was yummy!
Third we played outside. We played hula girls.
We watched *Happy Feet*. It was funny!
Then my Mom read us a story. Then we went to bed.

Maggie gives us six more pages of details, but you get the idea. Most striking is Maggie's intuitive understanding that emphatic and interesting words go at the end of the sentence—right before the period (or exclamation point). Look at the words she chooses to emphasize that way: *sleepover, blast, balloon fight, hoses, yummy, hula girls*, Happy Feet, *funny, story, bed*. No one taught Maggie to put cool language right before the period. She learned it from talking and listening and reading and being read to.

To build suspense, writers slow down the pace of the story. The best way to do this is with a series of short sentences. The more periods—the more full stops—the slower the reader will go. Ben Montgomery of the *St. Petersburg Times* does this with skill in the story of a high-school football championship game. Montgomery watches the match holed up in a local saloon with zealous Tampa fans. Here's the lead:

> Fourth quarter. Three minutes left. Nease High just went up
> 21–17 on Robert Marve and the boys from Plant.

I watched the game on television, and it had a thrilling conclusion. Throughout this brief narrative, Montgomery uses two strategies of delay that only heighten the suspense. He uses quotes from fans ("'South Tampa people,' says Marc, 'have a sense of pride'"). And he uses a series of short sentences, such as:

> Complete pass. Again. Clock's ticking. Again. Down the field
> they go. The kid can't miss. The Panthers are nearing the end
> zone....The whole place is on its feet. Ball's on the 5-yard line.
> Marve takes the snap. Drops back. Throws.

All those periods are stop signs. They slow the reader down. Way down. Leaving the reader in suspense. Until the very last moment. When we learn…

Building suspense is not the only reason to slow the pace of the reader. The writer may want to explain a complicated idea or process (say, derivative lending instruments). Or the writer may want to magnify the emotional power of a scene or feeling, as did author and poet Maureen Gibbon in her *New York Times* essay "My Rapist": "One day several years ago, I opened up my hometown newspaper and found a picture of my rapist on the Engagements page."

Her phrase "my rapist" seems compelling enough, but the idea of a photo of a rapist appearing in a wholesome setting like an Engagements page makes this lead irresistible and prompts questions that only a good story can answer: Would the victim confront her attacker? Would she get revenge by breaking up the wedding? Would she feel more empowered to take action—or more discouraged? My colleague Tom French calls such questions the "engines" of a story.

The essay is short but reads slowly. This effect comes from the brutal nature of the narrative but also, I would argue, from sentence length. Gibbon does not want you to breeze through her pain. Why would she?

Here's the second paragraph: "Maybe I shouldn't have been surprised. I knew he stayed in the area. But it still shocked me to see his photo. He was marrying a younger woman, one with a child, according to the article." Notice those four periods—four full stops. Here are the word counts of her first twelve sentences: 22, 6, 7, 9, 14, 8, 25, 19, 6, 23, 10, 7. The average length is thirteen words. The variation in length creates a rhythm and movement that prevents tedium. The writer has made an effective choice. Her short sentences magnify the emotional power of the piece, holding up a vision of enduring grief, so the reader cannot look away.

In 1971 a scholar named Virginia Tufte wrote *Grammar as Style,* a splendid volume reissued three decades later as *Artful Sentences: Syntax as Style.* Tufte's rhetorical approach to the elements of language makes her interpretation of texts persuasive and her analyses useful. Consider her take on short sentences:

> Ideas about the building of paragraphs from sentences usually concern "topic sentences" and the ordering of "subordinate ideas." Yet accomplished writers usually seem to have something else in mind when deciding how to put sentences together: the better the writers, of fiction and nonfiction alike, the more they tend to vary their sentence lengths. And they do it as dramatically as possible. Time and again the shortest sentence in a professional paragraph is brought up against the longest, or at least lodges among some much longer. This smallest sentence is often a basic sentence both grammatically and semantically, stating in simplest terms the central idea of the paragraph....Narrative prose may be fashioned on a somewhat different principle, a more dramatic one. It is still disposed into paragraphs most of the time, but short sentences when they do appear are less often a condensation of the topic than some narrowed, relaxed point of departure or a slamming start, a later point of rest, an abrupt turn or climax, or a simple close. Either way, however, as a topic sentence or as a kind of syntactic punctuation, a very short sentence can be effective.

As an illustration, Tufte chooses a paragraph by F. Scott Fitzgerald from the novel *This Side of Paradise:*

> The silence of the theater behind him ended with a curious snapping sound, followed by the heavy roaring of a rising crowd and the interlaced clatter of many voices. The matinee was over.

The short sentence—four words framed by two full stops— brings the action to a close.

## KEEPSAKES

- From now on think of the period as a *full stop,* and begin to look at the place right before the full stop as a hot spot, a point of emphasis.

• The more periods, the more stops, and the slower the pace of the work for the reader. Why would you want to set a slow pace?

> ✓ To create suspense; to keep the reader hanging (Oh, by the way, Plant High School won the big game.)
> ✓ To explain step by step
> ✓ To magnify an emotion

# 13

...

## Advocate use of the serial comma.

I have spent my career navigating between literature and journalism, trying to learn from both worlds. From my training and experience as an English professor, I carried into the newsroom the power of close reading, a respect for narrative, and a theoretical understanding of the writing process. From years of working with reporters and editors, I've gained a sense of craft, a respect for readers, and a compass that points me toward mission and purpose.

Though I embody these two language traditions in equal amounts, I have preferences, and some of them are passionate, even about the little things. So I say with the certainty of contradiction that when it comes to the serial comma, sometimes called the Oxford comma, the literary folks have it right, and the journalists have it wrong. The reader needs that final comma before *and* in a series. I need it.

Despite their common heritage in language, analysis, and storytelling, journalists and the literati belong to two different "discourse communities." There's that phrase again. I learned it from writing teacher and scholar Carolyn Matelene, and have found it one of the most useful concepts for understanding language. A simpler way to think of a discourse community is as a "language club," a place where members share the same lingo.

In my life—as a child, a parent, a brother, a Catholic, a New Yorker, a Long Islander, a baseball fan, a girls' soccer coach, a writing teacher, a medievalist, the grandson of immigrants, a resident of Florida, a rock musician, and so on—I've joined dozens of language clubs. If you are in a room with my mother when she's on the phone, you can tell from her conversation style whether she's talking to her Italian relatives on the Lower East Side of Manhattan or to her Jewish relatives in suburban New Jersey.

Philosophers form a language club (*epistemology, ontology, metaphysics*); so do baseball players (*blue dart, high cheese, can of corn*); so do jazz musicians (*riff, downbeat, syncopation*); so do trial lawyers, tax lawyers, and estate attorneys; so do medical doctors and witch doctors; so do scientists and Scientologists; so do drug dealers and gang bangers; so do straights and gays; so do Buddhist monks; so do kindergarten kids; so do runway models.

Believe it or not, we are back to the serial comma. For three decades, I have included that final comma in a series only to watch helplessly as my journalism editors pluck it out with tweezers. The absurdity of this situation will become apparent:

1. I will write an essay like this one, inserting serial commas wherever necessary.
2. Mallary Tenore, my editor at the Poynter Institute, which follows Associated Press style, will take them out for our website.
3. Tracy Behar, my editor at Little, Brown, which favors serial commas, will put them all back in for the book version.

Now check this out, the beginning of a personal essay by the same Ms. Tenore:

> The death we all know lives in hearses, bagpipes, and graveyards.
> The death I know lives in Maybelline mascara, 15-year-old cars,
> and oversized clothes. I've tried most of my life to save these things.

"Hey, Mallary. What's up with all those serial commas?"

"I like them," she says. "They make things clearer."

So the editor who takes out my serial commas fights to keep her own. It's like being a Yankee fan married to a Red Sox fan. You can't win.

To own a preference is one thing, to peddle it another, so let's test the value of the serial comma in a paragraph that contains two of them, from author Michael Paterniti:

> But the Mississippi isn't open for baptisms today. A momentary upriver thaw has set it loose with high water, and by the time it's made St. Louis, by the time it's been birthed from its first trickles out of Lake Itasca in northern Minnesota, picked up speed and caught the blue pulse of the St. Croix River south of St. Paul; after it's already borrowed the Rock River in Illinois, usurped Iowa's Des Moines, held up the Illinois, and sucked in the Missouri, it's one pissed and frothy mother rushing with alluvium, sturgeon, and pebbles from pre-history. (from *Driving Mr. Albert*)

I count ninety-seven words in that passage. The first sentence contains only eight words. That means the author is asking the reader to manage an eighty-nine-word sentence, a clever, flowing description, the length of which mimics the actions it describes. Just as a river needs banks, a sentence like this needs just the right punctuation to keep the meaning from flooding our ability to comprehend. That semicolon in the middle provides visual relief and lets the reader take a quick breath. The commas help the author organize two great lists: "borrowed the Rock River in Illinois, usurped Iowa's Des Moines, held up the Illinois, and sucked in the Missouri" and "rushing with alluvium, sturgeon, and pebbles from pre-history." Deleting the serial comma leaves holes in the trousers of the story. When I see that final comma followed by *and*, it alerts me that I'm coming to the end of the list and prepares me for the next one.

To use the serial comma well, it helps to ask what we mean by a series. Easiest to understand is the series of *words:* "The

1960s became famous for sex, drugs, and rock 'n' roll." Or a series of *phrases:* "Abraham Lincoln prayed that a government of the people, by the people, and for the people would survive and prosper, even after the devastation of the Civil War." Or even a series of *clauses:* "When hell freezes over, when all the rivers run dry, and when swallows forget to come back to you-know-where, that's when I'll vote Republican." In these examples, the final comma keeps each element of meaning in its place.

Robert J. Samuelson of the *Washington Post* thinks there's more at stake here than just a few missing squiggles on the page: "If all this involved only grammar, I might let it lie. But the comma's sad fate is, I think, a metaphor for something larger: how we deal with the frantic, can't-wait-a-minute nature of modern life. The comma is, after all, a small sign that flashes PAUSE. It tells the reader to slow down, think a bit, and then move on. We don't have time for that. No pauses allowed. In this sense, the comma's fading popularity is also social commentary."

An alternative view comes from the punk band Vampire Weekend when they ask the musical question "Who gives a fuck about an Oxford comma?" The answer, boys, is "I do."

## KEEPSAKES

- The longer the elements in a series, the more likely you will need the serial comma, even if you belong to a language club that reviles them.
- The serial comma can help you organize a series of words, phrases, or clauses.
- When you enter a new professional or academic community, make sure you know its preferences regarding the serial comma and other language issues. Learn what is expected before you attempt to violate those expectations.
- Fight to the death (or at least to the pain) for the serial comma.

# 14

...

## Use the semicolon as a "swinging gate."

My wife, Karen, worked with cancer patients for many years and taught me that an essential part of recovery is a good sense of humor. So when our pastor, Father Robert Gibbons, announced to the congregation that he'd need surgery for colon cancer, I rushed up to him after Mass with this happy thought: "Father, by the time they're finished with you, you may be the only man in America who knows how to use a semicolon."

The joke had the desired effect on the brainy cleric: it made him laugh.

Come to think of it, the semicolon does look a little like a colon with a polyp. In truth, it is probably used more often these days in winking emoticons ;-) than as an alternative to the period or the comma. Maybe because a period sits atop a comma in the semicolon, it sends off a "neither here nor there" aura, threatening me with its indifference.

Whenever I'm having unsettled thoughts about punctuation, I turn to the work of Tom Wolfe. It was in the 1960s, after all, when Wolfe and his buddies began to bust the boundaries of conventional nonfiction. Among those innovations was a tendency to use punctuation like hot spice in a Cajun stew. A little this!...A little that*!*!...Bada boom!!!

So, on a whim, I pulled out a copy of Wolfe's 1998 novel, *A Man in Full,* and thumbed through it until my eye caught this passage on page 262:

> Outside, Conrad threw the newspaper away in a receptacle on the corner. He now had two twenty-dollar bills, a five, a one, two quarters, a dime, and a nickel. He started walking again. Over there—a telephone. He deposited a quarter. Nothing; dead; it was out of order; he couldn't get the quarter back; he jiggled the lever; he pounded the machine with the heel of his hand. A panic rose up in him, and now his extremities seemed to shrink and grow cold. He walked all the way back to the first telephone he had found. His heart was beating much too fast. Gingerly he deposited his last quarter—and placed another collect call to Jill—and told her the whole sad story.

I admire this paragraph for many reasons, but especially for the ambitious varieties of punctuation, including ten periods, seven commas, five semicolons, and three dashes. I am especially intrigued by the unusual use of the semicolon in that central sentence:

> Nothing; dead; it was out of order; he couldn't get the quarter back; he jiggled the lever; he pounded the machine with the heel of his hand.

I admit that I would have been tempted to replace each semicolon with a period. In its current form, the sentence seems unparallel and out of joint. But then, isn't that the point of the sentence? In a panic, a man without a cell phone needs coins and a working pay phone to make an important human connection. By means of those semicolons, Wolfe describes a frantic series of actions that proceed in chronological order and together form a single sentence, a complete thought.

Abandoning Wolfe, I went from author to author looking for semicolons and was surprised to see the radically different preferences of writers, scholars, and critics. A collection of essays by twentieth-century philosopher Hannah Arendt revealed very few among hundreds of pages, while cultural critic Greil Marcus relies on them again and again, especially when he is trying to connect/divide two short important points: "Innocence is the colorless stain on the national tapestry," he writes in *The Shape of Things to Come.* "It violates the landscape; the only way to kill it is to cut it out."

Or "Alone, Madison plays a third video that has turned up. Like the first two, it opens in black and white; then in color it shows him kneeling on his bedroom floor."

Or "In his cell Madison has a vision of a house on stilts set in sand, burning; then the smoke and fire are sucked back into the house with a snap."

What strikes me about these uses of the semicolon is their arbitrariness, as if the semicolon were a mark of choice rather than of rule. Let me demonstrate the array of options inspired by the Marcus sentence "The Swede is the good son; Jerry is the bad son."

But why not "The Swede is the good son. Jerry is the bad son."

Or "The Swede is the good son, but Jerry is the bad son."

Or "The Swede is the good son, Jerry the bad son."

Or, with some subordination, "While the Swede is the good son, Jerry is the bad son."

If none of those possibilities is incorrect, then what impulse governs the writer? It sounds to me as if the writer is left with a musical decision. To the ear of Marcus, the semicolon without conjunction creates a balance achieved by simultaneous connection and separation.

What kind of object connects and separates at the same time? I suppose there are a number of correct answers, including the Cross Your Heart bra, but I'm thinking more of the swinging gate. That's how I see the semicolon in my own writing, as a gate that stands between two thoughts, a barrier that forces separation but invites you to pass through to the other side.

The French call the semicolon the *point-virgule,* which means something like the "point comma," and they have been fighting over it for a long time, as only the frisky and fractious French can. A French satirist named François Cavanna exclaims that the semicolon is "a parasite, a timid, fainthearted, insipid thing, denoting merely uncertainty, a lack of audacity, a fuzziness of thought." On the other side, reports Jon Henley of the *Guardian,* are those French triumphalists who see the semicolon as expressive of a nuance and delicate ambiguity of which Anglo writers are incapable.

New York standard-bearers went gaga when reporter Sam Roberts found a semicolon in this subway sign: "Please put it in a trash can; that's good news for everyone." Comments Roberts in the *New York Times:* "Semicolon sightings in the city are unusual, period, much less in exhortations drafted by committees of civil servants. In literature and journalism, not to mention in advertising, the semicolon has been largely jettisoned as a pretentious anachronism."

But one person's pretentious anachronism may be another's timely solution. So when would I use the semicolon in my own writing? My choices are governed more by sight than sound, especially on those occasions when the run of the sentence threatens to overflow the banks established by weaker forms of punctuation. Consider this autobiographical passage:

Growing up a baseball fan in New York in the 1950s was to be engaged in an endless debate with neighbors on who was baseball's greatest center fielder: Duke Snider of the Dodgers, who was a sturdy defender and one of the most reliable sluggers in the league; or Willie Mays of the Giants, one of baseball's first great black superstars, a man who on any given day could astonish you with his bat or his glove; or my idol, Mickey Mantle, the Yankee heir to the crown of Joe DiMaggio, who, when he was healthy, could run faster and hit the ball farther than anyone who ever played the game.

If I used only commas in that rambling and energetic sentence, there would have been ten of them, too many to help the reader keep track of its parts. When I substituted semicolons, the parts became clear. You can see them with your eye: a topic clause, followed by one part Duke, one part Willie, one part the Mick.

There remains a place for the semicolon even at a time, according to English professor Jennifer DeVere Brody, when the misunderstood mark "suffers nightmares from its precarious position" between the period and the comma. Perhaps it will be saved by the likes of poet Maurya Simon, who has her own peculiar dreams about punctuation:

> The semicolon is
> Like a sperm forever frozen in its yearning towards an
>   ovum,
> like a tadpole swimming upstream to rouse the moon's
>   dropped coin…

An author who likens a semicolon to a sperm—now that's what I call a sex symbol—is living a life deep inside the English language.

## KEEPSAKES

- The semicolon, long the subject of neglect and ridicule, may be making a comeback.
- It offers the writer choices other than the comma, period, or dash.
- Think of the semicolon as a "swinging gate," a tool that can connect and separate at the same time.
- A long passage with lots of commas may confuse the reader. Consider the semicolon a mark that offers the reader a visual clue as to how a passage is organized.

# 15

### • • •

## Embrace the three amigos: colon, dash, and parentheses.

Marks of punctuation can be friends of the reader and writer— or adversaries, blood clots in the body of the story. In a poem titled "The Lesson," John Ciardi satirizes the tendency of academic experts to interrupt their thoughts with endless digressions and parenthetical remarks, a sharp point he makes by rhyming a thick swarm of "fleas" with "parentheses." One thought or phrase embeds itself within another and then another until the poet requires a set of ten parentheses to enclose the final words of the poem, like this: ")))))))))."

While clarity flows best from straight one-two-three writing—subject, verb, object—authors find many reasons to nest one idea within another. The conventions of punctuation may govern how to separate some phrases and enclose others, but the writer usually has several options to choose from to give visible form to such strategic interruptions. Some prefer commas or semicolons. Journalists use the dash as a crutch. Scholars prefer the intellectual detours framed by parentheses. I like the colon. Here's why:

### THE COLON

I so much appreciate the colon and its uses that, on at least one occasion, I unleashed two colons in a single sentence, something like this: "There was only one thing that could get Sam French to clean out his car: a hot date for the Homecoming Dance, but it even surprised him that he was able to clean out 19 pounds of trash and clutter: his lunch from the first day of school, half a baseball bat, four light sabers, 32 CDs, leftovers of a turkey sub, a bow tie, a big bag of Purina Puppy Chow, and a copy of the Koran."

There are more mundane uses of the colon: to separate a title from a subtitle, to separate hours from minutes in a time stamp (10:41 a.m.), to mark the salutation of a letter or a message. But my affection for the double dot derives from the colon's more literary applications. As demonstrated above, the colon can be used to highlight or emphasize a word or phrase: "a hot date for the Homecoming Dance"; it can introduce a quotation, a statement, a question, almost serving as a trumpet flourish in a Shakespeare play; and it can signal to the reader the beginning of a list, even a very long one. Or a short one like this example from crime author James Ellroy:

The Gorman job: stymied, quicksand, sludge.

In that dense little fragment, the colon acts as a substitute for verbs, translating what could have been the longer and less pulpy version: "As for the Gorman job, we were stymied. It was like walking through quicksand and sludge."

## THE DASH

My friend and mentor Don Fry has waged a holy war against the dash. Not the hundred-yard dash or a dash of paprika, but the horizontal mode of punctuation. Don, known as an enthusiastic exaggerator, has drummed up his opposition to the dash to ramming speed, and, truth be told, I can't remember seeing a single instance of that miniflatline in his own writing. He argues that writers use the dash profligately as a substitute for another more precise mark, and that the failure to learn, say, the colon or semicolon has created a dependence on the dash as the fallback punctuation tool.

I followed Don's lead for a while and found that in most cases I was better off with something other than a dash. Then one day I sat staring at a sentence in frustration until my eyes went out of focus and my nose started bleeding. Suddenly it hit me: I needed a dash! Once liberated from Don's orthodoxy, I began to see useful dashes everywhere, especially in the work of some of my favorite authors. My reading reminded me that the dash has two important uses: (1) a pair of dashes can be used—like these two—to embed one sentence or important thought in another; and (2) a dash can be used for emphasis in sharp moments when you want to end a sentence with a snap—like this.

Verlyn Klinkenborg writes essays that often appear in the *New York Times,* as did this one about a striking coincidence concerning an infamous rocker of the 1960s:

> It has been nearly 40 years since the rocker Jim Morrison died. But last week—the day after Morrison would have turned 65—he appeared in the *New York Times* in two obituaries: his father's and that of the owner of the Los Angeles club, Whisky A Go Go, where Morrison's band, the Doors, got its big break.

Let's revise that second sentence using commas to replace the dashes:

> But last week, the day after Morrison would have turned 65, he appeared in the *New York Times* in two obituaries…

Those commas would pass Don Fry's abolitionist test, but I don't think they make the sentence better. Marking off the embedded clause with dashes sets it apart from the rest of the sentence and highlights an interesting set of coincidences. With sixty-five being the traditional retirement age, that clause contains a backstory and a moral lesson of sorts, reminding us of the great music Morrison might have created if a dissolute lifestyle had not led him to an early and much-visited Paris grave.

Klinkenborg wonders aloud about such lessons:

> You can play this kind of moral sudoku—finding the patterns —
> with the obituaries every day. Look at those summary lives. See
> how they fit together—or not.

To fit together his words and ideas in those three sentences, the author uses two dashes to embed "finding the patterns" and another at the end to emphasize "or not." So Don, I say with the love of a true brother, abolishing slavery was good, abolishing the dash not so good, especially when that tool is used with care. Get over it, dude.

## A PARENTHETICAL AFTERTHOUGHT

When writers have an afterthought, sometimes they stick it between the boundaries of two parentheses. You won't find an excess of parenthetical expressions in this book or in much else of my work. I favored them in my youth, usually as an opportunity to show how humorous or sarcastic I could be. "Holden Caulfield loved his little sister, Phoebe, and had dreams of saving children from falling off a cliff (which is all well and good, but couldn't he find a nice Yankees hat to wear around the city instead of that phony red hunting cap?)." I strive for an effect in my writing called *steady advance,* an invitation to the reader to keep moving forward without the need to stop, stutter, or turn back. Whatever is said inside parentheses better be meaty or funny or interesting, because otherwise they stand as roadblocks of meaning. In the end, you have to take a detour or just drive around them to get where you were headed in the first place.

I have a feeling that screenwriter Jason Reitman shares some of my hang-ups about parentheses. In his film *Up in the Air,* he carried the argument to a moral dimension when a young woman accused the George Clooney character of being an inauthentic human being, a mere "parenthesis" in life. "A parenthesis?" answered a puzzled Clooney. She meant that he was incapable of a commitment to home or to others; he was a digression in the narrative of life, absolutely beside the point. That was my first encounter with a mark of punctuation used as an insult. But consider the possibilities:

> "Why do you always come across as such a question mark?" he asked, stroking her hair.
>
> "Better a question mark than a goddam ellipsis," she said, stepping away.
>
> "Semicolon!" he yelled, making an obscene gesture.
>
> "ASTERISK!" she screamed, with emphasis on the first syllable.

## KEEPSAKES

• The colon can be used to introduce a statement or a quotation, to signal the beginning of a long list, and to highlight a word or a phrase at the end of a sentence: like this.

• Do not use the dash because you have not mastered other forms of punctuation, such as the colon or semicolon.

• Use two dashes to embed one interesting or important thought within another.

• Use a single dash to highlight an element at the end of a sentence.

• In general, limit the number of reader interruptions caused by the roadblock of parentheses. Strive, instead, for steady advance.

# 16

...

# Let your ear help govern the possessive apostrophe.

Language scholars have a word for the sound made by the letter *s*. They call it a *sibilant,* which is derived from the Latin word meaning "to hiss." Leave it to scholars to call something a sibilant when they could have as easily called it a hissy, but that term may have been mistaken for a synonym we in the South use for *tantrum.*

In fact, E. B. White once wrote of Florida: "The South is the land of the sustained sibilant. Everywhere, for the appreciative visitor, the letter 's' insinuates itself in the scene: in the sound of sea and sand, in the singing shell, in the heat of sun and sky, in the sultriness of the gentle hours, in the siesta, in the stir of birds and insects." I reread those sweet sentences aloud just to enjoy their alliterative music (go ahead, try it) and was surprised at how the passage sizzled without sounding all snaky.

Now hold your tongue and recite: "She sells seashells by the seashore." Sometimes excessive use of the letter *s* turns the tongue into flypaper.

This brings me to E. B. White's famous teacher William Strunk Jr., author of the original edition of *The Elements of Style.* Written in 1918, the little book on grammar, style, and usage begins with this advice: "Form the possessive singular of nouns by adding 's." What could be clearer? "The *book's* simplicity and utility have made it a classic." We also learn that an 's is all we need when the plural form of a noun ends in something other than *s*. "The *men's* room needs some cleaning."

We do run into sticky problems of sibilance in those tricky cases when we attach one *s* to another. Professor Strunk tells us to add the 's no matter the final consonant of the noun and cites as examples "Charles's friend" and "Burns's poems."

This makes great sense to me because it echoes the way we would speak the word aloud. So it puzzles me that the *Associated Press Stylebook*, an influential work for journalists, argues that a simple apostrophe suffices after proper nouns ending in *s:* as in "Agnes' book" and "Jules' seat." I don't know about you, but when I read those aloud, the missing *s* trips up my tongue, and on the page it bothers my eyes. I would say "Agnes's book" and "Jules's seat."

There are classic examples when adding an *s* gives you that Velcro feeling: I would not say "Achilles's heel. Achilles' will do fine, thank you, with the prepositional phrase a convenient escape hatch: the teachings of Socrates.

Why does this matter? In a recent edition of my hometown newspaper, a story contained these two climactic sentences: "In Wes' last act, he fed a stranger and gave him a place to rest. It cost him his life." As I read this compelling story, I stopped every time I encountered the possessive "Wes'." The discord between my eye and ear made the absence of another *s* stand out like an elephant without a trunk. No one I know would say "Wes' last act"; any reader would say "Wes's." The stylebook justifies the missing *s* based on the value of "consistency and ease in remembering a rule." To which I respond: What about the needs and experiences of the reader?

Most language experts advise writers to ignore restrictions that require you to write or say something awkward or ugly, especially something that offends the ear. In this case, let us match punctuation to speech. As long as the snake isn't swallowing its tongue, let the reptile hiss.

## KEEPSAKES

- To form a possessive singular, add an *'s:* "Sadie's ring."
- To form a possessive plural, in most cases, add an apostrophe after the *s:* "The Puritans' journey."
- If the plural of a noun does not end in *s,* add an *'s* to form the possessive: "The children's field trip."
- If a proper noun (a name) ends in an *s,* add an *'s* in most cases, but let your ear guide you through the tough ones: "Archimedes' experiment."
- On this issue and all others, make sure you know which style manual governs your work. It may change as you change classes and teachers or jobs and professions.

# 17

● ● ●

# Take advantage of the versatility
# of quotation marks.

Marks of punctuation would seem at first glance not to carry much ideological weight, but look a little closer. Direct quotations, bits of dialogue, a soliloquy, a special title, a creative emphasis, even a not-so-hidden message can be defined and enhanced by those sets of inverted, elevated commas. They help me make a big point in this brief essay:

> It came to me in a dream. I'm not kidding. A definition of narrative came to me in a dream. In my sleep I could see the whole thing from initial capital to final period, and when I awoke it was still there, still vivid, and ready to be committed to paper.
>
> Narrative is nothing more or less than taking what happened "then" and rendering it in the "here and now."
>
> Something happens, in the world or in the imagination. The narrator takes the stuff of the past and, using narrative strategies such as scenes and dialogue, renders it as if it's happening in the present.
>
> The author may be from another era or from my own, but my transaction with the text is the same. I am transported to another time and place. I am immersed in an experience that feels as if it's going on right here, right now.

Other writers may have written that definition of narrative without the quotation marks around the words "then" and "here and now." For me, those marks are meant to signal a story, all the events that have happened in the past that might be converted into the experience of narrative.

We encounter quotation marks in the work of children and in the novels of Nobel laureates. But their use in capturing human speech on the page leads to two distinctive and perhaps contradictory effects. Dialogue is by definition a form of narrative, a taut bowstring of action within a story experienced directly by the reader. Take this scene in which I'm joking with two children at a bagel shop:

> We started to talk about snow. Jessica, a Florida kid, had never seen it before, but Maggie was a well-traveled pro and described to Jessica how snow felt and tasted, and how it was "mostly water." I regaled them with a snowy Christmas song. Maggie recognized this spasm for what it was, a cheap ploy for attention, and mostly ignored it. But Jessica's eyes widened. She turned to Maggie and whispered.
>
> "He's weird."
>
> "That's normal Roy," said Maggie.

Contrast that dialogue to a direct quotation in a news or nonfiction story: "Just because a story is dull does not make it true." I first said that at an academic conference years ago during an argument about how some writers fabricate scenes and details to make a story more interesting. But my statement is never presented as dialogue, that is, as a response to another speaker in a particular place and time. As a quote it looks disembodied, out of time, displaced, the opposite of what we strive for when we use dialogue. Dialogue builds action; quotations suspend it.

Then there is the use of quotation marks to create a minieditorial, a veiled expression of opinion. I remember my anger when

I read this commentary by Michelle Malkin in the immediate aftermath of 9/11:

> The media snobs are at it again. Wrinkling their noses at flag pins and patriotic ribbons. Tiptoeing around the word "terrorist." Preening about their precious "objectivity," "neutrality," and "independence."

Those last six quotation marks are not just punctuation. They are editorial language in disguise, a substitute for the phrase "so-called," an accusation that the claims of righteousness are false.

Perhaps Malkin picked up that trick from the editorial page of the *Wall Street Journal*, which, according to Jonathan Chait in the *New Republic*, has mastered the technique. He calls them "scare quotes," a phrase that can be traced back as far as 1960:

> The *Journal* also uses the device to imply skepticism about phenomena it finds ideologically inconvenient. Thus terms like "the deficit" and "inequality," if they must appear at all on the *Journal* editorial page, are constantly set off in scare quotes.

Chait argues that such techniques "also serve as a shortcut for the inattentive reader":

> Imagine a busy manager, quickly skimming over an editorial. He might come across a phrase like "the deficit," and suppose it's a bad thing, or "affordable" health care, and suppose it's a good thing. The scare quotes would usefully signal the shortcut for the writers, allowing them to wallow in their ideological prejudices without spelling out their empirical premises. But maybe the *Journal* doesn't really consider this a "downside."

Such dirty punctuation tricks, Chait admits, are used by many writers across the political spectrum. His analysis should serve as a lesson to all who care about the language and the democracy: messages are conveyed by even the tiniest marks on the page.

## KEEPSAKES

- Use quotation marks before and after a direct quotation.
- Do not include any language inside quotation marks that is not part of a direct quotation, unless you signal a deletion with ellipses or an insertion with brackets.
- Use single quotation marks inside double quotation marks to indicate a quote within a quote. Take special care in proofreading such constructions.
- Quotation marks can be used to highlight a word, perhaps because it represents slang, dialect, or other unexpected usage. But take care: overuse can render this strategy ineffective.
- Use quotation marks for the titles of smaller, rather than larger, works: a poem, a song, an essay, a chapter in a book.
- Punctuate quotations this way:
  - ✓ Periods and commas go inside closing quotation marks.
  - ✓ Colons and semicolons go outside.
  - ✓ Question marks and exclamation points go inside if they punctuate the quotation but outside if they apply to the whole sentence.

# 18

### • • •

## Use the question mark to generate reader curiosity and narrative energy.

In my senior year in high school, 1966, I played the keyboard in a garage band called T. S. and the Eliots. We played at school dances and sock hops and dominated the school party scene along with our rivals the Aardvarks, led by my friend Joe Edmundson. Joe and I wound up in college together and joined forces to form Tuesday's Children, playing songs from the Beatles, the Doors, Jimi Hendrix, and our favorites, the Rascals.

Perhaps our greatest moment came at a dance concert at Bryant College, where we opened for one of the most interesting and oddly influential groups in rock 'n' roll history, Question Mark and the Mysterians. The lead singer, born Rudy Martinez, legally changed his name to Question Mark, and, in a move foreshadowing the symbol of "the artist formerly known as Prince," Question Mark preferred to render his name as the mark of punctuation. If you happen to have a 45 rpm record of the group's greatest hit, "96 Tears," you will see the band's name rendered thus: *? and the Mysterians.*

But who was Question Mark? And how did he become one of the godfathers of the punk rock movement? And why am I asking these questions in a book about grammar and language?

The answer has to do with the extraordinary power of the question mark.

Consider this paragraph from James Wood, author of *How Fiction Works:*

> In this book I try to ask some of the essential questions about the art of fiction. Is realism real? How do we define a successful metaphor? What is a character? When do we recognize a brilliant use of detail in fiction? What is point of view, and how does it work? What is imaginative sympathy? Why does fiction move us? These are old questions, some of which have been resuscitated by recent work in academic criticism and literary theory; but I am not sure that academic criticism and literary theory have answered them very well. I hope, then, that this book might be one which asks theoretical questions but answers them practically—or to say it differently, asks a critic's questions and offers a writer's answers.

That is a nifty paragraph, one I wish I had written myself. It has the basic structure required of classic paragraphs: a sharply drawn topic sentence at the start; by my count, eight examples of questions; a complicating turn in the middle (about the inadequacy of criticism and theory); and a resounding conclusion that gives me confidence that this author knows what he's talking about.

And look at all those questions, powered by all those initial question words: How? What? When? Why? Together, they serve as an unofficial table of contents. They act as little promises from the author: if you keep reading, I promise that these important questions, and others, will be answered for you.

The question mark, used well, may be the most profoundly human form of punctuation. Unlike the other marks, the question mark—except perhaps when used in a rhetorical question—imagines the Other. It envisions communication not as assertive but as interactive, even conversational.

The question is the engine of debates and interrogations, of mysteries solved and secrets to be revealed, of conversations between student and teacher, of anticipation and explanation. There are Socratic questions, of course, where the interrogator already knows the answer. But more powerful is the open-ended question, the one that invites the other to act as the expert in telling his own experience:

> *Q:* What was your first experience of anti-Semitism?
> *A:* It was when a lady spit at my mother in the street and called her "that Jew."
> *Q:* What was your reaction?
> *A:* I was shocked. I thought we were all Catholic. I didn't realize at the time that my grandmother was Jewish.

Questions can be theological and metaphysical and tend to be the form in which human beings examine their place in the universe. Why is there so much violence in the world? Do human beings really exercise free will? Does life continue in some spiritual form after death? If God is all good and all powerful, why did he create hurricanes and earthquakes that cause so much suffering? Is there life elsewhere in the universe? Is this all there is? Such questions, and the knowledge of our own mortality, separate us from all other creatures on the planet. Or am I being too hard on my dog, Rex? There are times when I see questions in his eyes: Am I going to have to stand next to this cabinet door all day before you give me a cookie? Are you going to finish that, or will you deign to give me a taste? Will you ever open that back door, or am I going to have to pee on the rug?

For the reader and writer, it is the great question that gives energy to a narrative. Fans of the Harry Potter books will remember the list of questions we had stored up as we waited for J. K. Rowling's final book in the series of seven: Who will live, and who will die? Is Headmaster Dumbledore really dead? Is Professor Snape good or evil? Will Ron and Hermione ever hook up? What will happen to Hogwarts School of Magic?

We feel the power of such narrative questions as we enjoy—

and at times endure—many expressions of popular culture: Will the bluesy guy with the gray hair become the next American Idol? Will the Cubs ever win the World Series? Will baseball slugger Barry Bonds become the all-time home-run leader, or will revelations about steroid use destroy him? Did Michael Jackson ever... well, you fill in the blank.

In "Enrique's Journey" Sonia Nazario retraces the perilous odyssey of a teenage boy traveling from Honduras through Mexico to the United States to find his mother. The book version arrived as America struggled to reassert its identity and find its cultural soul in its great debates over immigration, sovereignty, and the security of its borders. As I began reading the story of Enrique, I was struck by the transparency of the author's narrative direction. Here's the final paragraph of her prologue:

> Children who set out on this journey usually don't make it. They end up back in Central America, defeated. Enrique was determined to be with his mother again. Would he make it?

A popular aphorism reminds us that it's about the journey, not the destination. With narrative, that slogan rings false. It's about the journey *and* the destination, the payoff, the solution to the mystery, the answer to the question.

"Would he make it?" That question will drive me for most of three hundred pages to find out.

Which brings us back to my earlier questions about *? and the Mysterians.* According to a variety of online sources, the punky garage band formed in 1962 in Bay City, Michigan. They were best known for the hit "96 Tears," which horny teenage boys assumed was an inversion of their sacred number 69. A Japanese science fiction movie called *The Mysterians* may have inspired the band's name.

The birth name of "?" was Rudy Martinez, who became the leader and songwriter for one of the first Latino rock groups to achieve wide popular success. He continued in the music business for many years, long after the Mysterians broke up, but maintained his identity as Question Mark, refused to appear without his sunglasses, and claimed that he had invaded Earth from the planet Mars after years of living with the dinosaurs. I suppose there are more questions to be asked, but we'll leave those to his spiritual adviser.

## KEEPSAKES

Master the practical uses of the question mark as a signal of the interrogative mode:

- Answers to "frequently asked questions" help readers learn about a new service or experience.
- The best interview questions are open ended, which means the interviewer does not know the answer in advance.
- Questions often imagine another person, inviting a response or a continuing conversation.
- The best stories are formed around a question that the story answers for the reader: Who did it? Guilty or not guilty? Will she win the money? Will he get the girl?

# 19

...

# Reclaim the exclamation point.

Among mystery writer Elmore Leonard's ten guidelines for authors is this advice on exclamation points: "You are allowed only three," he reminded me in a buffet line at the Tucson Festival of Books, "in every one hundred thousand words of prose."

Before I either pile on the exclamation point, or throw my body over it for protection, allow me to recall one of the first pieces of research I read on the effects of word processing. It came from a professor who contrasted the work of students writing on Apple computers with those using IBM personal computers. The good professor concluded that while the Apple kids wrote cleaner-looking stories, the PC kids produced better writing.

More than a quarter century later, any person who sits at a computer to write can control how the text will look on the screen or the printed page. On a Royal Standard typewriter (kids, ask your grandparents), my choice was limited to upper-case and lowercase type, margin settings, and perhaps a ribbon that could produce black or red type. Now your humble servant can control white space, typeface, type size, italics, bold-face, borders, underlining, color, the style of bulleted lists, and much more.

I suspect that the liberty to influence how the page looks has altered writing in our time. I've run into contemporary books in which the author has added design elements—some of them dramatic—to what otherwise would have been considered an inviolable text. Such experimentation can be traced back to eighteenth-century novels such as *Tristram Shandy,* in which the author, Laurence Sterne, interrupts the text with plot diagrams and one dramatic page of mourning printed in black.

More than two centuries later, *The Emigrants,* a novel by German author W. G. Sebald, includes everything from dozens of family photographs to copies of handwritten messages. *The Curious Incident of the Dog in the Night-Time,* a novel by Mark Haddon written in the voice of an autistic boy, contains dozens of flowcharts, maps, mathematical formulas, signage, schedules—all rendered in a variety of typefaces. One of the odd pleasures in reading the work of the late David Foster Wallace is the opportunity to escape from the main text to explore epic footnotes, always rendered at the bottoms of pages in thickets of tiny type.

Amid all the bells and whistles of modern bookmaking, even the exclamation point is enjoying a comeback.

After a brief revival during the New Journalism of the 1960s—during which punctuation often looked like an LSD hallucination—the exclamation point was eschewed by serious writers. That little phallic bat and ball exposed itself mostly in children's literature and romance novels. Elmore Leonard assumed the usual position with this advice to writers: "Keep your exclamation points under control.... If you have a knack of playing with exclaimers the way Tom Wolfe does, you can throw them in by the handful." The secret message broadcast by the likes of Leonard is that the exclamation point reveals a flighty or playful personality.

Times have certainly changed. An e-mail I recently received contained a six-word sentence followed by eleven (yes, eleven!) exclamation points. The message, written by a man, challenges the way in which gender distinctions influence the use of punctuation.

Originally aired on October 7, 1993, an episode of *Seinfeld* included this exchange between Elaine Benes and her boyfriend, Jake, about his failure to demonstrate appropriate enthusiasm in a handwritten message:

> *Elaine:* Well, I was just curious why you didn't use an exclamation point?
> *Jake:* What are you talking about?
> *Elaine:* See, right here you wrote "Myra had the baby," but you didn't use an exclamation point.... I mean if one of your close friends had a baby and I left you a message about it, I would use an exclamation point.
> *Jake:* Well, maybe I don't use my exclamation points as haphazardly as you do....
> *Elaine:* I just thought you would be a little more excited about a friend of mine having a baby.
> *Jake:* Ok, I'm excited. I just don't happen to like exclamation points.
> *Elaine:* Well, you know Jake, you should learn to use them. Like the way I'm talking right now, I would put an exclamation point at the end of all these sentences! On this one! And on that one!
> *Jake:* Well, you can put one on this one: I'm leaving!

Later in the episode, Mr. Lippman, Elaine's boss at Pendant Publishing, notices that her final edit of Jake's manuscript contains an inordinate number of ... you guessed it!

> *Elaine:* Well, I felt that the writing lacked a certain emotion and intensity.
> *Lippman:* Oh, "It was a damp and chilly afternoon, so I decided to put on my sweatshirt!" ... You put an exclamation point after sweatshirt?

Which brings us to the *emoticon*. That new word was created by blending *emotion* and *icon*. The *AHD* defines it as "a series of keyed characters used especially in e-mail to indicate an emotion, such as pleasure [:-)] or sadness [:-(]." Something weird just happened on my computer screen when I typed those two emoticons. Like a scene out of *2001: A Space Odyssey,* my computer attempted to replace my typed images with smiley and sad faces: ☺ ☹. Which leads me to the suspicion that some virus has filled my word processor with a petri dish full of emoticons. Just as the Rosetta stone helped us translate Egyptian hieroglyphics, a simple Internet search will lead you to dozens of emoticons to signify everything from humor, to lust, to mischief. ;-)

In the land of the emoticon, the exclamation point seems downright weighty, a staff of sturdy stuff.

## KEEPSAKES

• If you want to be considered a serious writer, never, ever use emoticons in e-mail messages. The occasional exclamation point is fine.

• If you are tempted to use an exclamation point, read the passage aloud. If the content contains excitement or emotional intensity, perhaps you don't need the exclaimer.

• The more serious the story, the fewer exclamation points will be appropriate.

• The less serious the story, the more liberty you can take with !!!!!!!!

• The most practical use of exclaimers is after a quotation or a bit of dialogue that expresses excitement or intense emotion: "The Russians are coming!"

• In a story, a single exclamation point can go a long way.

# 20

## ...

## Master the elliptical art of leaving things out.

The ellipsis remains among the most underappreciated and versatile tools of punctuation. The singular is *ellipsis,* the plural *ellipses.* Derived from the Greek word meaning "to fall short," an ellipsis is usually represented by three dots, with a space before and after each ellipsis mark or point ( ... ). The basic function of an ellipsis is to signal to the reader that something has been left out. But that is just one of the practical and creative uses of those three little dots.

Here is an excerpt from my book *Writing Tools:*

> I love the wisdom that the best writers write not just with their hands, heads, and hearts, but with their feet. They don't sit at home thinking or surfing the Web. They leave their houses, offices, and classrooms.... Writers, including writers of fiction, collect words, images, details, facts, quotes, dialogue, documents, scenes, expert testimony, eyewitness accounts, statistics, the brand of the beer, the color and make of the sports car, and, of course, the name of the dog.

That ellipsis in the middle indicates that I have left something out of this quote, and indeed I have: "The great Francis X. Clines of the *New York Times* once told me that he could always find a story if he could just get out of the office." In a report or scholarly study, an ellipsis tells us that the writer has omitted a number of words or sentences, presumably to spare the reader from unnecessary information. Like a photographer who crops a photo to omit extraneous images and improve composition, a writer has an ethical obligation to "ellip" (don't bother looking; I made that up) responsibly, that is, to omit words or sentences in such a way that the spirit and meaning of the original text are not altered.

The game changes when we turn from formal reports to narrative writing. The clearer the shift from report to story, the more freedom the writer has to use ellipsis points to create special effects. In the vampire novel *Fledgling,* author Octavia Butler uses ellipses to dramatize dialogue, a technique that leaves nothing ambiguous:

> I said, "Someone found me as I was waking up in the cave. I don't know how long I'd been there. Several days, at least. But finally, I was regaining consciousness, and someone found me. I didn't know at the time that it was…a person, a man. I didn't know anything except…I killed him."

Real people and fictional characters do speak with pauses, here indicated with ellipses, which can signal everything from hesitation to thoughtfulness to forgetfulness to…dramatic emphasis.

The use of ellipses, in partnership with other marks of punctuation, turns out to be a powerful tool of narrative, a strategy that can communicate an urgent or suspenseful message and reflect back on the creativity of the writer. In this passage from "The Long Fall of One-Eleven Heavy," Michael Paterniti re-creates the final seconds before the crash of a jetliner filled with passengers. The pilot's name is Urs:

> Urs radioed something in German, *emergency checklist Air conditioning smoke.* Then in English, Sorry? .-.-.- Maintaining at ten

thousand feet, his voice urgent, the words blurring. The smoke was thick, the heat increasing, the checklists, the bloody· checklists -.-.-.- leading nowhere, leading—We are declaring emergency now at, ah, time, ah, zero-one-two-four -.-.-.- We have to land immediate—

The instrument panel—bright digital displays—went black. Both pilot and copilot were now breathing frantically.

Then nothing.

The author is using all the tools available to him to build drama and make meaning, from his own words to dialogue from the cockpit to verbal punctuation to italic typeface to sentence fragments to straight narration to short paragraphs to shorter paragraphs to an innovative form of elliptical punctuation.

Ellipses also can deliver a sense of uncertainty, not as a foil to clarity or understanding but as an acknowledgment that not everything can be known, a feeling of mystery captured in the famous ending of *The Great Gatsby:*

> Gatsby believed in the green light, the orgiastic future that year by year recedes before us. It eluded us then, but that's no matter— tomorrow we will run faster, stretch out our arms farther. . . . And one fine morning——
>
> So we beat on, boats against the current, borne back ceaselessly into the past.

I've read that passage dozens of times but have never before focused on the punctuation. Now I notice the nuances: the dash between "matter" and "tomorrow" with no period in sight, the spaces between the ellipsis points, the long dash after "morning"— all enhancing the crazed sense of love, power, wealth, and loss at the heart of the American experience.

However versatile the ellipsis, it is not the sole method of omission. I remember from the comic books of my youth those hilarious moments when a character would, say, run into a wall. The offended nose would swell to ten times its normal size, and symbols like these #*%! would stand in for the profanity.

For more serious contexts? Enter the humble hyphen.

Where an ellipsis can take the place of words and sentences, the hyphen steps in for letters. When I first taught writing as a graduate assistant at Stony Brook University, I noticed that some of my Jewish students would not spell out the name of God. Instead, they rendered the name of the Almighty with a hyphen in place of the vowel: *G-d*. I've been told that many observant Jews still follow this practice, which can be traced to the biblical story of Moses. When God appears to Moses in the form of a burning bush, Moses asks his name. God responds with four letters—all consonants—a word unpronounceable by vowel-burdened human beings but translated in the Bible as "I am who am." The lesson: God is so holy, so worthy of reverence, that mankind cannot even speak his name. The Greek word for "four letters" is *tetragrammaton* (notice the hint of that magical word *grammar* hiding in the middle). The sacred four letters are sometimes represented as YHWH, giving us the name Yahweh; sometimes as JHVH, giving us Jehovah.

Much more often, hyphens serve to make the profane barely acceptable, as when general-interest publications, so as not to offend, render the N-word as n-----, or the F-word as f---. Daring or mischievous editors sometimes just take out the vowel. I understand the strategic compromise behind the use of those hyphens, a desire to inform the public of what was said or written, but in a veiled fashion, the way some bookstore racks obscure part of the cover of a girlie magazine. The fun starts when a politician or football coach rips off a string of expletives slapped in the newspaper as:

> If that f------ a------ speaks to me like that again, I'm going to shut his m------------ mouth with my size 16 shoe, and if he doesn't believe that, he can take his skinny m------------ a-- and walk right out that door.

It might take a crossword master the likes of Merl Reagle to puzzle out such a passage. But remember this: if you must leave something out of your text, whether for brevity, taste, or dramatic effect, the humble hyphen and the elegant ellipsis are among your best friends.

## KEEPSAKES

- One set of three dots is called an *ellipsis*. Two or more sets are called *ellipses*.
- The dots in an ellipsis are called *ellipsis points* or *ellipsis marks*.
- Ellipses indicate the places in, say, a research paper, where part of a quoted text has been left out for the sake of brevity, clarity, or focus.
- Ellipses can help characterize the nature of speech in a direct quotation or a bit of dialogue.
- Ellipses can help slow down the text, signaling suspense or delay.
- Creative authors can, in special cases, play with the form of ellipses to produce special effects.
- Use a period at the end of a complete sentence, then an ellipsis, like this....
- Hyphens can be used to substitute for letters in words, sacred or profane.
- One professional organization of language scholars suggests that when words are omitted from a quoted text, the author should use not just an ellipsis but a bracketed ellipsis [...]—as if scholars needed another tool to disfigure academic prose.

...

# 21

# Reach into the "upper case" to unleash the power of names.

During my days as a newspaper writer, I would often receive from readers handwritten letters of complaint or protest. Some were pages and pages long, with all kinds of eccentric and slightly alarming forms of penmanship, including the use of different-colored inks. The references to Scripture, for example, might appear in red. But the angriest phrases were always carved into the page in capital letters. As in: MR. CLARK, YOU SHOULD BE ASHAMED TO CALL YOURSELF A WRITER! A friend told me about the day she received an e-mail message written with lots of capital letters and sent this response: "Please stop shouting at me." So one use of "all caps" is to shout at the reader, as captured on this bumper sticker: "Don't Make Me Use UPPERCASE..."

When we first learned about the uppercase (a reference to where typesetters stored those capital letters), the message was much softer: "A sentence begins with a capital letter and ends with a period." It doesn't take long, however, for the young reader and writer to learn that there are many, many, MANY more uses of the capital letter—along with sets of rules about proper and improper usage.

But within the light of a grammar of intent, the capital letter becomes a tool, a way to create meaning and emphasis, distinguish style and voice, and unleash the power of names. Consider this delightful passage from *On Boxing* by Joyce Carol Oates on the brutal but poetic names of boxers:

> [F]or the most part a boxer's ring name is chosen to suggest something...ferocious: Jack Dempsey of Manassa, Colorado, was "The Manassa Mauler"; the formidable Harry Greb was "The Human Windmill"; Joe Louis was, of course, "The Brown Bomber"; Rocky Marciano, "The Brockton Blockbuster"; Jake LaMotta, "The Bronx Bull"... Roberto Durán, "Hands of Stone." ...More recent are Ray "Boom-Boom" Mancini, Thomas "Hit-Man" Hearns, James "Hard Rock" Green, Al "Earthquake" Carter, Frank "The Animal" Fletcher, Donald "The Cobra" Curry, Aaron "The Hawk" Pryor, "Terrible" Tim Witherspoon, "Bonecrusher" Smith,...Hector "Macho Man" Camacho. "Marvelous" Marvin Hagler changed his name legally to Marvelous Marvin Hagler before his fight with Thomas Hearns brought him to national prominence.

The poet loves the names of things, and Oates carries that literary sensibility into fiction and nonfiction prose. She proves that all writers can take advantage of proper names and proper adjectives to tantalize and inform readers.

The workbook *Writers Inc* offers this nice list of commonly capitalized names:

Days of the week: Tuesday
Months: September
Holidays, holy days: Thanksgiving
Periods, events in history: the Renaissance
Special events: the Boston Tea Party
Political parties: the Republican Party
Official documents: Declaration of Independence
Trade names: Oscar Mayer hot dogs
Formal epithets: Vlad the Impaler

Official titles: Mayor Rick Baker
Official state nicknames: the Hoosier State
Geographical names: Australia, Ireland, Ohio, El Paso,
Park Avenue, the Sahara Desert, Pumpkin Creek,
Yellowstone National Park

Let's see how one writer, Erik Larson, takes advantage of the capital letter in his nonfiction book *The Devil in the White City* (notice how the first word and all the key words in that title are capitalized):

In Paris on the Champ de Mars, France opened the Exposition Universelle, a world's fair so big and glamorous and so exotic that visitors came away believing no exposition could surpass it. At the heart of the exposition stood a tower of iron that rose one thousand feet into the sky, higher by far than any man-made structure on earth. The tower not only assured the eternal fame of its designer, Alexandre Gustave Eiffel, but also offered graphic proof that France had edged out the United States for dominance in the realm of iron and steel, despite the Brooklyn Bridge, the Horseshoe Curve, and other undeniable accomplishments of American engineers.

The names bring the passage to life: the name of the city, the street, the fair, the designer, and the American engineering accomplishments. It is the specificity of the names that gives the paragraph authority and their beauty that lends it style.

The American answer to France was the 1893 World's Columbian Exposition in Chicago, and Larson's description makes use of proper names in all their variety:

Visitors wore their best clothes and most somber expressions, as if entering a great cathedral. Some wept at its beauty. They tasted a new snack called Cracker Jack and a new breakfast food called Shredded Wheat. Whole villages had been imported from Egypt, Algeria, Dahomey, and other far-flung locales....

A single exhibit hall had enough interior volume to have housed the U.S. Capitol, the Great Pyramid, Winchester Cathedral, Madison Square Garden, and St. Paul's Cathedral, all at the same time....Never before had so many of history's brightest lights, including Buffalo Bill, Theodore Dreiser, Susan B. Anthony, Jane Addams, Clarence Darrow, George Westinghouse, Thomas Edison, Henry Adams, Archduke Francis Ferdinand, Nikola Tesla, Ignace Paderewski, Philip Armour, and Marshall Field, gathered in one place at one time. Richard Harding Davis called the exposition "the greatest event in the history of the country since the Civil War."

The author is not dropping names to impress the reader with his knowledge. Each name is strategically suggestive, to convey the facts of history and also to evoke a culture filled with the energy of events, places, people, and products.

In my own recent travels, I came across *The Language of Names: What We Call Ourselves and Why It Matters* by Justin Kaplan and Anne Bernays. Along with countless interesting stories about names, Mr. Kaplan and the saucy Ms. Bernays provide us with a rich cultural context for writers' fascination with names. They quote Sigmund Freud from *Totem and Taboo:* "A human being's name is a principal component in his person, perhaps a piece of his soul."

This paragraph sealed the deal:

Names are what anthropologists call cultural universals. Apparently there has never been a society able to get along without them. They are among the first things we ask or learn when we meet someone new, and we use them to form immediate but often unreliable conclusions about personality and ethnicity. Names shape the language of the daily drama of gesture, avowal, and inference that is part of our social life. Full personal names, first and last taken together, stand at the intersection of opposing pulls: they set the bearer apart as an individual but also provide the bearer with family and extended kinship ties, and so focus both the present and the past. And beyond this, they have an occult associative and symbolic power. They are charms.

And charming, like the glamour of grammar. So never forget in your research to get the name, not only of the person but also of the dog and cat, the flower on the windowsill, the street behind the house, the village, the founder of the town.

## KEEPSAKES

• Capitals are called uppercase letters because typesetters would store them in the "upper case." Small letters were kept in the "lower case."

• Sentences begin with a capital letter and end with a period, or full stop.

• Capitals have a variety of effects on the reader, and full capitals may suggest that the writer is shouting.

• Capital letters unleash the power of naming, an act central to all literary experiences.

• Capitalize the names of people, places, holidays, historical periods and events, official documents, trade names, official titles, and geographical places. Such names fall into the category of "proper nouns."

• • •

# 22

# Vary your use of punctuation to create special effects.

Whenever we concentrate on the *rules* of grammar and punctuation, we run the risk of veiling the creativity and flexibility
available to authors who think of them as *tools* of meaning and
effect. Let's take as an example a splendid passage from Laura
Hillenbrand's bestselling book *Seabiscuit,* a stirring narrative
history of one of America's legendary racehorses. In this scene,
Hillenbrand describes the mystical glory of Seabiscuit's last great
stretch run in the 1940 Santa Anita Handicap:

> In the midst of all the whirling noise of that supreme moment,
> Pollard [the jockey] felt peaceful. Seabiscuit reached and pushed and
> Pollard folded and unfolded over his shoulders and they breathed
> together. A thought pressed into Pollard's mind: *We are alone.*
>
> Twelve straining Thoroughbreds; Howard and Smith in the
> grandstand; Agnes in the surging crowd; Woolf behind Pollard,
> on Heelfly; Marcela up on the water wagon with her eyes squeezed
> shut; the leaping, shouting reporters in the press box; Pollard's
> family crowded around the radio in a neighbor's house in
> Edmonton; tens of thousands of roaring spectators and millions
> of radio listeners painting this race in their imaginations: All this
> fell away. The world narrowed to a man and his horse, running.

Consider all the tools of language used—and not used—to create this startling, cinematic slow-motion effect. Not used, for example, are commas to break up what might look like a run-on sentence: "Seabiscuit reached and pushed and Pollard folded and unfolded over his shoulders and they breathed together." You will find three independent clauses in that sentence without the hint of a comma. You could argue that the brevity of these clauses makes punctuation unnecessary, even intrusive. I would suggest a more literary effect. That the sentence describes a continuous, flowing action of horse and jockey: first horse, then jockey, then both together. The action, if you will, is running on. And so is the sentence.

Then something startling happens, marked by the sentence "*We are alone.*" The author considers this thought so important, so dramatic, that she emphasizes it in three ways: she expresses it in the shortest possible sentence; she places it at the end of a paragraph, next to a bar of white space; and she sets it apart with italic type. (Perhaps in an online multimedia version, we could make the words flash and glow on the screen to the accompaniment of an angelic chorus of synthesized harps.)

What follows is an exercise in literary and cinematic time management, a slow-motion effect that expands the moment in the cause of suspense. Each of eight phrases leading to the final main clause ("All this fell away") happens in an instant as the camera pans from the track to the grandstand to the stables to the press box to a house in Canada to an audience of millions around the world. Unlike the earlier sentence, this is not one continuous motion, but simultaneous action, the literary equivalent of a cinematic montage. Here commas would not be strong enough to enclose the distinct actions. Periods would insult their spontaneity. The solution: that oft-maligned expression of Aristotle's golden mean, the icon that graces the cover of this book, the semicolon. Seven to be exact.

The final, startling insight comes in the form of one triumphant sentence: "The world narrowed to a man and his horse, running." The movement is from a big noun ("world") to two particular nouns ("man and horse") resolving themselves in a single word, a present participle ("running") that, standing at the end of the sentence, connotes perpetual motion... immortality.

Speaking of immortality, I conclude this section on punctuation with a letter from John Adams to Thomas Jefferson, as quoted in David McCullough's biography of our second president.

> I never delighted much in contemplating commas and colons, or in spelling or measuring syllables; but now... if I attempt to look at these little objects, I find my imagination, in spite of all my exertions, roaming in the Milky Way, among the nebulae, those mighty orbs, and stupendous orbits of suns, planets, satellites, and comets, which compose the incomprehensible universe; and if I do not sink into nothing in my own estimation, I feel an irresistible impulse to fall on my knees, in adoration of the power that moves, the wisdom that directs, and the benevolence that sanctifies this wonderful whole.

Now there's a man living fully inside the English language—writing to another.

## KEEPSAKES

Find a passage from a story that works for you as well as the *Seabiscuit* passage works for me. Do a close reading of the passage, focusing on punctuation. Ask yourself:

- What is the passage trying to accomplish, and how does the punctuation help?
- Does the author use a little punctuation or a lot?
- How rich a variety of punctuation exists in the passage?
- Are there alternate ways to punctuate the passage?

# PART THREE

...

# Standards

When most people think of grammar, they think of rules. But that word *rule* means different things for the "descriptive" grammarian than it does for the "prescriptive." Native English speakers begin to understand the rules that govern our language at an early age. We've learned from linguists like Noam Chomsky that those deep structures, or rules, ingrained in every language, allow us to generate millions of sentences throughout our lives. Each one of us uses these deep rules to make meaning, even if we don't recognize them as such, even if we don't know we are using them.

Another set of established rules continues to influence the use of written English and the formal uses of spoken English. Together they create something called Standard English. In almost every case in this book, I follow the standards of Standard

English, but I do so recognizing that this prescriptive approach exaggerates the value of certain kinds of usage and the dangers of others, such as splitting infinitives, using double negatives, and ending sentences with prepositions.

Enforced in the most heavy-handed way, the prescriptive approach creates the impression that these "mistakes" represent some failure of understanding, when, truth be told, famous writers have ignored or broken these rules with impunity for centuries and continue to do so. You should also feel free to break them, with one proviso: first you must learn them. Once mastered, these "rules" become "tools" and their violation becomes strategic.

It is always helpful to undertake a formal study of the common mistakes and misunderstandings that all of us fall victim to at one time or another. With some focused attention you can avoid subject-verb disagreement; pronoun-antecedent disagreement; confusing different words that sound alike; using the wrong (subjective or objective) case; failure to write complete, well-punctuated sentences; misplaced modifiers; and a few more.

This section will help you sidestep the traps that can lead to distracting variations from standard usage. You'll learn how to identify the sources of ambiguity, how to balance gender fairness with traditional usage and style, and even how to tell the difference between *lie* and *lay*.

You will often be judged, fairly or unfairly, on your use of language, both written and spoken, so it makes sense to learn the standards that teachers, editors, and potential employers are inclined to expect. Grammar may be magical, but remember this: a magician is an illusionist, someone who learns the strategic uses of physics and engineering.

# 23

•••

## Learn to *lie* or *lay,* as well as the principles behind the distinction.

In his famous essay "Politics and the English Language," George Orwell asserts that grammar and syntax are of no importance, "so long as one makes one's meaning clear." Yet I cannot recall a single lapse in old George's language that would require the application of a hickory stick to the seat of his anti-imperial pants.

As a writer I may want to stretch the language to the snapping point for effect, but as a reader I demand attention to Standard English, not just for clarity but also to avoid distractions that would make the act of reading less fluent. On the other hand, when a bank robber yells, "Lay on the floor facedown with your hands over your head," I'm disinclined to respond, "Excuse me, sir, but don't you mean 'lie'?"

There's *lie,* there's *lay,* and there's even *lei.*

I have played in rock bands since 1964 and over the years have seen more than an occasional gig with a Hawaiian theme: tropical fruit punch, shirts with images of hula dancers, papier-mâché volcanoes, twangy tunes from the Ventures. At some point a host or hostess approaches with a ring of flowers and asks mischievously, "How about a lei?" Which, of course, is a naughty play on *lay,* common slang for having sex.

That spicy introduction leads me to one of the most confusing grammatical distinctions of all time: the difference between *lie* and *lay*. It took me years, I'm embarrassed to say, to master it. But here's the good news: By solving this problem, I learned some language tools I have been able to use in other meaningful ways. That's right. I've turned a language problem into a language lesson.

Here's the simplest way to remember the difference: *lie* means "to recline"; *lay* means "to place." As in "I lay the cushions on the floor so I can lie in comfort." (You can use the vowel sounds as a memory aid: *lie* / recline; *lay* / place.)

Confusion sweeps in when we move from the present tense to the past. Alas, the past tense of *lie* happens to be *lay:* "When I heard the news, I lay on the bed in disbelief." And the past tense of *lay* is *laid,* as in "The bank robbers laid their weapons on the ground."

Two important language tools will help you master the distinction between *lie* and *lay,* words that, according to the *AHD,* have been confused for at least seven hundred years. (Don't you feel better?) The first is to remember the *principal parts* of the verb. Learning the parts of a verb helps you avoid mistakes that occur when those parts are *irregular,* that is, different from the usual pattern.

Take a verb such as *help.* The principal parts are the simple present (*help*), the simple past (*helped*), and the past participle (*helped*). So today I help. Yesterday I helped. In the past, I have helped. Easy enough because the verb is *regular.*

Not so with a verb such as *run.* The simple past, we know, is not *runned,* although a smart child might say that, applying the rule for a regular verb. The principal parts are *run, ran, run.* Today I run. Yesterday I ran. In the past decade, I have run ten marathons.

Both *lie* and *lay* are irregular and hence more confusing.

> *Lie:* Today I *lie* on the bed. Yesterday I *lay* on the bed. I
> have *lain* on that bed so many times there are holes in
> the mattress.

*Lay:* Today I *lay* my cards on the table. Yesterday I *laid* my cards on the table. I have *laid* my cards on the table so many times that I was bound to win.

Learning the principal parts of verbs will help you communicate your meaning and avoid unintended confusion.

Another useful grammar tool is the distinction between transitive and intransitive verbs. The word *transitive* derives from the Latin and means "to go across" or "to pass over." Thus, a transitive verb is one in which the meaning passes over from the verb to a direct object. Verbs such as *hit* and *pummel* almost always take an object.

Lots of verbs are tricky and have the ability to work as both transitives and intransitives. The verb "ran" is transitive in this sentence because it takes an object: "Gorgeous George ran his opponent from the wrestling ring into the crowd and pummeled him till he bled." But the same word can cross over to intransitive in a similar context: "Gorgeous George ran from the wrestling ring into the crowd."

Some verbs, such as *flirt,* take no object and are thus intransitive. You don't *flirt* a waiter or waitress, you *flirt with* a server. Which, I suppose, brings us back to where we began: The nineteenth and final definition of *lay* in the *AHD* is, you guessed it, "vulgar slang" for "to have intercourse with." Congratulations if you've followed this to the end. You deserve a lei.

## KEEPSAKES

• So now you've got it. *Lie* means "to recline" and is intransitive. It takes no object. *Lay* means "to place" and is transitive. It takes an object. You must lay the book on the table, or the coins on the counter, or the rifle on the stand. If you know your verb takes an object, use some form of the verb *to lay.*

• Remember that *lie* and *lay* are both irregular verbs and that the past tense of *lie* happens to be *lay.*

• *Lay* is a word that also points to the remarkable influence of prepositions on the meaning of a verb. The technical term for this is *phrasal verb* and includes such examples as *lay away, lay by, lay aside, lay into, lay off,* as well as such idiomatic expressions as *lay it on thick.*

# 24

...

# Avoid the "trap" of subject-verb disagreement.

My errors in grammar and usage are bigger and more embarrassing than yours. Like the preacher caught with the prostitute, like the dentist with bad teeth, like the loony psychiatrist, the ungrammatical language expert becomes a laughingstock.

My mistakes come from inattention, haste, or careless proofreading, but some come from ignorance. Not long ago, a friend asked me to intervene in an argument about a grammatical usage: "He was one of those actors who lives the part." I argued in favor of the writer, who thought that usage was correct. But when I checked several sources, I learned that the verb should be *live*, not *lives:* "He was one of those actors who live the part." In other words, the relative pronoun "who" refers back to the plural "actors" and takes the plural verb "live." I now realize I've been making that mistake for more than thirty years without correction from a teacher or an editor. So yes, as Caligula says in Lloyd Douglas's book *The Robe:* "So!—the Empire makes mistakes, then! Perhaps you will be foolhardy enough to say that the Emperor himself might make a mistake!" Yes, Majesty, emperors, even grammar emperors, make mistakes.

(When you find a mistake in my work, and you will, please alert me at rclark@poynter.org.)

While I try to learn from my mistakes, I admit to one that I make over and over again. I can fail to recognize it in my text until months or even years after publication. In early drafts of this book, I and my copyeditor caught it several times. I call this problem "the trap." I bet you fall into it, too. To see how it works, consider this sentence:

> Her collection of Dalí's art, which includes paintings, sculptures, posters, glass, jewelry, and knickknacks, impress even the most discerning experts.

The writer of this ungrammatical sentence (me!) has fallen into the trap. Singular subjects require singular verbs; plural subjects plural verbs. That's what we mean when we say that the subject "agrees" with the verb. But in this example they disagree. The subject of the sentence is "collection," which takes "impresses" as a verb: "The collection impresses." Singular subject. Singular verb.

In all such cases, I set a trap for myself by placing words and phrases between the subject and the verb. The greater the distance between subject and verb, the more likely the writer will make a mistake, or even worse, confuse the reader. In my example, the incorrect verb was contaminated by its proximity to plural nouns that were not the subject. "Impress" would be correct if, say, "knickknacks" had been the subject.

You can imagine that an inexperienced writer, or someone learning English as a second or third language, would be vulnerable to falling into the trap: "It is believed that these hills emerged from the sea with a thick cover of clay and is comparatively young at around sixty million years." Eleven words stand between the plural subject "hills" and the singular verb "is." Only on a comedy show would Julie Andrews have sung: "The hills is alive with the sound of music..."

Here a young writer falls into the trap: "A *slate* of capital improvement projects, estimated at $200 million, *include* a new community center and a rebuilt Highland Recreation Complex, as well as several sewer upgrades."

Even the most accomplished authors, supported by a squadron of editors, fall into the trap. Ben Yagoda begins one of my favorite recent books about language this way:

> In the end, it came down to two potential titles. Number one, *When You Catch an Adjective, Kill It.* Number two, *Pimp My Ride.* I have to admit that I carry a torch for number two—which alludes, of course, to the popular MTV series in which a posse of automotive artisans take a run-down jalopy and sleek it up into an awe-inspiring vehicle containing many square yards of plush velvet and an astonishing number of LCD screens.

What a cool way to kick-start a book on the soporific parts of speech. But can you find the trap? (I'll give you a minute.) Here it is:

> ...the popular MTV series in which a posse of automotive artisans take a run-down jalopy...

If you recognize that *posse* is a collective noun—grammatically singular, even though the sense is plural—you also see that the verb *take* does not agree. "A posse" (that "a" should be a hint) does not "take." A posse takes. The prepositional phrase "of automotive artisans" contaminated the verb. Ben Yagoda is one of America's best writers. If he and his editors can fall into the trap, so can you. And so have I. (Ben, to his credit, offers an escape hatch, noting I fell into *his* trap by not noting that the Brits tend to use plural verbs with collective nouns. "I was being self-consciously British!" he wrote, as in "Manchester United are going to win.") Another example of the pernicious influence of the Brits?

[I interrupt this chapter to bring you a brief message from my proofreader, who tells me that the emperor has once again made a mistake. She informs me that the *Chicago Manual of Style* accepts as correct singular and plural verbs with collective nouns, depending on whether the sense of the noun is singular or plural. That means that Ben Yagoda could correctly write "a posse ...takes" if he meant to emphasize the group, or "a posse...take" if he meant to empha-size the individual workers. Yeesh.]

Collective nouns pose a challenge when it comes to issues of number agreement. Words like *collection, posse, class, squadron,* and *gaggle* always give me agita. I once learned that these "col-lective" nouns have a plural sense (you can't, for example, have "a gaggle of goose") but take a singular verb. Now I'm not so sure. Suddenly I feel as if there is a trap inside a trap. You may stumble occasionally, but the key is to remain attentive. When using collective nouns and subjects such as *couple, everyone, ev-erything, all, anybody,* I need to be sure about whether the sense of the word is singular or plural. If I cannot, I try a different wording.

Some choices are easy: "All is well." "Everything is beautiful in its own way" (that sentence has a strong singular sense). But this strikes me as plural: "All of you make my life miserable." But what about *couple?* "The couple, newly wed, is headed for the motel." Or, "The couple, on their honeymoon, are headed for separate beaches." If you can't figure it out, ask your Magic 8 Ball which path to follow. When I asked mine, it answered, "Reply hazy, try again."

## KEEPSAKES

• During revision and proofreading, pay special attention to sentences in which subject and verb are separated.

• If you fall into the trap, record the sentence in a notebook as a reminder of your vulnerability.

• Even if separated subject and verb agree, try to rewrite the sentence in a way that brings them closer together to assist the reader.

• Get away from a draft of your story for a few minutes, even when on deadline. Your proofreading eye will sharpen with some distance from the text.

# 2 5

• • •

## Render gender equality with a smooth style.

When I was a young assistant professor of English at a small college in Alabama, we began talking about sexist language. That
was 1974. It suddenly seemed absurd to call Guinavera Nance the
chairman of the English department because she wasn't a chair
and she wasn't a man. Things got a lot easier when she became
dean, vice president, and then chancellor. But back in the day, we
thought nothing of writing gender-bending sentences such as
"The chairman showed off her new high heels." So if not *chairman*, then what? Chairwoman? Charwoman? Chair? Loveseat?

You would think we'd have this all figured out by now, that
forty years would have brought us to the reconciliation of fairness and aesthetics, but I have never met a writer for whom this
was not a struggle.

As I thought about the problem, I ran into a television promo
for an episode of the medical drama *ER:* "A fan favorite draws
their final breath." The sentence, of course, violates the standard
that pronouns should agree with antecedents in number: the
plural "their" disagrees with the singular "favorite." Part of the
challenge here is that the writer wants to conceal the gender
of the dead character, and "he or she" was deemed too, well, un-
promotional. But more and more we are seeing examples of

"they" used instead of "he or she." Call it the "singular they."

Consider this passage from J. K. Rowling's *The Tales of Beetle the Bard:* "Once a year, between the hours of sunrise and sunset on the longest day, a single unfortunate was given the chance to fight their way to the Fountain, bathe in its waters, and receive Fair Fortune forevermore." What is lost in number agreement is gained in singularity of subject ("a single unfortunate") and in story logic: that person could be male or female. But still...

Not long ago, I found a battered old friend at a used-book store. Titled *Writers Inc* (1990), this handy guidebook targets writers from high school to college, and contains everything from a six-year calendar to a glossary of computer terms. The section that caught my eye is titled "Treating the Sexes Fairly." The prologue raises the stakes for language high above correct grammar and proper usage to the level of equality and justice:

> When you box people in or put them down just because of their sex, that is called "sexism." When you identify all human virtues with only one sex, or when you identify one sex with the whole human race, that, too, is sexism. And when you bring in sexual distinctions where they don't belong, that, too, is sexism. Sexism is unfair. And it hurts. Ask anyone who has been a victim of it.

And then to the implications for language:

> To change our centuries-old habits of sexist thinking, we must try to change our language, for our traditional ways of speaking and writing have sexist patterns deeply imprinted in them. The assumptions built into our language teach even little children who they are and how they relate to others. For their sakes and our own, we must seek a language which implies equal value, equal potential, and equal opportunity for people of either sex.

It would take several books to grapple with the implications of those two paragraphs. On the negative side, in some academic circles such ideas have created a hypersensitivity to language that can make useful discussion about race and gender almost impossible. I remember reading, for example, a complaint from an Arizona professor about the use of the word *seminar*. He pointed out, correctly, that the word comes from the Latin for "seedbed" and carries the same root as *seminary* and *seminal*. And, as *semen* describes the male essence, he believed that any derived word is patriarchal and exclusionary. Such zealotry is rightly dismissed under the rubric of political correctness and does not help anyone seeking fair, equitable, and pragmatic solutions to real problems of language.

During one public forum on the issue of sexist language, an older woman stood and endorsed a proposal for the creation of a gender-neutral pronoun, something like *herm*. I love neologisms, new words for new purposes, and the history of the language reveals that pronouns are as subject to change as any other part of speech. But *herm* clearly never made the grade, perhaps because it is a man's name, after all, and rhymes with *germ* and *sperm*.

More-sensible solutions have come along and stuck. These include the choice of gender-neutral names to describe work functions. *Flight attendant, firefighter, letter carrier, police officer,* and *insurance agent* all describe jobs performed by men and women and do it with a practical elegance.

Now to the real fun: the so-called *universal masculine*. This problem is not that hard to solve if the translation is from *all mankind* to *all humanity*—though that revision changes the meter and has "man" in the middle. But why do I get so fidgety when I read in *Writers Inc:* "Don't use masculine pronouns—he, his, him—when you want to refer generically to a human being." The authors argue that you should not write: "A politician can kiss privacy goodbye when he runs for office." Three remedies are offered:

*Reword the sentence:* Campaigning for office robs a politician of privacy.

*Express in the plural:* Politicians can kiss privacy goodbye when they run for office.

*Offer optional pronouns:* A politician can kiss privacy goodbye when he or she runs for office.

I am now ready to offer another possible remedy, the usage that is becoming more common, even if it is condemned by some as blasphemous:

A politician can kiss privacy good-bye when they run for office.

Please do not throw this book out your nineteenth-story window. It may hit someone on the head. Stick with me. In a usage note for *every*, the *AHD* makes a helpful distinction about what is appropriate in common speech versus what is grammatically correct. The sentence "Every car must have its brakes tested" is correct, even though the plural sense of the subject might lead a speaker to say, "Every car must have their brakes tested." But a car, unless given a human name by its driver, is neuter, neither masculine nor feminine. The introduction of people adds the issue of gender fairness, as when J. K. Rowling writes in the Harry Potter series: "*Everybody* got to *their* feet and divided up." That is the British way.

Imagine this scene in a story in which a teacher says to the students: "Someone here has left the key to their locker where anyone can get at it. If this person comes forward now to claim this key, their punishment will be mild. But if this person refuses to take responsibility for their carelessness, they will be sent immediately to the assistant principal."

The grammatical problem, of course, is that the plural pronouns "they" and "their" do not agree in number with the singular antecedent "person." Given that clear violation of standard usage, why would anyone encourage it? There are at least two good, if not persuasive, reasons: (1) These days, gender equality trumps the arithmetic logic of formal grammar; (2) that's the way we talk.

When we speak, we often reach for the particularity of a singular subject: a teacher, a golfer, a carpenter, a nurse. But that sense of the singular, in enlightened usage, need not be exclusionary. In my book *Writing Tools,* my editor, Tracy Behar, and I tried to solve this problem by using the universal masculine in one chapter and the universal feminine in the next, an imperfect solution, to be sure, but one offered in good spirit.

If you don't think pronouns are subject to change, ask yourself why we no longer use *thee* and *thou* except in references to Elizabethan writing or the Lord's Prayer. In our own time, the pronoun has become a central issue for the discussion of language by such young transgender authors as Scott Turner Schofield and S. Bear Bergman. I sat in the audience at a club in Atlanta called Java Monkey when Bear walked to the stage to read from an essay. "I'm Bear," said the writer (notice that I used "writer," not *he* or *she*). "How many of you think I'm a *he?*" asked Bear. A few hands went up. "How many of you think I'm a *she?*" A few more hands. "How many of you have no fucking idea?" Most of the hands went up. "And that's the way I like it."

In his book *Butch Is a Noun*, Bergman argues that the culture would benefit from the creation of more neutral personal pronouns. While I can't get behind his suggestions *ze* and *hir*, I do understand what this dilemma means for him as a writer, particularly one for whom traditional gender identity is a prison.

> It is very difficult, as any closeted person who has ever tried to explain what ze did over a weekend will certainly tell you, to say even a few sentences about another person without using gendered pronouns. You end up constantly using the person's proper name and sounding like you are being translated from English to some other language and back again....Some people opt for the plural-pronoun-as-singular option: "Well, I went with my friend...so they could get a new car. They'd had this old one for more than ten years, so they really needed something newer. They got a 2002 Camry, and they seem really happy with it."

Bergman expresses dissatisfaction with that solution: "But that always sounds to me as though either you are dating someone with multiple personalities or you're polyamorous, either of which is a dandy thing as far as I'm concerned, but not what we're aiming at here."

If you have not yet had a conversation with a transgender person, you will. When you do, the problem of the pronoun will become pronounced. *So,* you must be thinking, *what are you suggesting? Are you slouching toward blasphemy in approving number disagreement?*

My answer is an enthusiastic but limited yes. When we are quoting someone, or writing dialogue, or speaking, or writing in less formal settings, I say go for it. In more formal settings, such as this book, I want to find ways to be inclusive that do not call attention to themselves by violating standard usage. It's a simple equation, really: Formal settings require formal usage. Informal settings permit some informal usage. Know when to wear your tuxedo and when to wear your cutoff jeans.

Another answer is to write from your heart. Here is fourteen-year-old Travis Stanton writing in support of his father, Steve Stanton, who made a very public transition to Susan Stanton:

> Throughout my whole life, I thought my dad was really a tough guy. He went out with the cops and busted bad guys. He shot guns, fought fires. He was an aggressive driver. He liked football and lots of sports.
>
> Then one day my thoughts changed about him when we had a family meeting and he told me how he felt about himself. He said he felt like a woman on the inside and was going to change into one. He said he tried his best to be a manly guy, but he couldn't stop his feelings to become a girl.
>
> At first, I thought I was in a dream. I thought he was 100 percent manly man, more manly than most guys.
>
> After a few days, I thought about it. I knew he was making the right choice to become a girl. Although I can't relate to his feelings, it must be really hard to hide something like that. It would be like having $1 million and not be able to spend it. After just so long, your feelings would take over and you would spend it....
>
> I think that everyone should be who they are and not try to be the same as other people. If you ask me, this has got to be the most manliest thing he has done in his whole life. It takes a real man to come out of his shell and say, "Hey, I am who I am."
>
> Now he is who he is meant to be. He is himself.

This letter, reprinted in the *St. Petersburg Times,* moved me greatly when I first read it. It reminded me of how moral courage can be expressed by the words on the page, especially by a young person. And it demonstrated how small-minded grammar etiquette can be when it is judged outside the context of what is being communicated. In the context of this letter, "most manliest" does not offend me as a redundant superlative. It moves me as an authentic, loving intensifier. And the subject-verb disagreement "I think that *everyone* should be who *they are...*" has never seemed more appropriate.

## KEEPSAKES

If you run into a problem that involves gender universals and/or number agreement, these questions may help you find a good solution:

- Am I writing formal or informal English?
- Can I find a way to be inclusive in my language but also aesthetically pleasing?
- If I'm stuck between two choices, can I come up with a third way?
- Can I show it to another person to see if he or she feels included or excluded?
- How can I avoid sexist language *and* the gooey trap of political correctness?

# 26

...

## Place modifiers where they belong.

I remember the morning I encountered this subheadline to an article about the nation's financial crisis:

> Bernanke defends unpopular actions
> to counter the crisis in a town hall meeting

It took me a few seconds to make sense of this—always a danger sign. Here's what the writer meant: Ben Bernanke, Federal Reserve chairman, spoke at a town hall meeting and defended his unpopular actions concerning the nation's economic crisis. But when I first read it, I thought the crisis involved the town hall meeting. Perhaps protesters disrupted the meeting, or disagreements arose as to who was allowed to speak. It turns out that the modifying phrase "in a town hall meeting" was in the wrong place, a problem corrected with this revision: "In a town hall meeting, Bernanke defends unpopular actions to counter the crisis." Why didn't the writer choose that version? I'll bet it's because headlines usually begin with subjects and verbs, but in this case form frustrated function.

I once had the pleasure of coaching a young soccer player named Dee Ehler who routinely lost her equipment, especially her shin guards and cleats. Her mom would get impatient with her for losing her stuff, but Dee always preferred the idea that they were misplaced rather than lost. "They're hiding," she liked to say.

Certain errors like to hide inside our prose as well. And they can be hard to find, even for the most dutiful proofreader. One of the trickiest hiders is the *misplaced modifier*—aka the *dangler.*

Speaking of tricky, we've already learned how parts of speech can shift their shapes. When a verb functions like an adjective, we call it a *participle,* which can act in either the present or the past. A present participle looks like this: "The house, *crumbling* from old age, was condemned by the city." A past participle looks like this: "*Condemned* by the city, the house was crumbling from old age."

At times, such versatility in parts of speech can lead to problems in grammar, syntax, and comprehensibility. I occasionally put the participle in the wrong place, hence the term *misplaced modifier.* I misplace my keys, my cell phone, my glasses, my wallet, my car in the parking garage, a daughter at the mall, my ethical compass, and an occasional participle or two.

It can look something like this: "*Condemned* by the city, a demolition team tore down the old and crumbling house." In the intended meaning, the city is condemning an old house, and a demolition team is doing the work. But the sentence could mean something quite different. What if the house has some historical value? Perhaps the city wants to see it preserved. City leaders may be condemning the action of the demolition team hired by a greedy developer. In either case, the writer has not given us a clear sentence.

Consider these alternatives: "*Condemned* by the city, the old house was torn down by the demolition crew." Or, if you prefer the active voice: "A demolition crew tore down an old and crumbling house *condemned* by the city." In both cases, I have taken the modifier (the past participle) and placed it right next to its soul mate.

Here is what makes the misplaced modifier hard to find: Often the brain of the reader or listener or writer revises the sentence—essentially replaces the participle—to make sense of the sentence from context. The writer already knows what she is trying to say so proofreading her own work does not reveal the error. But the consequences of not correcting this problem can be devastating, creating a confusion that can be serious—even potentially libelous:

> Reeling from accusations of child abuse, the minister attacked what he called a complacent and enabling church hierarchy.

Is the minister reeling or is the church hierarchy? It could say something like:

> The minister attacked "a complacent and enabling church hierarchy" already reeling from accusations of child abuse.

All such examples should lead us to this language strategy: to avoid confusion and ambiguity, put things next to each other that belong together. To do otherwise is to risk contamination by proximity.

## KEEPSAKES

• Verbs cross-dressing as adjectives are called *participles* and can work in the present: "He jumped to the top of the fence, *catching* the ball in the web of his glove"; or in the past: "He marched to his room, *caught* in the web of lies he told his mother."

• Beware of participial phrases that dangle at the beginning or end of a sentence. Double-check to make sure that the participle modifies the intended word.

• You may have to replace the modifier or rewrite the sentence to avoid confusion.

• Put things next to each other that belong together.

# 27

...

# Help the reader learn what is "essential" and "nonessential."

Certain fields of study, such as medicine, philosophy, and, yes, grammar, were built on a foundation of Greek and Latin, which is why we have to deal with specialized language uncommon in the everyday world, words such as *ablative, conjugation, predication, apposition,* and *amelioration,* just to name a few. On occasion, useful revisions come along that translate the Latin into easier Anglo-Saxon, as on that glorious day when an "auxiliary verb" became a "helping verb."

There was one language distinction I found almost impossible to master until I tripped over an alternate terminology: the difference between a *restrictive* and *nonrestrictive* relative clause. *Restrictive* and *nonrestrictive* sound a little like the language you might see in ads for girdles or jockey shorts.

Let's begin with the punctuation requirements:

- A nonrestrictive clause requires a comma or commas.
- A restrictive clause requires no comma.

But what is being restricted? The meaning.

Let's examine this sentence: "The soccer player who knows how to score goals is often a fan favorite." And this one: "The soccer player, who knows how to score goals, is often a fan favorite." Without commas, this is a generalization about soccer players: that those who score goals tend to be fan favorites. With commas, the focus is on one particular player, one fan favorite who happens to be a prolific goal scorer.

These contemplations plagued my daily life. One morning I was having breakfast at McCabe's Irish Pub in Naples, Florida, and was taken by the authenticity of the place. It turns out that the owner had pieces of the pub shipped to the Sunshine State from the Emerald Isle. On the menu, there was a paragraph that began with this sentence:

The pub, next to the church, is the center of Irish life.

I glanced at the sentence with such speed that I needed to read it a second time to discern the meaning because my first reading removed the commas, as in: "The pub next to the church is the center of Irish life." That made me imagine a particular Irish pub adjacent to a particular Irish church. Isn't it interesting to see how generality is transformed to particularity with the simple inclusion of those two minicroissants we call commas? Their contribution makes us imagine the importance to Irish life of two great institutions: the public house and the house of God.

The phrase "next to the church" has one of two technical names: restrictive or nonrestrictive. Because I can never keep these straight, I never use them and was fortunate to bump into alternatives: essential and nonessential. These terms make more sense to me, which means I'm less likely to mix them up. Simply put, in the first version, "the pub, next to the church, is the center of Irish life," the phrase "next to the church" is nonessential, which means the sentence can make some sense without it. But in the second version, the one without the commas, we need to know which pub in town is the center of Irish life. In our case, it's the pub that's next to the church.

In an essay about magazine fact-checkers, John McPhee described the problems posed by his text "Penn's daughter Margaret fished in the Delaware." Suddenly, McPhee confronts a problem, not just with punctuation, but with factual accuracy. Should there be commas or no commas around Margaret?

> Penn's daughter Margaret fished in the Delaware.
>
> *or*
>
> Penn's daughter, Margaret, fished in the Delaware.

According to McPhee, "The presence or absence of commas would, in effect, say whether Penn had one daughter or more than one. The commas—there or missing there—were not just commas; they were facts, neither more nor less factual than the kegs of Bud or the color of Santa's suit. Margaret, one of Penn's several daughters, went into the book without commas." The name of the particular daughter was deemed essential to understanding the meaning of the sentence and thus required no commas. If she were his only daughter, then her name would have been nonessential to the reader. This helps me to remember: If the phrase *is not* essential, then a comma or commas *are* essential.

I think I finally understand these distinctions. Good, because once again we've run into the same important lesson about language, that the smallest of decisions—comma versus no comma—can mean a world of difference.

## KEEPSAKES

A word, phrase, or clause can be in *apposition* to another, which just means that it sits next to it, offering more information about it. Consider these examples:

- *A word:* "Bruce Springsteen, *rocker,* can still fill a stadium at age sixty."
- *A phrase:* "Bruce Springsteen, *New Jersey's favorite son,* has never lost the spirit of his first gigs in Asbury Park."

- *A relative clause:* "Bruce Springsteen, *who was once declared the future of rock and roll,* is determined never to become its past."

Words in apposition can be either *essential* to the meaning of the sentence or *nonessential.* If they are not essential, they need to be kept in a frame set off by commas. If the words are essential, no commas are required.

# 28

...

# Avoid case mistakes and "hypergrammar."

I grew up in the 1950s and early 1960s, a time that would spark ridiculous debates about the grammar used in television commercials. "Winston tastes good like a cigarette should" was attacked, not for luring the young to eventual lung cancer and emphysema but for ruining their grammar. To the grammazons of that era, the correct usage was "Winston tastes good *as* a cigarette should." They were trying to enforce the distinction between *like* and *as,* the former used with phrases, the latter with clauses: "It hurt like hell" versus "It hurt as only a paper cut can."

Before Johnny Carson became an American icon as star of *The Tonight Show,* he hosted a comedy quiz show called *Who Do You Trust?* I can remember teachers pointing out that the creators of that show had the case wrong, that it should have been *Whom Do You Trust?* Coincidentally, just this morning I found that sentence in a sports column about whether the owners of a baseball team had credibility with the fans: "Before you decide how you feel,... you must first answer this: Who do you trust?" And then there was this recent quote from cranky old relief pitcher Troy Percival after a bad outing: "I've just got to set my sights on whoever is next."

When I read that sentence, I wondered if it was grammatically correct. To be honest, I forgot whether the preposition or the verb governed the case of the pronoun. If "on" was in charge, then the word might be *whomever,* as object of the preposition. But if "is" was the boss, then the subjective case would be correct: "whoever is…" *Who* is used in the subject position; *whom* when it serves as an object of a verb or a preposition.

But let me return to those thrilling days of yesteryear when the little sister of a friend would answer the telephone this way: "Witanowski residence. To whom do you wish to speak?" Her brother and I would imitate and ridicule her precociously pompous "whom." Clearly, as I would learn later, this was a case of hypergrammar, a level of correctness that called attention to itself, which is why, I think, Patricia T. O'Conner titled her cool book on grammar *Woe Is I*. "If you've ever been picked on by the pronoun police," writes O'Conner, "don't despair. You're in good company. Hundreds of years after the first Ophelia cried 'Woe is me,' only a pedant would argue that Shakespeare should have written 'Woe is I' or 'Woe is unto me.'"

In trying to pin down the distinction between *whoever* and *whomever,* I began with a dusty old copy of *A Dictionary of Modern English Usage* by H. W. Fowler, one of the most useful and delightful books about language ever written. In his essays on *who* and *whom,* he excoriates the journalists and sportswriters of his day (1927) for their ignorance, especially their tendency to fall back on *whom* in questionable cases to protect themselves from a likely mistake: "That every *whom* in those quotations ought to be *who* is beyond question," writes Fowler, "and to prove it is a waste of time since the offenders themselves would admit the offence; they commit it because they prefer gambling on probabilities to working out a certainty." In other words, the writers used *whom* because they were afraid of making a case mistake and didn't bother learning the logic governing conventional grammar. Something very different has happened in our own time, a decided shift toward *who* as the default position. *Whom* is not dead, but who could deny that it has fallen out of favor and will one day rest in peace with *thee* and *thou* and other archaic and obsolete usages.

Which brings us back to Troy Percival's declaration "I've just got to set my sights on whoever is next." It turns out that the whole clause "whoever is next" serves as the object of the preposition "on." The clause governs the case; that is, *whoever* is the subject of *is*. The subjective case is solved. Old Troy's got it right. I'm sure he'll be delighted to know—in between squirts of chewing tobacco.

But if Troy is right, then Philip K. Howard, the author of the book *Life Without Lawyers*, must be wrong: "...that society will somehow achieve equilibrium if it placates *whomever* is complaining." The object of the verb "placates" is the whole clause. The correct word would be *whoever*, subject of the clause.

By all accounts, President Barack Obama speaks and writes well and knows what it means to live inside the English language. But he makes a common case error, especially in off-the-cuff remarks, a boo-boo shared by many. Mr. President says things like "What a warm greeting you have given to Michelle and I." Because that last phrase is the object of the preposition "to," it is correct to say "Michelle and me." The same would be true for "It is our daughters who keep Michelle and I grounded." Make that "Michelle and *me*." Is this something that the president should work on, or is it a case of hypergrammar? Begin listening for case errors in the words of politicians, celebrities, and sports figures.

## KEEPSAKES

• These pronouns are used as subjects: who, whoever, I, you, we, he, she, it, they.
• These are used as objects: whom, whomever, me, us, him, her, it, them.
• *Who* is used in the subject position, but as an object *whom* is the right choice, at least in more formal speech and writing.
• Your ear will guide you to avoid *hypergrammar,* usages that are technically correct but that diverge widely from common usage.

# 29

...

# Be certain about the uncertain subjunctive and other "moody" subjects.

I begin this lesson on a difficult grammatical concept called the *subjunctive mood* with a memory of one of the first naughty films I ever saw. It was called *The Secret Sex Lives of Romeo and Juliet* (1969) but by contemporary standards would barely raise even a highbrow eyebrow.

Back in the day, it was considered hot stuff, a bawdy parody of the Bard in which the young star-crossed lovers get it on without the covers. I remember the hilarious send-up of the balcony scene in which Romeo stares up at the stargazing Juliet and speaks Shakespeare's actual words:

> See how she leans her cheek upon her hand!
> O, that I were a glove upon that hand,
> That I might touch that cheek.

At just that moment, the camera pans down to reveal a gloved female hand on Romeo's bare bottom.

Which brings me, of course, to the subjunctive mood.

Verbs wear different costumes for different kinds of masked balls, and we call these verb forms *moods* or *modes*. The most common have names, as provided by this simple *AHD* definition of *mood:* "A set of verb forms or inflections used to indicate the speaker's attitude toward the factuality or likelihood of the action or condition expressed. In English the indicative mood is used to make factual statements, the subjunctive mood to indicate doubt or unlikelihood, and the imperative mood to express a command." Add to this the interrogative mood, in which the speaker asks a question, and we've covered most of the territory.

When I feel in the indicative mood, I indicate my thoughts or ideas to the reader or listener. In this mood, I make straightforward statements, which is why the great majority of sentences in, say, the *New York Times* or the *Encyclopedia Britannica* or *War and Peace* are indicative.

> Emma Woodhouse, handsome, clever, and rich, with a comfortable home and happy disposition, seemed to unite some of the best blessings of existence; and had lived nearly twenty-one years in the world with very little to distress or vex her.

So begins Jane Austen's novel *Emma,* rolling over the English countryside in the indicative mood.

Interrogative sentences ask questions, of course, and can be used by writers to generate not just answers but also mystery or narrative energy. In an old photo studio in El Paso, Texas, more than fifty thousand portraits—without names—were discovered from as early as the 1920s. Stephanie Simon writes in the *Wall Street Journal:*

> Claudia Rivers is a librarian by trade, but lately she has become a detective hot on the trail of 50,000 mysteries.
>
> Her quarries are the names behind the faces in 50,000 antique negatives left in the town's shuttered Casasola photography studio.
>
> Who was the middle-aged matron flirting under a sombrero? Why did the young man with the butterfly tattoo pose bare-chested, clutching a can of spinach? What became of the grim-faced bride?

The interrogative mood reminds us that we are all curious creatures. But the interrogative can be tricky business, for a question can act as a statement or even as an order, as when my dear wife asks, "Are you going to leave your socks on the floor like that?" She had a choice between that question and the indicative: "You always leave your socks on the floor." Or the imperative: "Pick up your darn socks!"

Parents are well versed in the use of all three of these moods:

> *Indicative:* "I've told you a million times that you cannot
>     go to R-rated movies without my permission."
> *Interrogative:* "Do you think money grows on trees?"
> *Imperative:* "For the thousandth time, clean up your room!"

But then comes the moodiest of moods, that mood à la mode, the uncertain subjunctive. The word *subjunctive* relates to *subjective,* which suggests a state of mind that may be conditional or contrary to fact. What I am about to describe is tricky and complicated, but if you work to grasp it you'll avoid some common grammatical mistakes.

The speaker or writer uses the subjunctive—which in our own time can seem either archaic or erudite—to express a degree of uncertainty or a condition that is contrary to fact. You are most likely to recognize subjunctive verb forms in your reading when you come upon a verb that you think could not possibly be correct, as in the old subjunctive clause "If it be true," or "If it were true," as opposed to the more contemporary "If it is true."

Fear and prejudice led opponents of Barack Obama to assert, contrary to fact, that Obama was an Arab or a Muslim. Such misinformation was denied and proved inaccurate time and again, which led CNN's Campbell Brown to wonder aloud: "So what if Obama were a Muslim?" Notice the appropriate use of the subjunctive "were," rather than the indicative *was.* Because Obama is not a Muslim, the sentence is contrary to fact and requires the subjunctive.

The most common pattern of subjunctive statements comes

with adverbial clauses, especially ones beginning with "if." "If I were you, I would leave town this minute." But I'm not you, so, because it is contrary to fact, the sentence requires the subjunctive forms "were" and "would."

"If he is a child molester, why hasn't he been arrested?" We don't know whether he is a molester or not, so the statement is not contrary to fact and can be expressed in the indicative mood. If we knew the man to be innocent, this sentence in the subjunctive would have made sense: "If he were a child molester, he would have been arrested already."

Verb forms like *could, would,* and *should* are part of the subjunctive posse because each describes the world with a degree of uncertainty:

> "We could go to that party, but should we?"
> "I don't know. Would you like to go?"

Now let's return to the starstruck Romeo: "See how she leans her cheek upon her hand!" That sentence happens to be in the imperative mood because Romeo insists that we observe Juliet from his point of view. "O, that I were a glove upon that hand..." He is not a glove, of course, so the subjunctive form "I were" is required, even though my crack computer grammar checker wants Shakespeare to revise "were" to *was.* "That I might touch that cheek." But you're not a glove, Romeo, so you won't, and now I'm laughing again thinking about that cheeky moment forty years ago in *The Secret Sex Lives of Romeo and Juliet.*

## KEEPSAKES

The grammatical term *mood* describes verb forms that help indicate the factual or uncertain nature of the action described in the sentence.

- The indicative mood is the most common, a straightforward expression of fact: "Rumpelstiltskin is my name."

• The interrogative mood helps the speaker or writer ask questions: "Is your name Harry?"

• The imperative mood makes a demand or gives an order: "Give me your first-born child as you promised!"

• The subjunctive mood helps the writer make statements that may be contrary to fact. "If I were a wizard, I'd spin all the straw into gold myself."

# 30

...

# Identify all sources of ambiguity and confusion.

Poet and scholar William Empson was only twenty-four years old in 1930 when his book *Seven Types of Ambiguity* was published, which is why I resent him; not for the influence of his scholarship, but that so wise a study of literature should come from so young a writer. (On the flip side, I am intrigued by his roguish personal life: he was banished from Cambridge University after a housekeeper found condoms in his room.)

Ambiguity, it seems, has great value in certain discourse communities. In diplomacy, ambiguity enables compromise by inviting each side to interpret language for partisan benefit. In the famous legal decision *Brown v. Board of Education,* an oxymoron—"with all deliberate speed"—set the clock ticking in the hope that enlightened leaders would have the time needed for the peaceful desegregation of public schools. Opponents used the phrase to justify resistance.

In the experience of literature, ambiguity reflects a multilayered world, allowing the reader to hold on to multiple meanings at the same time. Empson defines *ambiguity* as "any verbal nuance, however slight, which gives room for alternative reactions to the same piece of language." As an example, Empson offers Shakespeare's Sonnet 73, in which an aging poet encourages his younger lover to love the older man with passion while there is still time. It begins:

> That time of year thou mayst in me behold,
> When yellow leaves, or none, or few, do hang
> Upon those boughs which shake against the cold,
> Bare ruined choirs, where late the sweet birds sang.

In the closest of close readings, Empson explores the levels of meaning generated by "bare ruined choirs." In short, he asks, "How is an aging lover like a tree in autumn and like the ruins of a monastery?"

Here's Empson:

> The fundamental situation ... is that a word or a grammatical structure is effective in several ways at once. [In the case of] "bare ruined choirs," [the comparisons make sense at a variety of levels]: because ruined monastery choirs are places in which to sing, because they involve sitting in a row, because they are made of wood, are carved into knots and so forth, because they used to be surrounded by a sheltering building crystallised out of the likeness of a forest, and coloured with stained glass and painting like flowers and leaves, because they are now abandoned by all but the grey walls coloured like the skies of winter, because the cold and Narcissistic charm suggested by choir-boys suits well with Shakespeare's feeling for the object of the Sonnets, and for various sociological and historical reasons (the protestant destruction of monasteries; fear of puritanism), which it would be hard now to trace out in their proportions; these reasons, and many more relating the simile to its place in the Sonnet, must all combine to give the line its beauty, and there is a sort of ambiguity in not knowing which of them to hold most clearly in mind. Clearly this is involved in all such richness and heightening of effect, and the machinations of ambiguity are among the very roots of poetry.

Such rich and detailed interpretation reveals the creative uses of ambiguity. For less skilled and experienced writers, however, ambiguity may not be a prize at all, or even an intended effect of the prose. Unintended multiple meanings creep into texts, even short ones, often producing disastrous or hilarious results. Consider these actual headlines, gathered over the years by the *Columbia Journalism Review:*

Starving Angolans eating dogs, bark
Disney keeps touching kids
Lay position proposed by bishop for women
Change found in subways: Panhandling is down
Gas levels high in Beantown
Torch relay runner dies after his leg
Cubans march over 6-year-old
Prostate cancer more common in men

In place of Empson's seven types of literary ambiguity, I will describe seven common ways in which writers stumble into unintended double meanings.

1. *Failure to account for homonyms.* Homonyms are two words that sound the same and are spelled the same but have different meanings. That helps create the laughable confusion of "Starving Angolans eating dogs, bark." In their desperation, the starving people are eating domestic animals and tree bark. That latter meaning of *bark* derives from the Old English, but a different meaning—to voice a sharp sound—comes from Old Norse.

2. *Confusion of parts of speech.* Using the same example, we see that though the writer intended to use "bark" as a noun, its ludicrous meaning derives from a verb form.

3. *Contamination of meaning by juxtaposed words.* It is almost impossible to see the word "bark" next to the word "dogs" without imagining Lassie trying to save Timmy from falling into the well. The headline about "gas" would seem sophomoric or scatological because of its association with the nickname for Boston, Beantown.

4. *Colliding denotations and connotations.* In "Disney keeps touching kids," we see an excellent example. "Disney," of course, is the name of a famous cartoonist and entrepreneur, but it is also the name of several places, including Disney World. The word *touch,* in a neutral sense, means to make contact with the hand, but here it carries conflicting connotations: a warm feeling in the heart, and inappropriate or illegal sexual contact with a child by an adult.

5. *Preposition mischief.* Added to a verb, a simple preposition can transform effect and meaning. It is the ambiguity in the preposition "over" that makes us wince when we read: "Cubans march over 6-year-old." The writer uses "over" as a synonym for *concerning,* not recognizing that "march over" could be mistaken for *trample.*

6. *The challenge of abstraction.* On rare occasions, the same word can be confused as either abstract or concrete. "Change" is one of them. It can refer to the jingle jangle in your pocket or to alms dropped in a tin cup. Or it can be used to challenge the status quo in a political campaign. "Change found in subways: Panhandling is down" is so bad, it's good. Next to the word "found," "change" feels like metal money, an impression reinforced by "panhandling." Unfortunately, the writer means the word as an abstraction, something like: "Things look different in the subways. Fewer people are begging for money."

7. *Failure to account for semantic change.* The meanings of words change, and then they change some more. If I invoke a cliché used innocently a century ago to describe a church dance, "A gay time was had by all," my intent may be frustrated by visions of San Francisco or Key West. Semantic change turns "lay position"—meaning a nonclergy position—into a sexual double entendre.

In the real world, most ambiguous messages become clear in context or practice. But just this morning I saw a television story with the headline "Plastic to become more expensive." For more than a few seconds I expected to learn that the cost of computers and cars would increase because of the rising cost of raw material. As it turned out, the story discussed increased interest rates for credit cards: "plastic." No animals or humans were injured during the writing of that headline, but a small cloud settled for a few seconds between my mind and the intended message.

## KEEPSAKES

Ambiguity can serve as a powerful creative force in the literary arts, offering audiences multiple shades of meaning from which to choose. But unintended ambiguity can corrode meaning, even turning serious content into something ludicrous. The sources for this negative ambiguity include:

- failure to account for words that sound alike
- times when one word can be used as more than one part of speech
- placing words next to each other in a way that confuses their meanings
- inattention to the connotations of words
- prepositions that change the meaning of verbs
- needless repetition
- words that can be abstract or concrete depending on context
- failure to account for changes in the meaning of a word over time

# 31

• • •

# Show what is literal and what is figurative.

Word confusion will always be a source of error, even for serious students of the language. Many people will say *prostrate* when they mean *prostate,* or *antidote* when they mean *anecdote,* or *appraise* when they mean *apprise.* (See a sample of such misused words in Appendix B.)

It's hard to imagine that word confusion would extend to antonyms, two words that have opposite meanings. How can you confuse *right* and *wrong,* or *right* and *left,* or *rich* and *poor?* But I agree with sports author Jack McCallum who observes how often writers and speakers confuse the antonyms *literal* and *figurative,* often expressed as adverbs, *literally* and *figuratively.*

A classic example: "Her head literally exploded from the excitement of the lecture." Now unless we're talking about blood, bone, and gray matter on the carpet and the walls, her head did not actually or literally explode. But it certainly may have exploded metaphorically or figuratively, which is to say that *explode* is used here as a figure of speech. In such a case, the writer might be describing the ideas or images or associations inspired by the lecturer.

I do not mean to be a scold—we'll save that role for the Brits—but I think the use of *literal* as a general intensifier has become a distraction, something that tears me away from the message and makes me doubt the messenger, even when he is a distinguished author such as Christopher Buckley. In a recent essay, Buckley, son of the late conservative writer William F. Buckley Jr., described the heat he and others received after turning against Republican presidential candidates: "As for Kathleen [Parker] she has to date received 12,000 (quite literally) foam-at-the-mouth hate e-mails. One correspondent, if that's quite the right word, suggested that Kathleen's mother should have aborted her and tossed the fetus into a Dumpster. That's Socratic dialogue for you." Now if Buckley wants to use "quite literally" to modify "received 12,000," I apologize. But I at first read him to mean that the hate e-mails were actually foaming at the mouth, which is impossible, or that their senders were foaming at the mouth, which he cannot know.

Another overused and misused word is *irony*.

My daughter is a huge fan of Canadian songbird Alanis Morissette, and so am I. Lauren got to meet Alanis before a concert and, bawling, exclaimed, "Thanks for getting me through my adolescence!" Alanis is a powerful singer and a clever songwriter, but I can't forgive her for "Ironic." This song is a great youthful anthem about how things in life don't work out as planned as described in the catchy chorus: "It's like rain on your wedding day, it's a free ride when you've already paid, it's the good advice that you just didn't take." Life can be a bitch, no doubt about it, Alanis. An old man can win the lottery and die the next day. You can find a blackfly in your Chardonnay. And maybe if you're looking for a knife, you might stumble into a room that contains ten thousand spoons, but, girl, what the heck are you doing looking for a knife in a spoon factory anyway?

The problem, it has been noted many times now, is not the unfortunate nature of these events. It's the description of them as "ironic." They may be unlucky, curious, sad, odd, interesting, coincidental, a sign that one's world is in disarray, but they hardly qualify as ironic. *Irony* is used so often and so loosely as a descriptor of unexpected events that it can be said to have suffered a form of semantic inflation, so overstuffed with responsibility as to be almost useless.

Words and even numbers get inflated or deflated to fulfill a variety of functions, some noble, some less so, including propaganda and marketing. Let's take the mature women's clothing store Chico's. It has created a system for sizing that includes only four sizes: 0, 1, 2, 3. A woman who might have once worn, say, a size 16 dress can rest in the knowledge that she's now wearing a 3. In other words, those sizes take in many more customers than they used to.

On the other side of the coin is Starbucks, which got us to buy cups of coffee at winelike prices by installing purple couches and giving its products exotic names: "I'll have a tall, double, half-caf, iced vanilla latte, please." But here's the catch. A "tall" drink translates to small or regular in common parlance. Yet instead of small, medium, and large, Starbucks has granted us tall, grande, and vente. This size inflation reminds me of a joke by Roseanne Barr about why men like to read maps: "They like anything where one inch equals a hundred miles."

Isn't that ironic? No, it's not. It's just funny.

So what, then, is the meaning of *irony*? And what represents responsible use of the word? Let's begin with our two favorite dictionaries. The *OED* defines *irony* as "a figure of speech in which the intended meaning is the opposite of that expressed by the words used; usually taking the form of sarcasm or ridicule in which laudatory expressions are used to imply condemnation or contempt," as when Christopher Buckley described hateful ravings as "Socratic dialogue." One of the earliest uses cited is from 1533 when a "naughty lad" is described as a "shrewd boy" and a "good son." The *AHD* essentially agrees in its first definition: "The use of words to describe something different from and often opposite to their literal meaning."

The *AHD* includes the word *ironic* with this list of synonyms: *sarcastic, caustic, satirical,* and *sardonic,* then adds this important advice in a usage note: "The words *ironic, irony,* and *ironically* are sometimes used of events and circumstances that might be better described as simply 'coincidental' or 'improbable,' in that they suggest no particular lessons about human vanity or folly." (Are you listening, Alanis?)

Here is the type of usage of which the panel disapproves: "When Don arrived in Florida, he went to work with Roy, who, ironically, had also been in the navy and studied medieval literature." This is more like it: "Roy rejected Don for the job because the candidate's expertise was in literature, not journalism. Ironically, Roy came to his job with exactly the same credentials." (In such cases, the adverb "ironically" is understood to mean "It was ironic that...")

*Irony,* a word we can trace back to Greek rhetoric and philosophy, has a different set of meanings in the world of serious literature than it does in popular culture and entertainment. In fact, books and academic courses have been devoted to the study of irony, an example of which comes from *The Rhetoric of Fiction* by Wayne C. Booth:

> All the great uses of unreliable narration depend for their success on far more subtle effects than merely flattering the reader or making him work. Whenever an author conveys to his reader an unspoken point, he creates a sense of collusion against all those, whether in the story or out of it, who do not get that point. Irony is always thus in part a device for excluding as well as for including, and those who are included, those who happen to have the necessary information to grasp the irony, cannot but derive at least part of their pleasure from a sense that others are excluded. In the irony with which we are concerned, the speaker is himself the butt of the ironic point. The author and reader are secretly in collusion, behind the speaker's back, agreeing upon the standard by which he is found wanting.

It has been said about irony—and also about satire—that the ability to detect it is the sign of a certain kind of intelligence. Literature and history are filled with examples of the misinterpretation of signs, messages taken literally when they were not meant to be taken so, from Jonathan Swift's "Modest Proposal" to solve the hunger crisis in Ireland by eating excess babies to the cover of *The New Yorker* picturing presidential candidate Barack Obama as an armed Islamic terrorist.

In a postmodern age, words like *ironic, sarcastic, satirical,* and *sardonic* seem to some insufficient to express the randomness of life on a dying planet, so make way for the word *snark.* The *AHD* defines *snarky* as slang for "irritable or short-tempered," derived from a Dutch word meaning "to snore, snort, or nag." But whole books are now being written about the snarkiness of American culture, and a website run by my young friends Robin Sloan and Matt Thompson is called snarkmarket.com.

Ruth Cullen in her pocket dictionary of slang, *The Little Hiptionary,* defines *snarky* as "a style of writing or speech infused with snide remarks that have humorous, not negative, connotation; witty, edgy, and sarcastic." But that definition scrapes some of the thorns off the word. When I hear *snark,* I hear less wit and more cynicism, not just a suspicion of authority but an inherent distrust of practical truth and sincere emotion. I'd be pleased for you to think of parts of this book as witty; not so pleased with the judgment that it's snarky, unless you are referring to my attitude toward British culture bullies who are invading America. Didn't Cornwallis surrender at Yorktown in 1781?

## KEEPSAKES

- Be cautious with use of the words *figurative, literal,* and *ironic.*
- When tempted to use *figuratively* or *literally,* complete the sentence, but try a revision in which you then omit it. In other words, let the context *show* you mean something figuratively. Don't shout it.
- Every time you use *literally,* double-check it to make sure you don't mean *figuratively.*
- Don't use the word *ironic* when you mean *coincidental.*

PART FOUR

•  •  •

# Meaning

So far we've explored the atomic energy of letters and words, the tendon strength of punctuation, and the trusty but rusting anchor of standard syntax. What comes next is meaning expressed when words work together to form phrases, clauses, and sentences.

We'll begin by considering how subjects and verbs serve as the dual locomotives of language energy, the one-two punch of making meaning with impact. A focus on verbs will include attention to active and passive voice, and to forms of the verb *to be*, how they work and why they matter. We'll consider the distinctions between the voice of a verb and the tense, categories that are often confused.

We'll switch to the sentence in all its variety, including the "verbless sentence," a mistake unless you intend it for a specific purpose. We'll look at each of the standard forms of sentences and how punctuation guides the writer and reader. The simple sentence is not as simple as it looks; the complex sentence helps connect unequal ideas; the compound sentence creates a balance of thought and meaning. We'll look at what happens when famous writers ignore these standards and what we can learn from their violation.

Prescriptive critics may condemn my recommendation that writers politely ignore the "crotchets" of purists who insist on old-school adherence to rules that have little influence on the making of meaning: splitting infinitives, beginning sentences with *and* or *but*, ending sentences with a preposition. Grammazons who profess that these are violations must face the counterevidence produced in the classic works of some of our most distinguished writers.

# 32

...

# Join subjects and verbs, or separate them for effect.

After millennia of language use and study, one powerful message persists: The creation of meaning—the expression of a complete thought—requires a subject and a verb, the king and queen of comprehensibility. And the king and queen are most powerful when they sit on adjacent thrones rather than in separate castles far away.

Consider the lead to this *New York Times* story about the downfall of an important political figure:

> Gov. Eliot Spitzer, whose rise to political power as a fierce enforcer of ethics in public life was undone by revelations of his own involvement with prostitutes, resigned on Wednesday, becoming the first New York governor to leave office amid scandal in nearly a century.

And then this accompanying story:

> Lt. Gov. David A. Paterson, a state legislator for 22 years and the heir to a Harlem political dynasty, will be sworn in as New York's 55th governor, making him the state's first black chief executive.

If you are counting, the writers put twenty-four words between subject and verb in the first sentence and fourteen words between subject and verb in the second. A simple diagram for both sentences might look something like this:

Subject —————————————— Verb ——————————————→.

These stories are so important, and the sentences so carefully constructed, that the curious reader will find a way through. But to clear the path, I'll follow an axiom of comprehensibility that requires stickum between subject and verb, a revision that would look more like this:

Subject Verb ——————————————————————→.

To achieve the new pattern, I'd rewrite the first lead this way:

> Gov. Eliot Spitzer resigned on Wednesday, becoming the first New York governor in nearly a century to leave office amid scandal. Having risen to power as a fierce enforcer of ethics in public life, Spitzer was undone by revelations of his own involvement with prostitutes.

The second sentence in that paragraph ("Having risen...") looks like this:

—————————————— Subject Verb ——————————→.

Whenever an author separates subject and verb, the reader can be led astray, as is the case in this clumsy rendering:

> A bill that would exclude tax income from the assessed value of new homes from the state education funding formula could mean a loss of revenue for Clark County schools.

Many obstacles to comprehensibility lurk in that sentence, but the separation of subject ("bill") and verb ("could mean") is a big one. Without a strong backbone, the sentence wanders in all directions, piling one bit of government jargon on another. I've tried to rewrite it, and the best I could do is this:

> Clark County schools will get less money from the state if the legislature passes a bill designed to lower property taxes.

It ain't no beauty, but it replaces a big mess of thirty words with a little mess of twenty-one words. Any time I can derive greater meaning from fewer words, I do.

It seems as if the subject and verb of a main clause can appear in almost any location and without much regard to the distance between the two. So a sentence could look like this:

Subject ——————————————————————————— Verb.

As in: "Hurricane Elene, rotating ominously in the Gulf of Mexico for two days, suddenly and unexpectedly turned left."

Novelist Robert K. Tanenbaum almost achieves that effect in a much longer and more ostentatious sentence:

> On Monday morning, Butch Karp and Marlene Ciampi and several hundred other assistant district attorneys, the district attorney himself and his aides and assistants, learned judges by the dozens and clerks and secretaries in the hundreds, and brigades of police, and regiments of witnesses and victims, the bored and the anguished, squads of jurors good and true, and uncounted lawyers, young and harried or suave and grave, depending on whether they worked for the poor or the rich, and the ladies and gentlemen of the press, merciless and cynical; and, of course, a varied mob of criminals, the cause and purpose of this whole cavalcade, the petty thugs, the thieves and robbers, whether by stealth or weaponry or clever papers, the whores of both sexes, the cold killers, the hot killers, the rapists and torturers of the helpless, the justly accused, the falsely accused,

together with their keepers, parole officers, social workers, ene-
mies, friends and relations, converged, all of them, on a single
seventeen-story gray stone building located at 100 Centre Street
on the island of Manhattan, there to prod into sullen wakeful-
ness that great beast, the Law. (from *Depraved Indifference*)

The author is showing off, of course, but the sentence is fun to
read the second or third time through. On the first try, it takes a
bit of work because that first element in the very compound subject, "Butch Karp," appears as the fourth and fifth words in the
sentence, but the verb "converged" is a bit tardy, showing up 151
words later.

Attention to the position of subject and verb does not require
the writer to create simple or childish prose. Here, for example,
is a paragraph from G. K. Chesterton, who often wrote about
religious themes:

> The world can be made beautiful again by viewing it as a battle-
> field. When we have defined and isolated the evil things, the
> colours come back into everything else. When evil things have
> become evil, good things, in a blazing apocalypse, become good.
> There are some men who are dreary because they do not believe
> in God; but there are many others who are dreary because they
> do not believe in the devil. (from *Charles Dickens*)

This passage rings clear as a bell, due in no small part to the
connubial nesting in all clauses of subjects and verbs. The single
separation is brief and dramatic, the place where "in a blazing
apocalypse" sits between "good things" and "become good."

Good language tools should offer the writer interesting
choices, creative opportunities to go against the grain. One such
choice is to offer the reader "happy interruptions," moments in
which modifying words and phrases enrich our sense of the
subject, thus preparing us for the verb. It may not have worked in
the story about Eliot Spitzer, but it's a device that captures the
bright scholarly style of my first college English teacher, the late

Rene Fortin. Here he writes about the ghost of Hamlet's father:

> The ghost, for all of its Christian credentials, imposes upon
> Hamlet a mission that is totally incompatible with the Christian
> moral system. And Hamlet, though he does entertain severe
> doubts about the nature of the ghost, wondering whether it is a
> "spirit of health or goblin damned," never once explicitly
> questions the mission of revenge, though revenge is abhorrent to
> Christian thought. Any suggestion that he is repelled by the task
> on moral grounds can only be inferred from his several vague
> remarks about conscience and scruples as causes of his delay.

Study, for a moment, the position of subjects and verbs (here
each dot represents an intervening word):

> The ghost......imposes
> Hamlet.........................questions
> Any suggestion..........can only be inferred

It was my old friend Dennis Jackson, scholar, writer, and teacher,
who introduced me to a term from language studies: the
*right-branching sentence*. To understand this useful concept, I had
to begin to imagine sentences in a different way, not as part of a
column of text but as a single line moving from left to right. To determine the direction of the branches, you first identify the subject
and verb of the main clause. So a sentence can branch to the right:

Subject Verb ——————————————————————————>.

Or to the left:

<——————————————————————————— Subject Verb.

Or from the middle:

<——————— Subject Verb ————————————>.

These—and many other variations—are all correct, but each version offers a different effect.

The right-branching sentence, for example, helps the writer make meaning early, which allows an infinite number of modifying elements to be added:

> A tornado ripped through St. Petersburg Thursday, tearing roofs off houses, shattering windows in downtown skyscrapers, snapping power lines and tree limbs, and sending children and teachers scurrying for cover from an elementary-school playground.

This sentence could go on and on effectively, all because the meaning comes early ("A tornado ripped") while all other elements branch to the right.

A left-branching sentence works, by definition, in the opposite direction. Subordinate elements pile up on the front end, with the main meaning arriving—at times in dramatic form—near the end, as in my prose summary of the first lines of Geoffrey Chaucer's *The Canterbury Tales:*

> When April comes with its sweet showers and pierces the dry days of March and soaks every root with such sweet liqueur that flowers jump up; when the sweet west wind has breathed upon the tender shoots in every wood and field, and the young sun has run its course halfway across the sign of the Ram, and small birds sing and sleep all night with eyes wide open—as Nature excites their little hearts—that's when English folks bust out to go on pilgrimages.

When this happens, when that happens, when the other thing happens, then off we go to Canterbury.

## KEEPSAKES

Examine the position of subjects and verbs in drafts of your stories. Look for trends by asking yourself these questions:

- In most cases, are subjects and verbs joined together, or do I tear them apart?
- If subjects and verbs are separated, what comes in between them, and why?
- How often do subjects and verbs come together near the beginning of the sentence?
- Are there opportunities for me to revise to bring subject and verb closer together?
- If I've separated subject and verb, is the interruption a happy one?

# 33

...

## Use active and passive verbs in combination—and with a purpose.

Even more than pubs, old movie houses, and ancient ballparks, I love bookstores. For me, a bookstore is like pizza: even when it's bad, it's good. My kind of bookstore has book carts out front, open to the elements, crammed with tattered and water-stained detritus, the ruined remnants of remainders. So it was that I approached A Cappella Books in the funky Little Five Points district of Atlanta, where doorways are shaped like skulls, and a whiff of something not quite legal wafts in the air.

There on the rack was a book I had been intending to read for a long time, *There Are No Children Here: The Story of Two Boys Growing Up in the Other America* by Alex Kotlowitz. I had recently met Alex at a writing conference and was impressed, and a bit intimidated, by his fervor for the craft. So I grabbed the copy, plunked down my $1.50, and soon turned to the first page:

> Nine-year-old Pharoah Rivers stumbled to his knees. "Give me your hand," ordered his older brother, Lafeyette, who was almost twelve. "Give me your hand." Pharoah reached upward and grabbed hold of his brother's slender fingers, which guided him up a slippery, narrow trail of dirt and brush.

"C'mon, man," Lafeyette urged, as his stick-thin body whirled around with a sense of urgency. "Let's go." He paused to watch Pharoah struggle through a thicket of vines. "Man, you slow." He had little patience for the smaller boy's clumsiness. Their friends had already reached the top of the railroad overpass....

Pharoah clambered to the top, moving quickly to please his brother, so quickly that he scraped his knee on the crumbling cement. As he stood to test his bruised leg, his head turned from west to east, following the railroad tracks, five in all, leading from the western suburbs to Chicago's downtown. His wide eyes and his buck teeth, which had earned him the sobriquet Beaver and kept his lips pushed apart, made him seem in awe of the world.

The passage is an example of a kind of prose writing once described by author Sir Arthur Quiller-Couch: "The first virtue, the touchstone of a masculine style," he explained to his Cambridge University students in 1915, "is its use of the active verb and the concrete noun." Active verbs. Concrete nouns. Almost a century has passed, but that preference has survived among many writers and teachers. Let's push aside, for the moment, the problems posed by the phrase "masculine style" (how about "muscular style"?) along with the fact that the great professor uses a form of the verb *to be* to hawk the value of active verbs. Instead, let's test the passage above for its virtue.

Using a scene, setting, and dialogue—the building blocks of narrative—Kotlowitz yanks us from our easy chairs and into the challenging lives of these children. He creates, in a few short paragraphs, a richly symbolic landscape, where two brothers lag behind as they struggle up the hillside, and where the young boy sees the tracks stretched out toward a city—a way of life—he will never attain.

And look at the verbs: *stumbled, ordered, reached, grabbed, guided, urged, whirled, paused, clambered, scraped, stood*. All active, all specific, all pushing the story forward toward the next revelation. But what makes an active verb active? If you can get a handle on that, you'll be able to heat up a cold academic distinction to solve problems and achieve your purpose.

By definition, an active verb describes an action performed by the subject of a clause:

> Residents *poured* from their homes as the procession *advanced.* The hearse *passed* families sitting on the hoods of their cars, their children wrapped in colorful blankets. One couple *stood* at the side of the road, their heads bowed. A boy on horseback *watched* with his dog near a barbed-wire fence. A man in a rusty pickup *stared* from atop a grassy hill. [my emphasis]

This passage from the book *Final Salute* by Jim Sheeler reveals five different subjects, each performing the action of a distinctive verb:

> Residents poured...
> The hearse passed...
> One couple stood...
> A boy on horseback watched...
> A man in a rusty pickup stared...

Notice that not all actions described by active verbs are equal. "Poured" denotes great energy, but "passed" is quieter. And "stood," "watched," and "stared" might be perceived by witnesses as no action at all. It turns out writers have in their word closet supercharged active verbs: *shred, snatch, grimace, dissect, inoculate;* and mild-mannered ones: *go, get, have, move, own.*

As you read this next passage from Sheeler, notice the variety of actions—some large, some small, some obvious, some subtle—all described by verbs in the active voice:

> Beside the road, three tribal chiefs in feathered headdresses *waited* on horseback, along with a dozen other riders and a small empty wooden wagon.

The procession *arrived* from over a hill, and as the Marines *got out,* the two bands of warriors *nodded* to each other. The Marines *lifted* the flag-draped casket from the new Cadillac hearse, *transferred* it to the old pinewood wagon, and *fell* in line, issuing clipped commands under their breath. They *stood* at attention in spotless dress blue uniforms, white gloves, and shiny black dress shoes. The Oglala Sioux escorts *wore* blue jeans, windbreakers, and dusty boots. They *spoke* to their horses in the Lakota language.

"*Unkiyapo,*" someone *said.* "Let's go." [my emphasis]

It is unwise and useless to attribute some absolute benefit to one syntactical choice over another. It will not get us anywhere to demonize the passive voice or forms of the verb *to be* while we lionize the active. George Orwell argues persuasively that the corrupt and powerful often use the passive to avoid responsibility for actions: "The report has been studied, and it must now be admitted that mistakes were made." If you took all the statements made by politicians under investigation and ran them through a computer program to count the most common sentence, my guess is that at the top of the list would be "Mistakes were made." The passive voice allows the reader or speaker to sidestep any mention of who read the report and who made the mistakes.

Take, for example, a sentence such as "The woman's teenage son stole valuable jewelry from her purse." "Jewelry" is more specific than "mistakes," but a little research could turn that word into "a gold charm bracelet worth more than $20,000." But if I did not know who stole the bling or wanted to hide the identity of the thief, I could resort to the passive: "A gold charm bracelet worth more than $20,000 was stolen Thursday from the purse of Mary Jane Adams." In other words, the passive voice lets me hide, if I want to, the agent of action.

That effect—along with the occasional wordiness and indirection of passive constructions—has given the passive voice a bad rap, which is unfair to both the construction and the author. In other words, when you want to place the receiver of action in the limelight, the passive voice is for you.

When Herman the chimpanzee was killed by another chimp at a zoo in Tampa, Tom French wrote a story for the *St. Petersburg Times* in the form of a eulogy for a fallen king. Along the way, he told the story of Herman, how he was kidnapped from his mother by trappers and then orphaned. And then there is this:

> He was carried across an ocean, installed inside a cage, taught to depend on the imperfect love of strangers.

As a victim, Herman receives the action of the verbs, which drives the writer to use verbs in the passive voice: The chimp "was carried," "[was] installed," and "[was] taught." But by the next sentence, Herman becomes a survivor, an actor rather than a victim, so it's no surprise that the author turns to active verbs: "He charmed Jane Goodall, threw dirt at the mayor of Tampa, learned to blow kisses and smoke cigarettes, whatever it took to entertain the masses." In two sentences the writer uses three passive verbs and then three active verbs, each snug to the meaning of the text.

These distinctions go back to the beginnings of Western literature. It was, after all, the ancient Greek dramatist Aeschylus who wrote in "The Persians":

> So in the Libyan fable it is told
> That once an eagle, stricken with a dart,
> Said, when he saw the fashion of the shaft,
> "With our own feathers, not by others' hands,
> Are we now smitten."

That passage smites the hell out of me, he said actively.

## KEEPSAKES

• All verbs can be sorted into one of three categories: active, passive, or a form of the verb *to be* (or other linking verbs).

- The voice of verbs should not be confused with their tense. There is no such thing as the active or passive tense.
- The active voice kicks in when the subject of a sentence performs the action of a verb.
- Writers have traditionally expressed a preference for active verbs.
- Active sentences tend to be shorter and more direct than passive ones.
- Use the passive to place emphasis on the receiver of the action.
- Don't be fooled by those who use the passive to hide who does what in a sentence.
- Caution: Just because some *to be* words appear in a sentence does not mean that the verbs are passive (that is, not active). Passive forms always need a form of *to be* as a helper; progressive forms of the active voice also use *to be*.
  - ✓ "John Donne *was* a metaphysical poet." That's a form of *to be*, pure and simple.
  - ✓ "John Donne *was riding* his horse westward on Good Friday." The verb is active and progressive because it uses the *-ing* form.
  - ✓ "One of his greatest religious poems *was inspired* by this journey." The verb is passive.

# 34

...

## Befriend the lively verb *to be*.

I don't like name-droppers, so with discomfort I'll drop a big one. Here goes: Oprah. Oprah Winfrey is such a big-name person that—like Elvis and Madonna—she doesn't even need a second name. I've met Oprah—twice. Her producers invited me to be part of two shows: one on truth and lies in memoirs, the other on truth and lies in government. I actually got to sit in the "greenroom," and it was there that I was visited by several attendants, including a "Lint Lady" and Mimi, a makeup artist with a French accent. As Mimi tried her best to make me look a little better, she blurted out her frustration: "Your skeen," she said, "it ees so dry!"

"Uh, I use a little moisturizer every day," I whimpered.

"It ees not enough!"

It was Mimi's pronunciation of *is* ("ees") that got to me. It was so French and so sure of itself, so deconstructive, so Jean-Paul Sartre, that it filled me with a kind of existential dread: There was No Exit from the greenroom.

God *is* Love. We *are* the world. I *am* yours. The verb *to be* means a lot to us, which is why we call ourselves human *beings*. "Let there be light," says God in the book of Genesis. The Gospel of Saint John begins: "In the beginning was the Word, and the

Word was with God, and the Word was God. He was in the beginning with God. All things were made through him, and
without him was made nothing that has been made. In him was
life, and the life was the light of men. And the light shines in the
darkness; and the darkness grasped it not."

At first the Word of God does nothing. He just *is*. And his
being, his is-ness, comes through in the biblical text by the repetition of *was*—seven times in all. When the evangelist finally
gets to a concrete subject and an active verb, when the "light
shines" in the darkness, the power is almost overwhelming.

I took Spanish in high school and always struggled to distinguish between the verbs *ser* and *estar*. Either verb can be
translated as "to be," though Spanish distinguishes between the
essence of something and its temporary status. The sentence
*"Estoy Roy"* makes no sense, but *"Soy Roy"* (please refrain from
laughing) expresses my essence: "I am Roy." Roy could also
properly say *"Estoy aqui,"* meaning "I am here," because sooner
or later I'll be someplace else. Not to get too philosophical, but
this suggests the distinction between Being and Becoming.

The verb *to be* is so powerful that it can stand on its own:
"You are a nincompoop." Or it can be used to help an active
verb: "He is running around like a nincompoop"; or a passive
verb: "He has often been called a nincompoop." (Having used
this silly word three times now, I'm dying to know its etymology, but the *AHD* says "Origin unknown," although it offers the
more abstract version in *nincompoopery.*)

With Mimi's Gallic "ees" still smarting on my dry skin, I
went on a search for interesting literary examples of the verb *to
be*. I struck gold with three very different writers. The first was
Philip Roth and the opening paragraph of his novel *Everyman:*

> Around the grave in the rundown cemetery *were* a few of his
> former advertising colleagues from New York, who recalled his
> energy and originality and told his daughter, Nancy, what a
> pleasure it had been to work with him. There *were* also people
> who'd driven up from Starfish Beach, the residential retirement

village at the Jersey Shore where he'd been living since Thanksgiving of 2001—the elderly to whom only recently he'd been
giving art classes. And there *were* his two sons, Randy and
Lonny, middle-aged men from his turbulent first marriage, very
much their mother's children, who as a consequence knew little
of him that *was* praiseworthy and much that *was* beastly and
who *were* present out of duty and nothing more. His older
brother, Howie, and his sister-in-law *were* there, having flown in
from California the night before, and there *was* one of his three
ex-wives, the middle one, Nancy's mother, Phoebe, a tall, very
thin white-haired woman whose right arm hung limply at her
side. [my emphasis]

That's only half of the paragraph, but it establishes a grammatical
pattern with deep thematic implications, where weakness
equals strength, and strength weakness. Writers generally think
of a prepositional phrase as a weak construction, but the novel
begins with two of them: "Around the grave in the rundown
cemetery..." The main clauses are mostly built around verbs
such as "was" and "were," a sign that the reluctant mourners are
not agents of grief. They are just there. Active verbs like
"recalled," "giving," "flown," and "hung" appear only in subordinate elements—especially relative clauses.

Things change, but only at the end of that first paragraph:

> ...There *was* only one person whose presence hadn't to do with
> having been invited, a heavyset woman with a pleasant round
> face and dyed red hair who had simply appeared at the ceme-
> tery and introduced herself as Maureen, the private duty nurse
> who had looked after him following his heart surgery years
> back. Howie remembered her and went up to kiss her cheek.

The pattern seems to reassert itself with the verb "was" until the
sympathetic apparition with dyed red hair and an Irish name
asserts herself. Maureen is a mood-altering character who turns
verbs into actions. Howie remembers her and kisses her cheek.

I now call as a witness one of my favorite writers, Nora Ephron, in defense of my skin that *ees* so dry:

> In my bathroom there are many bottles. There are also many jars. Most of these bottles and jars contain products for the skin, although none of them contain something that is called, merely, "skin cream." Instead they contain face cream, or hand lotion, or body lotion, or foot cream. Remember when we were young? There was only Nivea. Life was so simple. I know in my heart that all these labels on these bottles and jars are whimsical and arbitrary and designed to make vulnerable, pitiable women like me shell out astronomical sums of money for useless products; on the other hand, you will probably never see me using foot cream on my face, just in case. (from *I Feel Bad About My Neck*)

Notice how the verb "shell out" changes the paragraph from an inventory into a rant with an escape hatch? The effect comes in part from the forms of the verb *to be* leading up to it. I count six of them.

I decided to test the power of the verb *to be* by picking up a collection of verse called *Erotic Poems*. Surely such poems, expressing centuries of desire, would be filled with verbs like *caress, drown, blush, devour,* and *hung*—and I found plenty. But check out this passage from D. H. Lawrence's poem "Figs":

> Every fruit has its secret.
>
> The fig is a very secretive fruit.
> As you see it standing growing, you feel at once it is
>     symbolic:
> And it seems male.
> But when you come to know it better, you agree with
>     the Romans, it is female....
>
> There was a flower that flowered inward, womb-ward;
> Now there is a fruit like a ripe womb.

It was always a secret.
That's how it should be, the female should always be
    secret.

As I type these words my palms begin to sweat, and I can feel my heart beating a bit faster. What is it? The image of the inward flower? The taste of sweet ripe fruit. Or is it the persistence of the verb *to be:* so essential, so secretive, so ... copulative.

## KEEPSAKES

• Forms of the verb *to be* are among the linking verbs (such as *seem* and *appear*) that show no action but identify one thing with another, as in "You are a fabulous copyeditor."

• Because they express relationships rather than actions, forms of *to be* have been mischaracterized as weaker than active constructions.

• Vary the three types of verbs—active, passive, and linking—and use each for its intended purpose.

• And if you are wise, never tell a writer his skin is dry. You may turn up in a book someday.

# 35

...

## Switch tenses, but only for strategic reasons.

A problem I share with younger writers is a tendency to shift tenses for no obvious reason. At times the shift infects a particular sentence:

> Timothy Leary experimented with LSD and declared that the mind is as expandable as the cosmos.

Written in the historical past using verbs like "experimented" and "declared," the sentence goes awry with a shift to the present tense: "the mind is." I must remind myself, time and again, that if the verb in the main clause is in the past tense, the verb in an indirect quote usually shifts to past tense.

An unintended effect of such writing is a kind of disorientation, a dreamlike state you might find in a Dalí painting or a pretentious European movie. Radical experiments in narrative time can be found as early as the picaresque eighteenth-century novel *Tristram Shandy*, in which the plot moves backward in time from a climactic moment of passion interrupted when Tristram's mum asks his dad to wind the clock. They include movies such as the Japanese classic *Rashômon* in which different versions of the same event are told over and over; to edgy postmodern classics such as *Memento* and *Pulp Fiction*. Time and space are relative—thank you, Dr. Einstein—and story time can be unleashed, uncorked, thawed out, looped backward or forward, distorted, tended, distended, mished, mashed, or moshed.

To use a phrase that will date me, such experiments, well done or half baked, make a work feel "avant-garde" and an author worthy of a cigarette holder and a beret.

I usually get tense over tense during the drafting stage of a story, when the narrative line has not been clearly drawn, and when it's easy to get time unintentionally out of whack. Perhaps I'll begin a story in the present tense with a desire to make it seem more immediate or urgent:

> I am at one of my favorite events—the antiquarian book fair—and I'm staring down at the back cover of a book, a biography of the great prizefighter Joe Louis. But the image I'm staring at is not a photo of the Brown Bomber but one of his first biographers, a 21-year-old woman named Margery Miller, who looks more like a college debutante than a down-and-dirty chronicler of the pugilistic arts.

Then, without intent, my prose feels the gravitational pull of that old narrative workhorse, the historical past. "After trying to ignore the young Miss Miller and her boxing book, I made several turns around the auditorium, doing my best to repress my curiosity: What would make a young woman from Williams College in 1946 want to write a boxing biography? And what the heck became of her? Before you know it, I had snapped up the book with a ten dollar bill." Only during revision do I note the jump from the present tense back into the past, a shift with no rhyme or reason.

In most cases, I force myself, and my students, to stick to one tense, either the present or, more often, the historical past. This is not to say that I'm incapable of switching tenses to create a specific effect. I'm thinking of a personal essay I wrote in 2007 about an unusual encounter in the men's room of our local Catholic church:

> The stall door swings open, and out comes a boy—maybe 8 years old—all dressed up in his Sunday suit: white shirt and tie, dark blue slacks and jacket, a right proper little lad. But he has a problem. For this young man has clearly outgrown this outfit, so that his pants barely contain his lower frame. "Mister, I can't pull up my zipper. Can you help me?"
>
> I'm in a Catholic church, in the middle of the greatest sexual scandal in the history of Catholicism, in the men's room, with a boy who wants me to help him with his zipper.
>
> What would you do?

At this point in the essay, I wanted the reader to stop and think, that is, to leave the immediacy of the narrative and take a moment to reflect, so I freeze the story and shift briefly into the past tense:

> I've asked this question of many friends and co-workers and have been surprised by their answers: Under no circumstances would I have touched him. Or, I would have gone and found his parents. Or, I would have passed a note so an announcement could be made from the pulpit. And my favorite: I would have found a woman to help him.
>
> In other words, men cannot be trusted with little boys.
>
> That's not the way I saw it. No, I believed with all my heart that helping him would be an act of male solidarity. I knew, in a pure way, what he was suffering. The embarrassment. The desperate hope that a stranger could help. And didn't Jesus prove in the story of the Good Samaritan that the stranger could be your neighbor? Hey, I was in church.

What follows is a return to the narrative and to the present tense. So that sounds to me like a kind of language tool: If you write a narrative in the present tense and want to create some suspense, step away from the story line and address the reader in the past tense. It's also possible to shift from the historical past to the present to make a particular scene stand out from the rest. But you must do this with a purpose and a plan.

One of the best nonfiction books ever written on boxing is by novelist Joyce Carol Oates, and one of her favorite moves is the use of the present tense to make you feel you are watching a fight as it is happening, second by second, punch by punch:

> Early in the second round, Tyson knocks Berbick to the canvas with a powerful combination of blows, including a left hook; when Berbick manages to get gamely to his feet he is knocked down a second time with a left hook to the head.... Accompanied by the wild clamor of the crowd as by an exotic sort of music, Berbick struggles to his feet, his expression glazed like that of a man trapped in a dream; he lurches across the ring on wobbly legs, falls another time, onto the ropes, as if by a sheer effort of will gets up, staggers across the ring in the opposite direction, is precariously on his feet when the referee, Mills Lane, stops the fight. No more than nine seconds have passed since Tyson's blow but the sequence, in slow motion, has seemed much longer.... The nightmare image of a man struggling to retain consciousness and physical control before nine thousand witnesses is likely to linger in the memory: it is an image as inevitable in boxing as that of the ecstatic boxer with his gloved hand raised in triumph. (from *On Boxing*)

With the present tense, the author transports us into the ring, but then, using the same device, she does something more: she creates a continuing present—an everlasting presence—that is likely to "linger in the memory," not just of the spectator but of the reader.

Inexperienced writers may look at such passages and be tempted to demonstrate their "mad skills" by switching tenses like the masters. In most cases, this should be avoided or at least limited to experiments in style. In other words, go ahead and try it, but be ready in revision to saddle up that old workhorse, the historical past tense.

I offer three reasons: (1) you are less likely to trip; (2) you are less likely to confuse the reader; (3) the past tense is often more compelling than the present. As an example of this last point, let's look at a passage from Don DeLillo's novel *Libra,* an imagined reconstruction of the assassination of JFK, including an elaborate description of the shooting, in all its gruesome detail:

> Agent Hill was off the left running board and moving fast. There was another shot. He mounted the Lincoln from the bumper step, extending his left hand to the metal grip. It was a double sound. Either two shots or a shot and the solid impact, the bullet hitting something hard. He wanted to get to the President, get close, shield the body. He saw Mrs. Kennedy coming at him. She was climbing out of the car. She was on the rear deck crawling, both hands flat, her right knee on top of the rear seat. He thought she was chasing something and he realized he'd seen something fly by, a flash somewhere, something flying off the end of the limousine. He pushed her back toward the seat. The car surged forward, nearly knocking him off. They were in the underpass, in the shadows, and when they hit the light he saw Connally washed in blood. Spectators, kids, waving. He held tight to the handgrip. They were going damn fast. All four passengers were drenched in blood, crowded down together. He lay across the rear deck. He had this thought, this recognition. She was trying to retrieve part of her husband's skull.

Any writer who doubts the immediate power of the historical past tense need only read this passage and others like it. The effect on me is a suspension of disbelief: "Shit, this really happened." Compared to the reality created by the historical past, a passage in the present can seem gauzy and unreal, a dream vision rather than a vicarious experience.

## KEEPSAKES

- For most narratives and reports, prefer the historical past tense. Make it your workhorse.
- On rare occasions, use the present tense to give a sense of you-are-here immediacy to the reader.
- If you shift tenses, do it for a purpose, not just to show off.
- In your copyediting and proofreading, make sure your tenses are consistent.

# 36

...

## Politely ignore the language crotchets of others.

Some people who love the English language—including yours truly—develop "crotchets" about it, that is, "odd, whimsical, or stubborn notions." If we carry around too many crotchets for too long, we get crotchety, or perversely stubborn and judgmental, the way Ebenezer Scrooge managed the work of his clerk Bob Cratchit. Members of the crotchety crowd love one another and tend to turn their own preferences about grammar and language into useless and unenforceable rules.

One famous crotchet, going back more than a century, demands that the writer not split an infinitive. How then do we explain the enduring popularity of the language that opens the *Star Trek* adventures: "Space...the Final Frontier. These are the voyages of the starship *Enterprise*. Its five-year mission: to explore strange new worlds, to seek out new life and new civilizations, to boldly go where no man has gone before."

"To boldly go..." I'll say.

In the *New York Times* essay titled "Oaf of Office," Steven Pinker argues that it was a language crotchet that led the chief justice of the Supreme Court to botch the words of the presidential oath of office. In the process of swearing in Barack Obama, Justice John Roberts asked him to "solemnly swear that I will execute the office of president of the United States faithfully." But the order of those words differs from those in the Constitution: "Solemnly swear that I will faithfully execute," not "I will execute...faithfully."

According to Pinker,

> Language pedants hew to an oral tradition of shibboleths that have no basis in logic or style, that have been defied by great writers for centuries, and that have been disavowed by every thoughtful usage manual. Nonetheless, they refuse to go away, perpetuated by the Gotcha! Gang and meekly obeyed by insecure writers.
>
> Among these fetishes is the prohibition against "split verbs," in which an adverb comes between an infinitive marker like "to," or an auxiliary like "will," and the main verb of the sentence. According to this superstition...Dolly Parton should not have declared that "I will always love you" but "I always will love you" or "I will love you always."

Of infinitive splitting, Henry Fowler wrote in 1926: "No other grammatical issue has so divided English speakers." So if you face the temptation to mischievously split an infinitive, I say succumb to it.

Another crotchet concerns ending a sentence with a preposition, as in the song lyric "Do you know where you're going to?" To please the crotchety, you could cut off that last word, although that strategy would not work with "Where are you coming from?" "From where are you coming?" would mark you as a prig and a bore. I approve of responding to your crotchety critics by the addition of three little words, as in this vignette:

> "Where are you coming from?"
>
> "I won't tell you because you ended that sentence with a preposition."
>
> "OK. Where are you coming from, you pompous ass?"

Which leads me to this final crotchet: that a formal writer should not begin a sentence with *and* or *but*. This is another "rule" you can ignore as long as you are sensitive to the preferences of a teacher or an editor and to the general standards of a particular discourse community.

The problem for me is that *and* and *but* are lumped together as *correlative conjunctions,* that is, words that join other words together to create a relationship of balance. What exists on one side of the conjunction should equal what is on the other: the devil and the deep blue sea; Sonny and Cher; faith, hope, and love.

But for me the two words *but* and *and* are not equal and can and should be used for different effects. This occurred to me while reading *The Reader,* a novel written in German by Bernhard Schlink and translated into English by Carol Brown Janeway. I noticed that very few sentences began with the word *and* (*und* in German), and that *but* (*ader* in German) was used time and again at the beginning of sentences and even paragraphs.

I began to see a logic in this distinction. In most cases, the reader anticipates the *and,* that one word or thought will follow another, and another, and another. In other words, *and* becomes the default position. The word *but* does not have this effect. *But* doesn't add something to what has come before; *but* takes something away. At its most daring, it can feel like a Bat Turn, a 180-degree spin in the Batmobile. Make that a But Turn.

Here's an example in which the protagonist reflects on an experience with an older woman in his youth:

> I can also remember classes at school when I did nothing but dream of her, think of her. The feeling of guilt that had tortured me in the first weeks gradually faded. I avoided her building, took other routes, and six months later my family moved to another part of town. It wasn't that I forgot Hanna. But at a certain point the memory of her stopped accompanying me wherever I went. She stayed behind, the way a city stays behind as a train pulls out of the station. It's there, somewhere behind you, and you could go back and make sure of it. But why should you?

The grammar checker in my computer does not recognize "But at a certain point..." as a complete sentence and wants me to revise it, perhaps because it prefers the conjunction to be within rather than at the beginning of the sentence. The checker does not object to that final sentence, "But why should you?" But the first use of *but* reverses the energy and direction of the paragraph.

In one of the most dramatic lines in the novel, Hanna reflects on the consequences of having served as a female guard in a Nazi concentration camp:

> I always had the feeling that no one understood me anyway, that no one knew who I was and what made me do this or that. And you know, when no one understands you, then no one can call you to account. Not even the court could call me to account. But the dead can.

The logic of *but* in this novel transcends mere functionality. *But* turns out to be the conjunction of moral ambiguity, and that is at the heart of the book's argument as a young German man weighs his own choices in the cloud of his country's history.

## KEEPSAKES

Do not be afraid to:

- split infinitives or other verbs forms.
- end a sentence with a preposition.
- begin a sentence with *and* or *but*. Just as I argued that writers should appreciate the huge differences between *a* and *the*, the same should apply to *and* and *but*. In my logic, *and* is the default conjunction, the one that adds on to what is already written or said. *But* is the subtraction conjunction. This distinction and its consequences are well known in the fields of leadership and management. There are *but* folks in every group, people whose inclination is to argue against the proposal. An *and* culture permits you to add on to the ideas under discussion without the reflexive cautions of But Boy or But Girl.

...

# 37

# Learn the five forms of well-crafted sentences.

Letters represent sounds. Words are built from letters. A group of words makes a phrase. Add a subject and verb, and you have a clause. If that clause expresses a complete thought, we call it a sentence. But if that clause expresses an incomplete thought, it is called subordinate or dependent, and we have to attach it to a main clause or it will not be considered Standard English. One complete sentence, or even a fragment or a word, can serve as a paragraph. More often, though, several sentences join together in a paragraph to develop a thesis or idea. And several paragraphs, sometimes many, are required to write an essay, report, or chapter for a book. What an amazing process.

Ten sentences form that last paragraph, and I wrote it, in part, to illustrate the basic variety of sentence structures. As an experienced reader and writer, I think of these distinctions less often than you might imagine, but they are necessary to produce effective sentences with purposeful punctuation. At a more advanced level, they will provide you with some reliable tools to make meaning and tune your style.

Here are the five basic sentence structures:

1. **The intentional fragment.** This expresses meaning without a subject and verb: "What a woman!" The reader provides

the missing words that are understood: "I think she is a great woman."

2. **The simple sentence.** This is a complete thought expressed in one clause: "Rome has fallen to the barbarians." But a simple sentence can have more than one subject or verb: "Like a freight train, the fullback rumbled, tumbled, and stumbled into the end zone." And although a simple sentence can be very short ("Jesus wept"), it can be infinitely long: "I like pizza, French fries, fried chicken, cheeseburgers, potato chips, pretzels, coconut custard pie," ad infinitum.

3. **The complex sentence.** This includes one independent clause and any number of dependent clauses: "Where there is no justice, there can be no peace." That last clause can stand alone as a sentence, but the first one needs help.

4. **The compound sentence.** This sentence requires more than one independent clause linked in a variety of ways: "Madonna was once the holy name of the Blessed Virgin Mary, but then came along a young Italian girl singer from suburban Detroit." Either clause could stand alone. They can be linked with a comma and a conjunction, or with a semicolon.

5. **The compound-complex sentence.** This adds one or more subordinate clauses to a compound sentence, as in this revision of the sentence above: "Madonna was once the holy name of the Blessed Virgin Mary, but then came along a young Italian girl singer from suburban Detroit, who turned disco clubs into little houses of worship."

Let's break down the paragraph that opens this chapter:

- "Letters represent sounds." *Simple sentence, one independent clause*
- "Words are built from letters." *Simple sentence*
- "A group of words makes a phrase." *Simple sentence*
- "Add a subject and verb, and you have a clause." *Compound sentence, two independent clauses*
- "If that clause expresses a complete thought, we call it a

sentence." *The first clause depends on the second, giving us a complex sentence*

- "But if that clause expresses an incomplete thought, it is called subordinate, and we have to attach it to a main clause or it will not be considered Standard English." *Compound-complex sentence*
- "One complete sentence, or even a fragment or a word, can serve as a paragraph." *Simple sentence*
- "More often, though, several sentences join together in a paragraph to develop a thesis or idea." *Simple sentence*
- "And several paragraphs, sometimes many, are required to write an essay, report, or chapter for a book." *Simple sentence*
- "What an amazing process." *Intentional fragment (no verb)*

To review: Simple. Simple. Simple. Compound. Complex. Compound-complex. Simple. Simple. Simple. Fragment.

Writers and teachers often advise that varying sentence length and structure creates the effects we call style, voice, rhythm, and flow. The more straightforward and informational the writing, the more simple sentences you are likely to find. The more stylish and scholarly the writing, the greater the variety you are likely to discover.

Consider this paragraph from *Goldengrove,* a novel by Francine Prose:

> If all the clocks and calendars vanished from the planet [dependent clause], people, especially children, would still know [main clause] when Sunday came [dependent clause]. They would still feel that suck of dead air [main clause], that hollow vacuum created when time slips behind a curtain [dependent clause], when the minutes quit their orderly tick, and ooze away, one by one [dependent clause]. Colors are muted [main clause], a jellylike haze hovers and blurs the landscape [main clause]. The phone doesn't ring [main clause], and the rest of the world hides and conspires to pretend [main clause] that everyone else is baking

cookies or watching sports on TV [dependent clause]. Then Monday arrives [main clause], and the comforting racket starts up all over again [main clause].

Complex. Complex. Compound. Compound-complex. Compound. No simple sentences or intentional fragments in this passage, but still an interesting variety of lengths and structures, all suiting the author's narrative purpose.

## KEEPSAKES

• The *intentional fragment* can be a word, a phrase, or a clause but does not express the full thought of a complete sentence.

• A *simple sentence* is made up of one main clause and no other clauses.

• A *complex sentence* is made up of one main clause and at least one subordinate clause. (A subordinate or dependent clause has a subject and a verb but cannot stand alone.)

• A *compound sentence* has two or more independent clauses.

• A *compound-complex* sentence has at least two independent clauses and at least one dependent clause.

# 38

## • • •

## Make sentence fragments work for you and the reader.

I sit at this moment in my doctor's office staring at my choles-terol numbers, and they are not good. Too much pizza and Pepsi, I guess. I look up and notice two pieces of office art: a scale model of the human heart, and the head of a giant alligator. The gator looks like he is about to eat the heart. It is not a comforting image for a guy whose total cholesterol number is 70 points higher than his IQ.

I avert my eyes, which now catch the cover of a recent issue of *Time* magazine. The headline reads:

*Why the pope loves America*
*U.S. Catholics may confound him, but America doesn't.*
*On the eve of his papal visit, a look at how this country has shaped Benedict XVI.*

It occurs to me that the first and last of those sentences are frag-ments, which means that only the middle one can stand inde-pendently as a complete thought: "U.S. Catholics may confound him, but America doesn't."

Lots of meaning is packed into one complete sentence and two intentional fragments. The key word is *intentional*.

A college student once told me that she liked to use fragments in her writing but that her composition teacher corrected her every time. "Would you let me use fragments?" she asked, looking for ammunition she could use against her professor. I told her that I'd feel better about giving her permission if I knew that she understood the difference between an intentional and an unintentional fragment, that is, between a strategy and a mistake.

A useful insight about language reveals that some words—ones that would make a sentence complete—are understood by the reader or listener, even if those words are missing from the text. If I should yell "Go to hell!" the subject is understood to be "you." But what if I said or wrote, "When hell freezes over!"? That clause has a subject and a verb but cannot stand alone as a sentence. Yet its clarity and context keep it from being a mistake. The reader provides what is missing from information supplied earlier. "When hell freezes over!" can mean "I'll move to Florida when hell freezes over," or "I'll root for the Red Sox when hell freezes over."

So. The intentional fragment. Not a mistake. No sirree. More than that: the intentional fragment can carry several important strategic uses in a piece of writing.

### THE SHOTGUN BLAST

A fragment can explode upon the reader's sensibility to bring a shocking truth into sharp relief. Consider this passage from Mark Haddon's novel *A Spot of Bother*:

> He had removed his trousers and was putting on the bottom half of the suit when he noticed a small oval of puffed flesh on his hip, darker than the surrounding skin and flaking slightly. His stomach rose and he was forced to swallow a small amount of vomit which appeared at the back of his mouth.
>
> Cancer.

That fragment—serving as word, sentence, and paragraph—hits the reader like a shotgun blast.

## THE REST PERIOD

The fragment can offer relief, usually in the form of a resolution to a problem. Used as a single paragraph, the fragment offers a pause, especially when it follows a long sentence. Here Mark Haddon describes a man waking from a nightmare:

> He fixed his eyes on the tasseled lampshade above his head and waited for his heart to slow down, like a man pulled from a burning building, still not quite able to believe that he is safe.
> Six o'clock.
> He slid out of bed and went downstairs.

The fragment as a paragraph creates a snowbank of white space on the page that helps to relieve the reader's tension.

## THE INVENTORY

A series of short fragments helps the writer build a body of evidence for the reader, especially when the fragments read less like a list and more like details from a narrative. Consider this paragraph from an essay by Wright Thompson on the rise and steroid fall of baseball slugger Mark McGwire:

> Only ghosts remain at McGwire's boyhood home in Claremont, California. Bits and pieces of a former life, things left behind. The pink and white chairs in the living room. The white wrap-around couch. The blue wallpaper upstairs.

## THE INTENSIFIER

My friend Jennifer 8. Lee uses few fragments in her entertaining book *The Fortune Cookie Chronicles*. When she does reach for one, it always intensifies the effect she is trying to achieve. In this passage, she describes the search for a certain Chinese restaurant in Omaha, Nebraska:

I looked up the number online and dialed. A woman picked up.
I started out by introducing myself in Mandarin Chinese.
I receive the telephone equivalent of a blank stare.
I switched to basic Cantonese.
More blankness.
I tried English.
The woman cut me off. "We're Korean," she said in a thick accent. Then she hung up.

Notice how the single fragment "More blankness" helps Lee build the tension before that delicious punch line.

Turn to the back cover of Lee's book, and you'll discover that those trying to sell it understand the intensifying power of the intentional fragment:

One woman.
One great mystery.
One consuming obsession.
Forty thousand restaurants.

## STRIVING FOR INFORMALITY

You are unlikely to find many fragments in works of philosophy. That is because the fragment almost always expresses a degree of informality, except, perhaps, in works of poetry or oratory. But even in the most serious works of literature, the fragment is an irreplaceable building block of dialogue.

"Why not?"
"Because."
"Because of the sex?"
"Not just that."
"Then what?"
"Because of your mother."

I just made that up, but something tells me I've read a dozen scenes like it in novels and screenplays.

## THE OBJECTIVE CORRELATIVE

T. S. Eliot argued that the poet was always in search of the object that correlated to a feeling or emotion the poet wanted to express, hence the literary jargon "objective correlative." Watch how veteran journalist Jacqui Banaszynski uses the fragment to fulfill this purpose in her report about Turkish refugees:

> Toothpaste. And toothbrushes. Ten of them. One for himself, his wife and each of their eight children. Is that so much to ask? The man who calls himself Ali Ahmet wants to know.
>
> "They are trivial things, but they are important," Ahmet says. "When I was in my home, I cleaned my teeth, and my children cleaned, at least three times a day. Since one month, since I left my home, we have not cleaned. And please, tell the world we have not enough soap."

A fragment is a rare way to begin a newspaper story, but in this case the power of that first word "Toothpaste" serves as the physical manifestation of a man's search for dignity for his family.

I've checked my opinions about the intentional fragment against those of that great standard-bearer H. W. Fowler and his reviser Sir Ernest Gowers. In *Modern English Usage* Gowers offers practical advice on the use of what he calls the "verbless sentence." He admits that "a grammarian might say that a verbless sentence was a contradiction in terms." But, at least in this case, let the grammazons be damned:

> The verbless sentence is a device for enlivening the written word by approximating it to the spoken. There is nothing new about it. Tacitus, for one, was much given to it. What is new is its vogue

with English journalists and other writers, and it may be worth while to attempt some analysis of the purposes it is intended to serve.

Among those purposes, Gowers lists (with examples): a transition, an afterthought, a dramatic climax, a sharp comment, a picture, an aggressive opinion—in general, the creation of a livelier, more staccato style.

The authors of *Modern English Usage* stand among my heroes, early champions of a reconciliation of what came to be called prescriptive and descriptive grammar:

> Used sparingly and with discrimination, the device can no doubt be an effective medium of emphasis, intimacy, and rhetoric. Overdone...it gets on the reader's nerves, offending against the principle of good writing immortalized in Flaubert's aphorism "L'auteur, dans son oeuvre, doit être comme Dieu dans l'univers, présent partout et visible nulle part." ["The author, in his work, ought to be like God in the universe: present in everything, visible in nothing." —RPC]

## KEEPSAKES

The intentional fragment or verbless sentence can work for you and the reader, but only if you use it as a purposeful strategy. It can:

- shock the reader.
- provide a moment of relief.
- create an inventory of significant details.
- intensify the meaning.
- modulate a voice toward informality.
- focus the reader on a key point.

# 39

## • • •

# Use the complex sentence to connect
# unequal ideas.

All of us who express opinions about language sometimes write statements that others find startling or even alarming. One such statement comes from Robert Gunning, a well-known enemy of foggy writing. His recommendation is to "avoid complex sentences." On its face, this advice is ridiculous and impossible to carry out. Imagine my trying to avoid complex sentences in the process of writing this book or any text. It may be that Gunning does not mean what I think he means. He might be using the common meaning of *complex* rather than the technical one. If by *complex* he means "so complicated as to defy understanding," I embrace him as a brother. But if he means that I should not use subordinate clauses next to main clauses, we've got a problem.

A complex sentence is a wonderful tool for combining two thoughts by giving one of them more weight: "As public concern over high gas prices and climate change continues to grow, so too will the demand for alternative energy solutions." That sentence comes from a magazine advertisement designed to persuade you to invest your money in solar or wind power. The copywriter uses a complex sentence to make the case, beginning with a subordinate clause reminding you of what you already know: that people are worried and angry about high gas prices. That dependent clause leans on the main clause, the one that pushes you toward action.

If the complex sentence conveys unequal ideas, then we need a sentence structure to communicate equal ones, and that structure is called *compound:* "You will provide the information, or I will kill your entire family." That bit of dialogue from a thousand different action movies works because of the balance imposed by the sentence structure: do this, or I will do that.

One way I learned the elements of the English language—grammar, syntax, parts of speech, sentence structure—was by diagramming sentences. Curiously, I associate this discipline with two different schools of grammar: nuns teaching armies of Catholic kids in the 1950s, and contemporary linguists drawing trees with branches of language and meaning.

The diagramming of sentences was invented in 1863 and was a popular way of teaching syntax until the 1970s. (Kitty Burns Florey could spark a revival with her book *Sister Bernadette's Barking Dog.*) I remember spending hours diagramming sentences in elementary school, and it really did help me understand how sentences work at the basic level. Short simple sentences were, of course, the easiest to diagram. Linguist R. L. Trask offers this example, using the simple sentence "The police trapped the frightened burglar just behind the house":

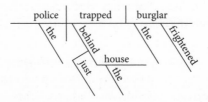

I will admit, though, that my patience and diagramming ability wore out quickly, especially when we moved from simple sentences to ones that were compound or complex. For some sentences, it might take a wall and an engineer to capture and render an accurate diagram. That thought came to me as I read the opening of a short essay by Brian Doyle in *Orion* magazine:

> The greatest nature essay *ever* would begin with an image so startling and lovely and wondrous that you would stop riffling through the rest of the mail, take your jacket off, sit down at the table, adjust your spectacles, tell the dog to lie *down,* tell the kids to make their *own* sandwiches for heavenssake, that's why god gave you *hands,* and read straight through the piece, marveling that you had indeed seen or smelled or heard *exactly* that, but never quite articulated it that way, or seen or heard it articulated that way, and you think, *man, this is why I read nature essays, to be startled and moved like that, wow.*

(We should note, in passing, how Doyle uses italics strategically— to mimic speech, to emphasize meaning, and to render both emotion and thought.) But I am not nearly smart enough to attempt to diagram such a show-offy sentence (I mean that in a good way) or even to give a label to its structure. I guess it is a compound-complex sentence, which means that it contains two independent clauses and at least one subordinate clause. One main clause starts with "The greatest nature essay *ever* would begin with an image." Another main clause (I think) seems embedded in the rest: "that's why god gave you *hands.*" The simple test of their independence is that either one can stand alone as a sentence. Not so the dependent clause that begins: "that you would stop riffling through the rest of the mail" or the one that begins "that you had indeed seen or smelled." That final clause in italics, "*man, this is why I read nature essays,*" can also stand as a complete thought.

The best sentences, even the most serious ones, are fun to write, coming from creative drafting and revision, not from some diagrammatic calculation. Consider this paragraph from Salman Rushdie's *Imaginary Homelands:*

> But human beings do not perceive things whole; we are not gods but wounded creatures, cracked lenses, capable only of fractured

perceptions. Partial beings, in all the senses of that phrase. Meaning is a shaky edifice we build out of scraps, dogmas, childhood injuries, newspaper articles, chance remarks, old films, small victories, people hated, people loved; perhaps it is because our sense of what is the case is constructed from such inadequate materials that we defend it so fiercely, even to the death.

It is not just the variation of structure that builds this argument, but the linking of elements of different length: a sentence of twenty-two words, followed by a fragment of eight words, followed by the longest sentence leading to the most powerful phrase "even to the death."

But the same ingenuity went into this sentence, a wonderful parody of the most dreadful examples of Ernest Hemingway's prose: "As his hands, calloused and cross-hatched from too many afternoons fighting the big fishes in the big ocean, slid down her firm but pliant body, he discovered the scar from a long-ago bullet just above her hip bone." If you are laughing somewhere, Mr. Gunning, know that you are laughing at one of those complex sentences you urged us not to use.

## KEEPSAKES

• *Complex sentences* create a connection between clauses that are unequal and dependent.

• *Compound sentences* balance the scales with clauses of about equal weight.

• The punctuation of a complex sentence depends on the position of the subordinate clause. That advice seems abstract, but the application is quite easy. If the weaker clause comes first, use a comma to separate it from the main clause. (As I just did.) You will usually not need a comma if the weaker clause comes at the end of the sentence.

• Equal clauses need stronger connectors than a comma. Tie one clause to another with a semicolon or with a comma plus a conjunction such as *and* or *but*.

# 40

...

# Learn how expert writers break the rules in run-on sentences.

You would think that one way to learn about the technical aspects of language is to read masterful writers, especially contemporary authors whose work is honored by critics and prize juries. So you should head for the archives of the Pulitzer Prizes or the National Book Awards, right? Not so fast. What you will find there, more often than not, are privileged authors whose status has given them a license to break the rules.

They have earned that right and so can you. But first, make sure you can identify common mistakes. You can't break a rule and turn it into a tool unless you know it's a rule in the first place.

Let's begin with two of the most common mistakes of sentence construction: the *run-on sentence* and the *comma splice*. Think of them as two sides of the same language coin. Some writers will construct sentences with multiple independent clauses, one clause running into another without benefit of punctuation. For example:

> I played the keyboard in dozens of rock bands but they wouldn't let me sing until I agreed to purchase the new sound system. The hand that rocks the cradle may rule the world but the hand that holds the mike rules the world of rock.

Most books on grammar, syntax, usage, and punctuation will tell you that the two main clauses in each of these sentences need something stronger than the conjunction "but." The writer has at least three ways to correct this error:

1. Place a comma before the conjunction.
2. Connect the clauses with a semicolon instead of using *but*.
3. Divide each sentence in two.

Now I've read a lot of student stories with sentences that looked like this: "I played the keyboard in dozens of rock bands, they wouldn't let me sing until I agreed to purchase the new sound system." My mistake here is that I spliced together two independent clauses with that wispy comma, which is not strong enough to hold them together.

So two classic mistakes: the run-on sentence and the comma splice. What, then, am I to make of this passage, describing a young man trying to escape a stalker outside a crowded baseball stadium?

> Their eyes meet in the spaces between rocking bodies, between faces that jut and the broad backs of shouting fans. Celebration all around him. But he is caught in the man's gaze and they look at each other over the crowd and through the crowd and it is Bill Waterson with his shirt stained and his hair all punished and sprung—good neighbor Bill flashing a cutthroat smile.

Or this one about the celebration inside the ballpark:

> But the paper keeps falling. If the early paper waves were slightly hostile and mocking, and the middle waves a form of fan commonality, then this last demonstration has a softness, a selfness. It is coming down from all points, laundry tickets, envelopes swiped from the office, there are crushed cigarette packs and sticky wrap from ice-cream sandwiches, pages from memo pads and pocket calendars, they are throwing faded dollar bills, snapshots torn to pieces, ruffled paper swaddles for cupcakes,

they are tearing up letters they've been carrying around for years pressed into their wallets, the residue of love affairs and college friendships, it is happy garbage now, the fans' intimate wish to be connected to the event, unendably, in the form of pocket litter, personal waste, a thing that carries a shadow identity—rolls of toilet tissue unbolting lyrically in streamers.

These two passages come from the novel *Underworld* by Don DeLillo, one of America's most celebrated fiction writers. I say "celebrated," even though that first passage contains three clauses that run on; even though the second passage contains five independent sentences spliced together by commas.

So who gets to break the rules? Clearly, one answer is Don DeLillo. And what are we to make of this paragraph from *The Road*, the apocalyptic novel by Cormac McCarthy?

They ate the little mushrooms together with the beans and drank tea and had tinned pears for their dessert. He banked the fire against the seam of rock where he'd built it and he strung the tarp behind them to reflect the heat and they sat warm in their refuge while he told the boy stories. Old stories of courage and justice as he remembered them until the boy was asleep in his blankets and then he stoked the fire and lay down warm and full and listened to the low thunder of the falls beyond them in that dark and threadbare wood.

McCarthy is capable of writing conventional prose as he demonstrates in that first sentence. But he sings his way out of his chains, to paraphrase Dylan Thomas, with a sentence that contains three run-on clauses, and then takes it to a higher level of rebellion with an intentional fragment that also manages to run on and on. Study McCarthy's work, and you'll get the feeling that he thinks marks of punctuation are like bedbugs: irritating, unsightly, worthy only of extermination. Even extended dialogue lacks quotation marks. And he doesn't give words like *won't* their standard apostrophe.

What does he get for all of these violations? A Pulitzer Prize for fiction, of course.

In spite of my admiration for both DeLillo and McCarthy, I must admit that their intentional violation of traditional standards can feel a bit precious at times. By *precious* I mean not "valuable" but "overrefined," a style that focuses too heavily on the lyrical gifts of the author rather than on the subject of the story. A much harsher analysis comes from critic B. R. Myers in *A Reader's Manifesto,* a work he describes as "an attack on the growing pretentiousness in American literary prose." As a prime example, he cites this passage from McCarthy's novel *Cities of the Plain:*

> For God will not permit that we shall know what is to come. He is bound to no one that the world unfold just so upon its course and those who by some sorcery or by some dream might come to pierce the veil that lies so darkly over all that is before them may serve by just that vision to cause that God should wrench the world from its heading and set it upon another course altogether and then where stands the sorcerer?

This passage does have the feeling of self-parody about it, staggering from an author who is word drunk and full of himself. "Try reading that passage out loud, and you'll realize why McCarthy is so averse to giving public readings," writes Myers. "His prose is unspeakable in every sense of the word." That is too harsh. But there is a way to make the paragraph more speakable, so to speak. Please, Cormac, sprinkle in some punctuation.

Study the masters, dear reader, and learn to appreciate their creative gifts and what they offer you. But don't turn them into idols. Use them, instead, as cautionary examples, writers who test your own sense of what is possible on the page, but who can also lead you into a bit of trouble. Recall that you run the risk of being punished if you use strategies for which privileged authors are rewarded.

# KEEPSAKES

In conventional descriptions of sentence mistakes, three are most common:

- The *unintentional fragment,* when the writer forgets to include a subject or a verb, or when the reader gets a wobbly dependent clause, not a clause that can stand by itself: "After her prom dress got caught in the door of the limousine."
- The *run-on sentence,* when independent clauses flow one after the other without any separation by punctuation or conjunction: "Her prom dress got caught in the door of the limousine but she didn't know it yet and then she leaned over to kiss her date and they both heard a rip and knew they were in trouble." This structure can work in high-level narrative prose, but it stands out for its rebellious resistance to punctuation. (If the two clauses are short enough, they can coexist without connectors: "She leaned over to kiss him and he heard the rip.")
- The *comma splice,* when independent clauses are separated only by a comma, which is not strong enough to do the job: "Her prom dress got caught in the door of the limousine, she leaned over to kiss him." The writer has several choices: use a semicolon rather than a comma; subordinate the first clause; make one sentence into two; or add to the comma a conjunction such as *but* or *and.*

PART FIVE

• • •

# Purpose

The history of my education is marked by a small number of stunning insights, usually passed along to me by a relative, friend, teacher, student, or colleague. These new ways of seeing the world are so powerful that they become the intellectual equivalent of getting cataract surgery, in which the cloudy old lenses are destroyed and brand-new ones implanted to return your vision to twenty-twenty.

Writing is not a magical talent but a rational process that can be learned by anyone willing to try; narratives are forms of vicarious experience; there is a direct connection between language abuse and political abuse. These are examples of theories that have helped me cultivate my own personal view of language and the world.

Here is another: there can be no perfection of craft without a noble purpose. That notion came to me through the late Cole Campbell, who dedicated his life to the improvement of journalism and the advancement of democracy. In a world divided by ideology, disinformation, propaganda, spin, and incivility, professing the nobility of language has even more importance. Without such high ideals, language can and will be used for mischief or worse. Even tyrants can learn to use the active voice and master rhetorical strategies such as emphatic word order.

This final section of *The Glamour of Grammar* considers the uses of language that bear significant social, cultural, and political consequences. We begin with the value of a strategic knowledge of nonstandard English, everything from slang to dialect to jargon to language that is considered taboo. You will discover important semantic distinctions between Standard and nonstandard English, between denotation and connotation, between concrete and abstract, the general and the particular. Key forms of figurative language will be analyzed for their strategic potential to describe, move, and persuade.

Living as we are in the midst of a technological revolution, we'll also take a look at how the Internet has changed the ways we experience communication, with special attention given to the formal requirements of an informal writing style. Many of the oldest strategies of grammar can remain glamorous, even in a hastily written blog post or a Twitter message of 140 characters. Back in the fourteenth century, when *grammar* was still *glamour,* a powerful magic spell was probably shorter than a Tweet.

# 41

...

## Master the uses of nonstandard English.

Because all of us belong to multiple discourse communities, or language clubs, all of us at one time or another rely on slang. I use sports slang and guy slang and musician slang and various ethnic slangs and the youth slang of those who grew up in the 1950s and 1960s. I know a little police slang (*perp, skell, snitch*) from watching cop dramas on TV. I don't know military slang or geek slang or nurse slang, so it's harder for me to get by in those little worlds without a translator.

The *OED* does not specialize in slang words, leaving room for the delightfully outrageous and compensatory compilation *Slang and Its Analogues,* but at least the *OED* defines *slang* and offers historical uses of the word dating back to 1756. *Slang,* in the Victorian view, was "the special vocabulary used by any set of persons of low or disreputable character; language of a low and vulgar type." Or, in a slightly different sense, "language of a highly colloquial type, considered as below the level of standard educated speech, and consisting of new words or of some current words employed in some special sense."

Such definitions come from the top of a class society and flow downhill, marking the speaker of slang as a person of low status. But there is also a bottom-up view of slang, apparent in this definition in the *AHD:* "A kind of language occurring chiefly in casual and playful speech, made up typically of short-lived coinages and figures of speech that are deliberately used in place of standard terms for added raciness, humor, irreverence, or other effect."

Could the definitions be more different? The *OED* gives us words such as "low," "disreputable," "vulgar." From the *AHD* we get "casual," "playful," "humor," "irreverence." Missing from both definitions is the "why" of slang, the sense in which slang defines a group, often a despised and marginal tribe. Knowledge of slang helps get you into a group just as slang can keep the un-initiated out of the clubhouse. The more marginalized the group—from prisoners to drug abusers to homosexuals to panhandlers to teenagers to gang members to a wide variety of ethnic groups living on the edge of the American mainstream culture—the more likely it is to produce its own nonstandard language.

Although both dictionaries define *slang* as a form of speech, the use of slang by authors goes back to Shakespeare and beyond. At a recent production of the American musical *Guys and Dolls,* I noticed how much of the gambler lingo I could not make out from characters such as Harry the Horse and Big Julie from Chicago. Some of the slang in the work of a writer such as Damon Runyon still sounds colorful, even though the meaning of individual words and phrases may no longer be available. The *AHD* is right. Many of the words coined into slang are "short-lived."

Here is Runyon describing his brief immersions into the "hobo" experience:

> I just thought it was the thing to do to steal rides on freight and passenger trains and to go places for no particular reason.... My transportation thefts were limited and I never went real far, but I picked up much of the lore of the road through contacts with real rovers and I accumulated considerable of their patter of that long-gone time.

I knew about "bindle stiffs" and "gay cats" and I had brief experience in some of the "jungles" or hobo camps, of those days, shelter spots in the woods or along rivers near towns where the 'boes "jungled up" and made common cause of "mooching" food in the towns and stewing it up in one big community pot over a camp fire.

I needed the *AHD* to teach me that a *bindle stiff* refers to a hobo who carries a bedroll, but I was delighted that the slang *mooch* survives to our time. (I've been known to mooch a ride or two from friends.)

All these reflections were inspired by a satirical piece in my morning newspaper written by Stephanie Hayes, a hip and versatile writer, capable of penning serious obituaries and edgy fashion pieces on the same day. She once wrote in the voice of Kellie Pickler, a young country music star discovered on *American Idol*. Pickler was having a bad hair day, a "scare-do":

> Howdy, y'all. It's me, Kellie Pickler, previously of American Idol, presently of boob job. Ain't they sumthin? POWZAM, DOLLY!...
>
> Anywho, I found myself in a real pickle trying to get to the 7th Annual Dressed To Kilt charity fashion show Monday. I was runnin' around lickety split trying to toast up some Eggos and get Taylor Swift off my couch. Girlfriend did not take the hint when I handed her some Folgers Mountain Grown in a styro-to-go cup. I'm all, PRINCESS ANGEL, Jonas McFace is not coming back! Pull yourself together, key his Benz and move on like Donkey Kong!

This send-up goes on for another three paragraphs, but you get the idea. What I like most about this fictional monologue is the way the writer draws on different forms of nonstandard English, not just slang ("key his Benz") but also the use of dialect to reflect the speaker's region and social class, along with the allusions to youth and commercial culture. You need a good ear and a good eye to pull this off, and, to avoid the stereotypes and cruel caricatures about "trailer trash," it helps to have a target who is now a wealthy public figure. There is a little bit of *OED* and *AHD* in Hayes's use of slang, a bit of snarky condescension along with a celebration of what's popular and crazy in American culture.

## KEEPSAKES

- Social groups on the margins often express themselves in forms of nonstandard English, including slang.
- From different points of view, slang can be framed as substandard language, unfit for educated use, or as a creative form of new expression, ripe for use by the talented writer.
- Strong writers master Standard English but also take advantage of opportunities to use nonstandard varieties to create special effects.
- Because the level of language is often tied to region or social class, the writer must take care that characterizations of speech do not cross the line into stereotype.

# 42

## • • •

## Add a pinch of dialect for flavor.

One of the trickiest and most tempting acts of writing is to render a person's style of speech. Each of us speaks—and sometimes writes—in a dialect, that is, a nonstandard form of English defined or influenced by national origin, region, ethnicity, and social class. There are standard dialects, sometimes referred to as the *koine* of the realm. The word comes from the name of an ancient Greek dialect that was once considered the standard for the Hellenistic world, but its modern usage, as defined by the *AHD*, is "a regional dialect that becomes the standard language over a wider area, losing its most extreme local features."

In England, at least since the time of Chaucer (about 1380), the standard dialect was the one spoken in and around London, the center of politics and culture. (Think, now, of the language of the BBC.) Chaucer and Shakespeare both put regional dialects in the mouths of some of their characters to distinguish or satirize their personalities. Chaucer, for example, took two foolhardy university students at Cambridge and had them speak in what would have been considered the unsophisticated dialect of the far north of England. In other words, he made them hicks from the sticks. One of Shakespeare's laughingstocks was a character in *Henry V* named Fluellen, a pompous fool who spoke in an undeniable Welsh accent.

In the United States, the standard spoken dialect is sometimes called "generalized American," the form of speech we are most likely to hear from our news anchors. In the dialect geography of American speech, it is not northern but southern language that has been ridiculed for its associations with simplemindedness and bigotry. This in itself is a form of language prejudice, which all writers must be cautious to avoid.

I learned long ago the hard lesson that there is nothing inherent in a dialect that makes it, in linguistic terms, superior or inferior to another. And yet when we hear or read dialect, it may provoke a powerful response based on our prejudices. Foreign languages and accents provide useful case studies. When I hear British English, I think *culture*. When I hear French, I think *romance*. When I hear Italian, I think *passion*. When I hear German, I think *dictator*. Why such associations? They come not from the language but from our feelings about the speakers of the language, and their culture and history—and ours.

Doug Williams was the first African American quarterback to lead his team to a Super Bowl victory. He started his pro career with the Tampa Bay Buccaneers but was let go in a contract dispute. The Bucs began to play poorly without him, and when asked by a reporter how he felt about his old team, Williams was quoted as saying, "I hope they be 0 and 16." In other words, he expressed the hope that they would lose all of their games.

In certain dialects, such use of "be," though nonstandard, is not a mistake. It expresses time, duration. It indicates that the speaker wanted the team to lose for the long haul. But the quote poses a problem for the writer. Some will read it and think the speaker is ignorant, even characterizing such language as "ghetto" or "Ebonics" or just "black." Of course, a writer could paraphrase the quote, but such cleansing drains the juice from the original. (Williams, by the way, is back with the Bucs in an executive position.)

Writers err when they decide to limit their use of dialect to only certain "colorful" characters in the culture. Marshall Frady, biographer of Alabama governor George Wallace, quoted the segregationist politician in dialect, using such words as "guvnuh," "reckon," and "whup 'em with a stick." The same author in the same book quoted Bobby Kennedy, who spoke in a distinctive Boston accent, without a trace of regionalism—as if he were Walter Cronkite.

This leads me to some useful advice from E. B. White in his part of *The Elements of Style:* "Do not use dialect unless your ear is good." He warns that phonetic spellings of speech can be easily misunderstood. "The best dialect writers, by and large, are economical of their talents: They use the minimum, not the maximum, of deviation from the norm, thus sparing the reader as well as convincing him."

When it comes to capturing patterns of human speech, Irish author Roddy Doyle has a great ear, and it shows in *The Commitments,* one of my favorite novels and movies, about a group of working-class musicians trying to bring American soul music to Dublin. Here is a typical scene in which the group goes after Deco, its obnoxious but talented lead singer:

> —Yeh were lookin' for tha', said Jimmy.
> —Wha' did I do now? Deco asked....
> —Yeh didn't introduce the group properly, said Jimmy.
> —I forgot.
> —Fuck off!
> —I was oney jokin'. Yis have no sense o'humour, d'yis know tha'?

In this brief passage, Doyle reveals one way of capturing the authentic dialect of working-class Dublin, and that is by using a phonetic rather than regular spelling to represent the spoken word. In this case, for example, the second person plural, which is simply "you" in Standard English, is represented by "yis," which might be "youse" in parts of New York City and "y'all" in the American South.

In addition to sound, dialect can also be expressed by distinctive variations in vocabulary. A classic example in the United States reveals the regional variations for describing sweet carbonated beverages in a can or a bottle. In the New York City of my youth, it was *soda*. When I went to school in New England, some kids from the Boston area called it *tonic*. When I moved south, it was either *pop* or a generic *coke*, representing all soft drinks, not just cola.

Here, for example, Pulitzer Prize–winning journalist Madeleine Blais captures the speech patterns of a young woman in prison for the murder of children under her babysitting care:

> I love young 'uns. I don't know why I done what I done. Young 'uns is real cute. They don't really give you no problem. They sleep most of the time. They is affection and you can cuddle them.... Everybody asks me, why you done it, why you done it. I keep askin' myself.

Blais characterizes the sound of the "killer babysitter" with spellings such as "askin'," and she uses a version of Southern speech with vocabulary such as "young 'uns" rather than "children." And she reflects the third element of dialect, which is nonstandard syntax, exemplified by phrases such as "done what I done" rather than "did what I did"; "They is affection" rather than "They are affectionate"; and the double negative of "They don't really give you no problem."

So remember that trinity of techniques: sound, vocabulary, and syntax.

Mark Twain brought brilliant transparency to this process in his explanation at the beginning of *Huckleberry Finn:*

> In this book a number of dialects are used, to wit: the Missouri Negro dialect; the extremest form of the backwoods Southwestern dialect; the ordinary "Pike County" dialect; and four modified varieties of this last. The shadings have not been done in a

haphazard fashion, or by guesswork; but painstakingly, and with the trustworthy guidance and support of personal familiarity with these several forms of speech.

I make this explanation for the reason that without it many readers would suppose that all these characters were trying to talk alike and not succeeding.

Twain may have been the first great American author to suppress some of his own language in order to stay true to the dialect of his characters. But I believe Flannery O'Connor was his equal in capturing versions of Southern speech. In a nonfiction essay about her raising of peacocks, the famous author from Milledgeville, Georgia, represents the speech of a farm family amazed by the sight of a peacock in full bloom:

"Whut is thet thang?" one of the small boys asked finally in a sullen voice.

The old man had got out of the car and was gazing at the peacock with an astounded look of recognition. "I ain't seen one of them since my granddaddy's day," he said, respectfully removing his hat. "Folks used to have 'em, but they don't no more."

"Whut is it?" the child asked again in the same tone he had used before.

"Churren," the old man said, "that's the king of the birds!"

What gives such writing its authority is O'Connor's characterization of her own speech. Referring to an ad for peacocks, she tells her mother, "I'm going to order me those." Later she tells a lineman from the telephone company to be patient for her peacock's grand display of tail feathers. "Nothing ails him. He'll put it up terreckly. All you have to do is wait." "Terreckly" instead of "directly" sends the message: This is my language, too. Nothing to be ashamed of.

## KEEPSAKES

- Each of us speaks in a dialect, a variety of English influenced by social class, ethnicity, and region.
- In most societies, one dialect, called a *koine,* is privileged and becomes the standard, with other variants considered to be somehow deficient.
- Authors going back hundreds of years have quoted characters speaking in dialect, usually as a form of social commentary or satire.
- While languages are not technically superior or inferior, we often make positive or negative characterizations about language based on our biases toward the speakers.
- Writers can develop character using dialect but must be careful that such characterizations do not hold the speaker up to ridicule based on social class, nationality, or ethnicity.

# 43

...

## Tame taboo language to suit your purposes.

Taboo language can be used crudely or with literary elegance. The crude uses are more common than ever. Some popular movies use the so-called F-word hundreds of times in a two-hour span. But if you live inside the English language, you'll realize that there are ways in which offensive language can be used to achieve a higher purpose.

1. *As an authentic expression of realistic human speech.* For both fiction and narrative nonfiction, we will at times want to reflect the world as it is, rather than as we wish it to be. The F-word can become deadened from overuse, but to create a pulp-fiction universe or a nonfiction rendering of a street corner or jail cell, it might be appropriate to let the dog out of its cage. In *The Commitments,* Irish author Roddy Doyle captures the working-class banter between a young band manager and a lead singer he is trying to recruit:

> —Are yeh in a group these days?
> —Am I wha'?
> —In a group.

—Doin' wha'?

—Singin'.

—Me! Singin'? Fuck off, will yeh.

—I heard yeh singin', said Jimmy.—You were fuckin' great.

2. *As a single, shocking, almost-out-of-context blow to the solar plexus.* A great example comes from *The Uncommon Reader,* a novel by British author Alan Bennett (playwright of *The History Boys*). The uncommon reader in the title turns out to be none other than the Queen of England—uncommon, indeed. When HRM discovers the joys of reading, she turns the monarchy and the nation topsy-turvy, so that her retainers conspire against her.

> The Queen said: "Yes. That is exactly what it is. A book is a device to ignite the imagination."
>
> The footman said: "Yes, ma'am."
>
> It was as if he were talking to his grandmother, and not for the first time the Queen was made unpleasantly aware of the hostility her reading seemed to arouse.
>
> "Very well," she said. "Then you should inform security that I shall expect to find another copy of the same book...waiting on my desk tomorrow morning. And another thing. The carriage cushions are filthy. Look at my gloves." Her Majesty departed.
>
> "Fuck," said the footman, fishing out the book from where he had been told to hide it down the front of his breeches.

3. *As a neutralizer to the poison of piety, fastidiousness, and erudition.* Since the Middle Ages, sexual and scatological language has been used to afflict the pretentious, be they lawyers, politicians, or preachers. Chaucer tells us the story of a fat and greedy friar who tries to swindle a jewel out of a dying man's bedclothes, only to have the man explode a fart in his hand.

Consider this passage by David Foster Wallace in which he questions the quality of John Updike's latest novel:

Updike makes it plain that he views the narrator's final impotence as catastrophic, as the ultimate symbol of death itself.... I am not shocked or offended by this attitude; I mostly just don't get it. Rampant or flaccid, Ben Turnbull's unhappiness is obvious right from the novel's first page. It never once occurs to him, though, that the reason he's so unhappy is that he's an asshole.

What might seem discourteous or uncivil to me in this critique may seem bold and edgy to others. In a passage that also mentions Blaise Pascal and Søren Kierkegaard, that final word is meant to deflate the reputation of one of America's most-honored authors.

4. *As a way of defining character.* People who, on occasion, use the F-word in public speech or writing may be revealing something interesting or significant about their characters. Excessive use of the word—like a body covered with tattoos—is usually associated with a lack of class. But be careful. Just as tattoos are no longer the sole possession of drunken sailors and prison lifers, so too the language of the lower classes has been appropriated by speakers who want to establish their street credibility or their cultural range from high to low. None other than Theodore Bernstein, the influential style czar of the *New York Times,* once published this opinion: "There is not...a single transitive verb in respectable or even in scientific language that expresses the idea of the slang verb *fuck.*"

An editor named Andy Barnes once told me that he thought you could get anything in print if you did it in the right way. So even if the F-word looks or feels wrong for your audience, never fear. There are hundreds upon hundreds of synonyms, metaphors, euphemisms, and dysphemisms that describe the sex act with a humor and originality to which we all may aspire. Evidence of this comes from a wonderful lexicon *Slang and Its Analogues* by J. S. Farmer and W. E. Henley, a work that sought to include all the fun stuff that Victorian sensibilities would not allow in the *OED.*

To understand Standard English, both spoken and written, we need to understand the nonstandard varieties, and they are spelled out by Ted Bernstein in the introduction to *Slang:*

> Strictly speaking, this monumental compilation is not a dictionary of slang, for it includes material that is not normally classified as slang, such as colloquial and informal language and nicknames. But there is no need to speak strictly; we can accept the compilers' broader scope to embrace everything that might come under the general heading of nonstandard language. Thus it includes *argot* (the speech of thieves and rogues, and, by derived meaning, the "inside" speech of any particular class), *jargon* (the language of a special group, of a science, sect, trade, profession), *dialect* (regional variations of language), and *casualisms* (relaxed, familiar, colloquial language).

Among its many charms, *Slang* is famous for its long (some might say endless) lists of synonyms for the most common offensive words and phrases. For reasons that are not clear, these treasure troves appear in almost random spots throughout the work, so that the synonyms for the F-word appear under the word *ride*. Drawing on classic literature and the language of the brothel, Farmer and Henley include these synonyms, and hundreds more:

> To accommodate, Adamize, ballock, belly-bump, bitch, block, bob, bore, bounce, brush, bull, bum, bung, caress, caulk, chuck, club, couple, cover, cross, cuddle, dibble, diddle, do, ferret, fiddle, flap, flimp, flutter, frisk, get-into, handle, have, hoist, huffle, hump, hustle, impale, jack, jape, jig-a-jig, knock, know, lay, mount, nibble, nick, nug, oblige, occupy, peg, perforate, pestle, phallicize, pizzle, plough, plug, poke... [etc., etc.]

If you need more and will be selling your next steamy novel in Paris, our happy lexicographers offer three full pages of synonyms in French.

In the glossary *Shakespeare's Bawdy* by Eric Partridge, we find endless evidence of the Bard's wit, poetic ingenuity, attention to character, and sensitivity to multiple audiences. Depending on context and purpose, Shakespeare can move from "make love" to "make one's heaven in a lady's lap" to "make one's play" to "make the beast with two backs" (Iago's cynical phrase) to "make the diseases." Hamlet talks with Ophelia of "country matters," a pun on the C-word.

Perhaps the most moving use of the F-word I ever encountered came in the documentary *9/11* by two French filmmakers about a firehouse in New York. During the filming, two jetliners flew into the Twin Towers, changing the way Americans look at the world. Even though the show ran on commercial television, we were given a chance to hear, uncensored, the rough emotional language of a fraternity of America's Bravest facing their greatest challenge. Real language. Real life.

## KEEPSAKES

Always use caution when using language some readers or listeners may consider taboo. But there are creative reasons to use such language:

- as a form of realistic speech
- to shock the reader to attention
- to burst the windy bag of pretension
- to define the character of the speaker

Remember to consider the alternatives: metaphors, euphemisms, or hyperbole in place of the most offensive forms.

# 44

...

## Unleash your associative imagination.

The Beat author Jack Kerouac, who died here in St. Petersburg, once said: "The only people for me are the mad ones, the ones who never yawn, or say a commonplace thing, but burn, burn, burn." People, of course, don't burn *literally* except in house fires, self-immolations, and cremation ceremonies. But some do burn in Kerouac's sense, the great ones like comets, others like meteorites, burning themselves out in a blaze of glory. It may not be obvious, but the word *burn* is a metaphor, an implied comparison, a close cousin to the simile, which is a more overt comparison, as in "like comets" or "like meteorites."

A simile uses *like* or *as:* "The moon, like Cupid's bow." A metaphor does not need *like* or *as:* "The moon's silver bow." But, as we'll see with the help of Northrop Frye, the differences are more significant than that.

It takes some practice and experience living inside the language, but many writers develop an associative imagination that allows them to use these figures of speech with power and meaning. And although these figures are more commonly associated with poetry than with prose, writers in almost every genre can take advantage of them. Consider the opening of the book *Ghosts of Manila,* in which Mark Kram describes the physical decline of world-famous boxing champion Muhammad Ali:

> Only his face remained as I remembered it. Eight years had elapsed since I had seen him spiral through the final, perilous years of his career, and even at age forty-two it still held at bay any admission of destruction. There was no zippered flesh, no blistered or pulpy ears, nor eye ridges that drop into sagging eaves; the nose remained agreeably flat without the distended bone or hammered spread. Always the centerpiece of vanity—this face, so instantly transportable into world consciousness—it was betrayed only by his eyes, his words. Where once his eyes publicly spilled with tumbling clowns, they were now a dance hall at daybreak. Where once the words streamed in a fusillade of octaves, they were now sluggish and groping.

Now consider this paragraph about Ali's greatest rival, Joe Frazier:

> Nearing the end of the century, Muhammad Ali still swam inside of Joe Frazier like a determined bacillus. Despite the advice of a few friends and some of his children, Frazier was keeping an obsessional hold on Ali, sometimes with a freefall into the void between regret and revenge; at other times his contempt just lay there hissing. Much time had passed since my visit with Ali, and if he had been a sonata of sometimes bewildered withdrawal, Frazier was a brass section insistent on sending out a triumphal arch of sound not consonant with his early self. The usually remote Frazier had taken on, ironically, the attitude and coloration of the Ali that had once stuck words on him as if he were a store window dummy.

Figurative language can compare and contrast two physical objects or experiences, but it can also illuminate the world of ideas by lending them the trappings of the concrete world. Let's revisit that passage from *Imaginary Homelands* by Salman Rushdie:

> But human beings do not perceive things whole; we are not gods but wounded creatures, cracked lenses, capable only of fractured perceptions. Partial beings, in all the senses of that phrase. Meaning is a shaky edifice we build out of scraps, dogmas, childhood injuries, newspaper articles, chance remarks, old films, small victories, people hated, people loved; perhaps it is because our sense of what is the case is constructed from such inadequate materials that we defend it so fiercely, even to the death.

A kind of puzzle or riddle stands behind the language of comparison: How is a human being like a cracked lens? How is the meaning of life like a shaky edifice? Even when the author provides some answers, he does not close the door to our own interpretations.

The language of comparison becomes less literary and more useful when it turns into *analogy,* an understanding of what is less known by holding it next to something that is more known. In his Pulitzer Prize–winning book *The Soul of a New Machine,* Tracy Kidder describes for a broad audience a system of "rings" that protects access to information in a computer:

> Picture an Army encampment in which all the tents are arranged in several concentric rings. The general's tent lies at the center, and he can move freely from one ring of tents to another. In the next ring out from the center live the colonels, say, and they can move from their ring into any outer ring as they please, but they can't intrude on the general's ring without his dispensation. The same rules apply all the way to the outermost ring, where the privates reside. They have no special privileges; they can't move into any ring inside their own without permission.
>
> Analogously, each ring defines some part of the computer's memory. How does the computer mediate a user's access to these

various areas? In the general case, it compares two numbers—the number of the ring to which the user has free access
and the number of the ring that the user wants to get into. If the
user's ring number is smaller than or equal to the number of the
ring that the user wants to enter, the user is allowed to go in.

The use of such devices of comparison and contrast reveals
much about the character of the author or speaker. We learn a lot
about the narrator of *The Reader* by Bernhard Schlink when he
uses analogy rather than metaphor to explain the power and
danger of love:

> When an airplane's engines fail, it is not the end of the flight.
> Airplanes don't fall out of the sky like stones. They glide on, the
> enormous multi-engined passenger jets, for thirty, forty-five
> minutes, only to smash themselves up when they attempt a
> landing. The passengers don't notice a thing. Flying feels the
> same whether the engines are working or not. It's quieter, but
> only slightly: the wind drowns out the engines as it buffets the
> tail and wings. At some point, the earth or sea look dangerously
> close through the window. But perhaps the movie is on, and the
> stewards and air hostesses have closed the shades. Maybe the
> very quietness of the flight is appealing to the passengers.
>
> That summer was the glide path of our love. Or rather, of
> my love for Hanna. I don't know about her love for me.

No critic wrote more engagingly about figurative language
than Canadian scholar Northrop Frye, who described the "mo-
tive for metaphor" in his book *The Educated Imagination*:

> As soon as you use associative language, you begin using figures of
> speech. If you say this talk is dry and dull, you're using figures as-
> sociating it with bread and breadknives. There are two main kinds
> of association, analogy and identity, two things that are like each
> other and two things that are each other. You can say with Burns,
> "My love's like a red, red rose," or you can say with Shakespeare:

Thou that art now the world's fresh ornament
And only herald to the gaudy spring.

One produces the figure of speech called the simile; the other
produces the figure called metaphor.

In other words, the metaphor asserts more power than the simile
because the author closes the distance between the two elements
of comparison. Being a light to the world is more powerful than
being like a light to the world.

Every tool, however useful, possesses a danger of misappli-
cation, as happens when you step on the teeth of a rake or slam
your thumb with a hammer. A literary tool such as the anecdote
can be abused to build a false case for the general from a misap-
propriated particular. For Frye, the same dangers lurk within all
metaphorical language:

> In descriptive writing you have to be careful of associative lan-
> guage. You'll find that analogy, or likeness to something else, is
> very tricky to handle in description, because the differences are
> as important as the resemblances. As for metaphor, where you're
> really saying "this *is* that," you're turning your back on logic and
> reason completely, because logically two things can never be the
> same thing and still remain two things. The poet, however, uses
> these two crude, primitive, archaic forms of thought in the most
> uninhibited way, because his job is not to describe nature, but to
> show you a world completely absorbed and possessed by the
> human mind.... The motive for metaphor, according to Wallace
> Stevens, is a desire to associate, and finally to identify, the human
> mind with what goes on outside it, because the only genuine joy
> you can have is in those rare moments when you feel that al-
> though we may know in part, as [Saint] Paul says, we are also a
> part of what we know.

My teachers always warned me: "Be careful with whom you
associate." That lesson applies to figurative language as well.

Compare and contrast to your heart's content, but always do so with caution and proportion.

## KEEPSAKES

• The simile, metaphor, and analogy are all figures of speech—that is, figurative language—that attempt to express a difficult truth through comparisons. In each, the purpose is to know something better by comparing it to something else.

• The *simile* does this by direct comparison, using the word *like* or *as:* "His words hurt like a hundred paper cuts."

• The *metaphor* identifies the two elements without using *like* or *as:* "That Roman orgy of a caucus was no place to select a presidential candidate."

• The *analogy* tends to be more explanatory, helping you to understand, say, distance and difficulty by comparison and contrast: "The path into the city was only the length of two football fields, but the roadside bombs would make the distance seem quite a bit longer."

• When you use any of these devices of association, be sure to consider not only how the elements are alike but also how they differ.

# 45

...

## Play with sounds, natural and literary.

There will come a time in the lives of most young writers when they will be inspired to use techniques of poetry in their prose. As we've seen, finding just the right metaphor, simile, or analogy can be hard literary work, heavy lifting. So it helps to build your muscles with the lighter weights, and the lightest of the light is *alliteration*.

In the song "That's Life," Frank Sinatra croons that he's been "a puppet, a pauper, a pirate, a poet, a pawn, and a king." The repetition of the *p* sound at the beginning of those five words is called *alliteration*, and it is a technique that can be traced back to the earliest forms of English poetry and echoed as late as 1877 by Gerard Manley Hopkins in his breathtaking religious poem "The Windhover":

> I caught this morning morning's minion, king-
> > dom of daylight's dauphin, dapple-dawn-drawn Falcon, in his
> > > riding
> > Of the rolling level underneath him steady air, and striding
> High there, how he rung upon the rein of a wimpling wing
> In his ecstasy!...

I first read this poem as a freshman at Providence College and admitted to my teacher Rene Fortin that even though I could not yet understand its meaning, I knew it was a great work of art because when I read it aloud, the sound of it moved me. The classical word to describe this effect in writing is *euphony*.

Perhaps the greatest master of prose alliteration was a man named Whiting Allen, who used his inexhaustible word-hoard to advertise the circus in the days before electronic media ruled. In a 1902 interview, Allen said,

> Alliteration is like the cable that grips a street car—it grips the mind and insensibly the mentality of the reader is caught by one word only to be gently but surely passed on to the next.

In describing a group of daredevil aerialists, Mr. Allen wrote: "In all man's struggles and strife in seeking supremacy by superiority in strength, skill, and strenuosity, there has never been anything like an approach to this fearful, frightful and fearless feat in rash and reckless risk of limb and life."

William Safire ranks a close second to Allen as a famous alliterator (my spell-checker wants me to change this to *obliterator*). As a newspaper columnist, Safire wrote about another type of circus: American politics. As a speechwriter for the Nixon administration, he attacked critics as "nattering nabobs of negativism" and "hopeless, hysterical hypochondriacs of history."

From mystical verse to circus hype, alliteration can be used to decorate the writing, even to the point of calling attention to itself. The aspiring writer should have a ball with it in experiments of style and voice, but the more experienced writer will use it judiciously.

Teaching a lesson on euphony, a writer named Arlo Bates offered this advice to students at Harvard more than a century ago:

> Excess of alliteration is the form of this fault which constantly besets young versifiers, and even poets of reputation are not always free of the charge of having carried this dangerous

ornament too far.... But properly applied this ornament in prose, as well as in verse, may be delightful.

Bates might have been anticipating something like the oratory of a Rev. Martin Luther King Jr.: "The ultimate measure of a man is not where he stands in moments of comfort and convenience, but where he stands at times of challenge and controversy." Writers must always remember that the sounds of language precede the symbols we use to represent those sounds on the page.

Many versions of the Batman story have been told over the past half century, but my favorite is still the parody of comic-book motifs produced in the 1960s television series starring Adam West as the alliterative Caped Crusader. I especially remember the fight scenes in which cartoon lettering exploded across the screen: Smash! Crash! Kerpow! Splat! In literary terms, the technique for making words echo sounds is called *onomatopoeia,* Greek for "coiner of names." The *AHD* offers *murmur* and *buzz* as examples.

When children are asked to write using words that echo sounds, they are inclined to exaggerate the effect, which is not a bad way to learn. An American poet laureate, Donald Hall, has encouraged writers to imitate, even parody, the forms they are trying to master. So it should not surprise us when sound-drunk kiddies write about puppies who bark, whine, whimper, and growl—all while the mutts are smashing and crashing and bashing the furniture.

Such exaggerated experimentation does evolve into something more mature and less noticeable. Consider this passage by Erik Larson describing a famous meeting of architects in 1891 planning the Chicago World's Fair:

> The light in the room was sallow, the sun already well into its descent. Wind thumped the windows. In the hearth at the north wall a large fire cracked and lisped, flushing the room with a dry sirocco that caused frozen skin to tingle.

At Hunt's brusque prodding the architects got to work.

One by one they walked to the front of the room, unrolled their drawings, and displayed them upon the wall. Something had happened among the architects, and it became evident immediately, as though a new force had entered the room. They spoke, Burnham said, "almost in whispers." (from *The Devil in the White City*)

What stands out in this passage are not just the words that reflect actual sounds—"thumped," "cracked," "lisped," "sirocco" (a hot wind), and "whispers"—but also the appeal of the description to multiple senses: to sound, sight (the play of light in the room), and touch (dry heat that causes frozen skin to tingle).

The writer can play with sounds, even in the most serious contexts, and what could be more serious in New York City than a memorial to the victims of 9/11?

Once more the leaden bells tolled in mourning, loved ones recited the names of the dead at ground zero, and a wounded but resilient America paused yesterday to remember the calamitous day when terrorist explosions rumbled like summer thunder and people fell from the sky.

That sentence opens a story by Robert D. McFadden of the *New York Times,* and I invite you to read it again, aloud this time. Go ahead, please. Read it aloud. I'll wait.

For such a story, on such a day, the news can read like poetry. The writer begins with the inherent drama and symbolism of ceremony. The tolling of bells and the reading of names place us in a familiar, but still emotional setting, fraught with history and meaning. Then come the sounds. In this passage and throughout the piece, details echo so effectively that they might serve as natural sound in a brilliant NPR story. The bells are leaden. They toll. The names are recited. On that dreadful day in 2001, explosions rumbled like summer thunder. (The poet would point out the repetition of those short *u* sounds, a device called *assonance.*)

The writer chooses words with care, and each reverberates with a solemn tone. Examine the language. Listen to it: *leaden, bells, tolled, mourning, loved ones, recited, names of the dead, ground zero, a wounded...America, summer thunder, fell from the sky.*

McFadden begins his story with three elements, a symbolic number that represents the whole. More interesting is the movement through the triad: from bells, to loved ones, to a resilient America—that is, from a symbolic object to powerful witnesses to an abstract representation of the nation as a whole. Finally, this sentence of forty-five words ends with a haunting, almost mystical image. The bloodless euphemism of people falling from the sky exemplifies decorum, a sensitivity that helps us look back with resolution and hope, rather than with bitterness and despair.

## KEEPSAKES

• *Alliteration* is an easy tool to teach and learn, but all figures of speech are best used with caution. With alliteration the writer or speaker repeats the initial sounds or letters in a word. So the names Marilyn Monroe and Mickey Mantle and Mickey Mouse alliterate. But many would argue that the name of the famous wrestler Gorgeous George alliterates because first and last name begin with the same consonant, even though they are pronounced differently. If you accept that premise, then alliteration (derived from the Latin word for "letter") is a figure of sight as well as a figure of sound.

• Many words are formed to imitate the natural or artificial sounds around us, words like *murmur, whimper, sizzle, moan,* and *click.* These words are examples of a long Greek word called *onomatopoeia,* pronounced on-uh-mat-uh-PEE-uh. But you can use simpler terms to describe them. Because of their imitative origins, they are sometimes called *echo words* or simply *sound words.*

• In the use of all these devices, moderation is a virtue—unless you are just trying to show off, and even then you'll look better by doing less.

# 46

...

# Master the distinction between denotation and connotation.

One of my favorite language lessons involves the story of a ceremony held at the Georgia Aquarium to mourn the death of a rare beluga whale. A reporter covering the story had written: "The crowd gathered and knelt around the 12-foot creature," which I, in a writing workshop, revised to "The crowd gathered around the 12-foot creature and knelt." One benefit of that revision, I argued, was to get the word *knelt*—with all its reverential connotations—in a more emphatic position.

Words have denotations and connotations, a distinction with a hundred applications for those trying to create or derive meaning. A word denotes its direct, literal meaning; in the case of *knelt*, the act of bending one's knee. A word connotes meaning indirectly through common associations, so with *kneel*, we may think of prayer, liturgy, mourning, or giving homage.

I first learned this distinction in 1972 when George McGovern ran against Richard Nixon for president. Some teacher pointed out to us the difference between these two sentences:

Richard Nixon was caught hiding in a limousine.
George McGovern was sighted striding into a sedan.

Neither of these sentences, it was clear, represented a neutral report. Their language loaded with associations, both sentences took the form of minieditorials. Nixon was "caught" while McGovern was "sighted." One was "hiding," the other "striding." A neutral report might have indicated that both of them "got into their cars," but the writers chose words with vibrating connotations. It is the common man or woman who rides in a sedan, but it is the privileged celebrity or mob kingpin who seeks refuge in a limousine.

It is often a battle of connotations that fuels political and cultural wars. Take, for example, the 2006 debate on the use of "civil war" to describe the struggles in Iraq. News outlets such as the *Los Angeles Times* and NBC began to include that phrase in their reporting. Other news organizations remained in a holding pattern with terms such as "sectarian violence." Tony Snow, speaking for the Bush administration, insisted that "civil war" overstated and mischaracterized the nature of the violence on the ground.

So what is a responsible writer or editor to do? The answer will be easier when we realize that the fair choice of words is one of the most important and common challenges in American speech, writing, and politics. Consider these words and phrases:

> *pro-choice* vs. *pro-abortion* vs. *anti-abortion* vs. *pro-life*
> *illegal alien* vs. *illegal immigrant* vs. *undocumented worker*
> *refugee* vs. *evacuee*
> *invasion* vs. *incursion* vs. *police action*
> *prisoner of war* vs. *enemy combatant*
> *Islamo-fascist* vs. *jihadist* vs. *terrorist* vs. *Muslim fanatic* vs.
>    *Iraqi insurgent*

The gravity of these word choices weighs heavily on the writer, as it should. For in politics, each term carries ideological meaning, even as it appears to the world in the sheep's clothing of impartiality. My terrorist, as they say, is your freedom fighter.

In his famous essay "Politics and the English Language," George Orwell argued that political abuse and language abuse form the double helix of government corruption and tyranny. "In our time," wrote Orwell after World War II, "political speech and writing are largely the defense of the indefensible. Things like the continuance of British rule in India, the Russian purges and deportations, the dropping of the atom bombs on Japan, can indeed be defended, but only by arguments which are too brutal for most people to face, and which do not square with the professed aims of the political parties."

The corrupt create language, argued Orwell, that softens or veils the truth through euphemism and abstraction: "Defenseless villages are bombarded from the air, the inhabitants driven out into the countryside, the cattle machine-gunned, the huts set on fire with incendiary bullets: this is called *pacification....* Such phraseology is needed if one wants to name things without calling up mental pictures of them."

The political language of our own time has mutated a bit from what Orwell read and heard. Today, the debate is framed by simple phrases repeated so often to stay "on message" that they turn into propaganda slogans, another substitute for critical thinking. Each side develops "talking points." So one side wants to "stay the course," without settling for the "status quo," and condemns political opponents who want to "cut and run."

One job of the responsible writer is to avoid the trap of repeating catch phrases, such as "the war on terror," disguised as arguments, and to help the public navigate the great distances between "stay the course" and "cut and run." It turns out that they are not the only options.

Which brings us back to "civil war." The phrase itself is odd, almost an oxymoron. All other denotations and connotations of *civil* are positive, the antithesis of war. We long for "civility" in speech and behavior, which is a sign of a "civilization" populated by citizens and "civilians" who study "civics." The phrase "civil war" is almost ancient. One early use in English, dated 1387, describes the "battle civil" between two Roman factions.

Shakespeare uses the word *civil* at the opening of *Romeo and Juliet* to describe the violence between the Capulets and the Montagues. And the exact phrase "civil war" appears in 1649 to describe the struggle between the British parliament and King Charles I.

We should also remember that the American Civil War was once called the "War Between the States," which seems neutral when compared with the contentious language of North and South that created the "War of the Rebellion" and the "War of Secession." Likewise, we should remember that many terms we take for granted were applied retrospectively by historians or other experts. (I explained to someone just today how— ignorant of the term *The Great War*—I always marveled at the prescience of those who named the First World War, knowing that a Second World War was sure to come along.)

The phrase *illegal alien* turns people into criminal Martians, yet *undocumented workers* seeks to veil their illegal status. Which leads me to *illegal immigrants,* a compromise that seems clear, efficient, and, from my limited perspective, nonpartisan. Others will and should disagree.

I argued in 2006 that journalists—and all fair commentators and writers—should avoid the widespread and unreflective use of the term *civil war.* The phrase is too vague an abstraction to describe all that is happening on the ground in Iraq. The violence comes from Americans, from civilians, from militia, from various Muslim sects (against foreigners and each other), from mercenaries, from criminal gangs, from foreign jihadists. It is less the job of the foreign correspondent to summarize information in abstract language than it is to report, in concrete and specific terms, what is happening.

The reporters in war zones are, to my mind, men and women of great physical and moral courage, performing one of democracy's precious duties: to observe war as closely as possible and to report back to those of us who claim to govern ourselves. If those observations conflict with government claims, so be it. We'll argue the definitions back home, and the news media here can cover that, too.

Ideological and cultural battles are often fought on fields of combat mined with denotation and connotation. "Partial-birth abortion" is harder to defend than the technical medical description "intact dilation and extraction." Some evacuees from Hurricane Katrina objected to the designation "refugee" because of its connotations of foreignness and war.

I once asked a group of writers, "What is the difference between *naked* and *nude?*" A woman yelled from the back of the room, "Being naked is more fun." The denotation of each word is the same. In fact, the *AHD* uses the word *nude* to define *naked,* and *naked* to define *nude.* Sofa, couch; couch, sofa. Rock, stone; stone, rock.

But we know from experience and popular culture that a house is not a home. Words like *film* and *movie* may be used as synonyms, but *film* has a decidedly up-culture connotation, which is why we call *Smokey and the Bandit* a movie but *The Seventh Seal* a foreign film.

Art critic Lennie Bennett argues that the differences between *naked* and *nude* have wide implications for the worlds of commerce and art:

> Naked versus nude may seem like a small, irrelevant distinction.... But those two words represent important and very different ways not only in how we look at an image but how we judge its value and the value of those involved in its creation.

She refers to debate over a photographic image of model Carla Bruni taken in 1993 by Michel Comte. The photo shows a posed Bruni without clothes standing in a slightly awkward posture, knock-kneed, hands over her privates. (I'm trying to find a neutral, nonerotic, nonclinical, nonhumorous word, and *privates* is the best I can do. No one said it would be easy.) Fifteen years later, Ms. Bruni is Madame Sarkozy, the First Lady of France, hugging Michelle Obama. Christie's auction house estimated the value of the photograph at $3,000, but crazed bidding drove it to a sale price of $91,000. Debate goes on as to whether the interest and the price rose because the First Lady is nude or naked. If nude, the buyer is getting a photographic work of art. If naked, the buyer is getting a piece of soft-core celebrity porn.

Bennett quotes art historian Lord Kenneth Clark: "To be naked is to be deprived of our clothes, and the word implies some of the embarrassment most of us feel in that condition. The word 'nude,' on the other hand, carries, in educated usage, no uncomfortable overtone. The vague image it projects into the mind is not of a huddled, defenseless body, but of a balanced, prosperous, and confident body."

Bennett agrees: "Nude confers power; naked implies help-lessness." But connotation can be overpowered by the eye of the beholder. There was not, I assure you, any helplessness in one lady's assertion that "Being naked is more fun." (She may have said "nekkid.")

The distinction between *connote* and *denote* becomes especially important for any writer trying to craft a neutral report. Reporting is not just a job for journalists: police officers write reports; social scientists write reports; physicians write reports. One benefit to a report is a kind of strategic evenhandedness. The writer is not some robotic blank slate but tries to convey information through a process that limits bias and special interest.

The scholar who wrote most effectively about this was from the field of semantics, not the world of journalism. His name was S. I. Hayakawa, and in 1939 he wrote *Language in Action,* a work that is still in print as *Language in Thought and Action.* Hayakawa devotes an early chapter to the language of reports, noting that by definition a report is "verifiable." Remember, he wrote this in 1939, but his commentary has a contemporary feel: "With the emphasis that is being given today to the discussion of biased newspapers, propagandists, and the general untrustworthiness of many of the communications we receive, we are likely to forget that we still have an enormous amount of reliable information available." To earn reliability, the writer of the report must learn skills such as the exclusion of judgments and what Hayakawa calls "loaded words."

"In short," he writes, "the process of reporting is the process of keeping one's personal feelings out. In order to do this, one must be constantly on guard against 'loaded' words that reveal or arouse feelings. Instead of 'sneaked in,' one should say 'entered quietly';...instead of 'officeholder,' 'public official';... instead of 'crackpots,' 'holders of uncommon views.'"

To follow such a discipline of reporting, one thing is certain: The writer must be aware of the denotation of a word or phrase and its connotations as well, associations that may unfairly load what is supposedly a neutral text with all kinds of disguised opinion.

## KEEPSAKES

• The denotation of a word conveys its literal meaning.

• The connotation of a word describes the associations attached to the literal meaning over time.

• Connotation can often add a layer of opinion to what appears to be a neutral report.

• Many of our most difficult ideological divides include battles over language, with partisans choosing words that give their point of view the most positive spin while casting opponents in a negative light.

• Language corruption can lead to political corruption, which often results in more language corruption.

• The writing of an effective neutral report requires the use of unloaded language.

# 47

...

# Measure the distance between concrete and abstract language.

Almost a century ago, the great British scholar Sir Arthur Quiller-Couch advised his Cambridge University students to prefer in their writing concrete nouns and active verbs. Even in such an exalted academic setting, the professor proclaims a preference for the concrete over the abstract. Three decades later, S. I. Hayakawa popularized the "ladder of abstraction," teaching us that there is nothing wrong or right about the concrete or the abstract, but that all language can be placed on a ladder that extends from one semantic end to the other. At the low end skips my sixteen-year-old Jack Russell terrier, Rex. At the top are terms such as *reckless energy*, *disrespectful enthusiasm*, and *courageous loyalty*.

Writing teachers, including yours truly, speak about the power of showing (through concrete examples) over telling. Rubbing against this grain is Francine Prose, author of *Reading Like a Writer*:

> The passage contradicts a form of bad advice often given young writers—namely, that the job of the author is to show, not tell.... And the warning against telling leads to a confusion that causes novice writers to think that everything should be acted

out—don't tell us a character is happy, show us how she screams "yay" and jumps up and down for joy—when in fact the responsibility of showing should be assumed by the energetic and specific use of language.

This advice from Prose is a useful corrective for anyone tempted to apply one tool too rigorously, but I still admire those rare scholars who are able to work both ends of the ladder, as does Camille Paglia in her book *Sexual Personae:*

> Michelangelo's exaltation of maleness deforms his depiction of women. Like many Renaissance artists, he used male models for female figures, since a woman posing nude was scandalous. But from the evidence of his surviving drawings, Michelangelo never sketched any woman from life, dressed or not. Furthermore, the cross-sexual origin of his female figures has left a strong visual residue. The best examples are the Sibyls of the Sistine Chapel ceiling....The old Cumaean Sibyl is one of the most fantastic sexual personae in art. She has grim wizened features yet bursting breasts, fat as pumpkins. Her lumbering shoulder and arm are brawny beyond human maleness. She is witch, hag, wet nurse. She is Michelangelo's *Mona Lisa,* mother nature in the flesh, old as time but teeming with coarse fertility.

The fabulous Ms. Paglia gives us lots of language to linger over. At the beginning and end, readers find the language of ideas expressed in generalities and abstractions by a scholar: *exaltation, evidence, visual residue, beyond human maleness, fantastic sexual personae, mother nature, old as time, coarse fertility.* Such language would be intriguing enough, but flavored by specific, concrete examples—*bursting breasts, fat as pumpkins, witch, hag, wet nurse*—the passage gives off a sense of accepted authority, a feeling I like to call "gaining altitude."

Moving from sexuality to spirituality, I picked up an old copy of *Markings,* the diary of Dag Hammarskjöld, former secretary-general of the United Nations. Poet W. H. Auden, a friend of the author, helped in the translation from Swedish and wrote the introduction. Auden's language got me thinking again about the power of altitude and abstraction. Here are two examples:

> Geniuses are the luckiest of mortals because what they must do is the same as what they most want to do and, even if their genius is unrecognized in their lifetime, the essential earthly reward is always theirs, the certainty that their work is good and will stand the test of time....
>
> It makes me very happy to see that, in the last three years of his life, he took to writing poems, for it is proof to me that he had at last acquired a serenity of mind for which he had long prayed. When a man can occupy himself with counting syllables, either he has not yet attempted any spiritual climb, or he is over the hump.

Perhaps because of his poetic vision of the world, Auden gains altitude in his prose without leaving readers thinking that meaning is beyond their grasp. By using "geniuses," rather than the idea of "genius," he turns abstraction into a narrative characterization. And by juxtaposing "serenity of mind" with "over the hump," he rides a pogo stick between the mystical and the comical.

It's not just scholars and poets who know this move. I see it often in the work of critics such as Kyle Smith, writing for the *Wall Street Journal:* "No contemporary literary eminence wrote as many bad books as Norman Mailer." Even better: "Vainglorious, fatuous, fractious and breathtakingly pretentious, a rake, a mystic and a fool, Mr. Mailer wanted to be Hemingway plus Dostoevski times Tolstoy. Instead he found his fame steadily eclipsed by his infamy, having stabbed his second wife, Adele Morales, nearly to death."

When I see such smart writing, it saddens me that so many scholars of media studies write so obtusely. Part of the problem, of course, is that much research in the field derives from quantitative and social-science methods, creating a discourse community that working journalists and media professionals find difficult or impossible to enter. It need not be that way. Consider this paragraph written by the late Neil Postman in his book *The Disappearance of Childhood:*

> It is obvious that for an idea like childhood to come into being, there must be a change in the adult world. And such a change must be not only of a great magnitude but of a special nature. Specifically, it must generate a new definition of adulthood. During the Middle Ages there were several social changes, some important inventions, such as the mechanical clock, and many great events, including the Black Death. But nothing occurred that required that adults should alter their conception of adulthood itself. In the middle of the fifteenth century, however, such an event did occur: the invention of the printing press with movable type. The aim of this chapter is to show how the press created a new symbolic world that required, in its turn, a new conception of adulthood. The new adulthood, by definition, excluded children. And as children were expelled from the adult world it became necessary to find another world for them to inhabit. That other world came to be known as childhood.

What gives this paragraph altitude, I think, is that the abstractions are not so abstract, and that from the air we can still imagine a living landscape populated by folks working their presses, winding their clocks, dying from the plague. The paragraph even has a kind of narrative engine to it, a mystery about the meaning of childhood that the rest of the book will solve.

All of us who want to fully inhabit English should be on the lookout for language that builds a bridge between the world of things and the world of ideas. This passage comes from Marjorie Garber, author of *Shakespeare After All:*

> There has always been a productive tension between the idea of the play as a poem or a text and the idea of the play as a performance. Some portions of Shakespeare's plays are inaccessible to

us because they are made up of spectacles or performances rather than words. Examples include the masque in *The Tempest;* the apparitions in *Macbeth;* the tilt, or challenge, in *Pericles;* the descended god Jupiter in *Cymbeline;* and music throughout the comedies.... Battle scenes, like those in the English history plays and in *Antony and Cleopatra,* are also moments of high visual interest and onstage action, important to the tenor and pace of the play, and easy to underestimate (or skip over entirely) if one reads the plays as literature rather than visualizing them as theater.

To understand the brilliance and utility of such prose, a reader need only take a taste of the bad stuff, which I will now spare the reader. You're welcome.

The nonfiction writers I learn from already have two practical ways for gaining altitude. The first is something called the *nut paragraph,* a device for linking a scene or a character to higher categories of news or meaning. Editors may not tolerate the anecdote of a young woman, her face covered with soot, in a morgue, her husband keening over the body, unless we identify that woman as a victim of an underground mine disaster, and connect her death with the idea that as women move into traditional male workplaces, they come to share with men not only the benefits but also the vulnerabilities.

A distant cousin of the nut paragraph is the *conceptual scoop.* In short, this comes from the ability of the writer to sift among confusing data, information, and phenomena, see a cultural pattern, and give it a name: the "soccer mom" or the "dynastic presidency." I'm about to work on an essay that will argue that Americans often confuse incompetence with corruption. That theory will require specific evidence, of course, but all the proofs will hang on the tree of an idea, a theory, an explanation, an analysis of American politics and culture.

The ability to think or work through abstractions connects us at the highest level to a world that can only be described by metaphysics or theology, from the debates between Plato and

Aristotle over things and ideas, to Freud's argument that the true gift of the Jews to humankind was not monotheism but the belief in an invisible God, which inspired human beings to think more abstractly.

When some gurus of new information technologies describe the potential of the Internet, they often minimize journalists as mere content providers and data dumpers. Most of the writers and storytellers I know don't think of themselves that way. Instead, they seek to report what matters, to tell stories that change lives, and, more and more I hope, help us gain a little altitude along the way.

## KEEPSAKES

• Many words exist on a metaphorical ladder, with abstract words (*freedom*) at the top, and concrete words describing examples ("Roy's 1966 Mustang convertible") at the bottom.

• To gain full understanding, readers often need to move from top to bottom (abstract to concrete) or from bottom to top (concrete to abstract).

• Abstractions denote categories of ideas: *pirate wealth, venial sin, gay fashion.* Concrete words exemplify those abstractions: *pieces of eight, a dirty magazine shoplifted from a newsstand, a mauve tie with matching pocket hanky.*

• If you offer a reader an abstraction, anticipate the reader's inevitable desire: "I wish she could give me an example of that." If you begin with a concrete case, many readers will want to follow you up the ladder, reaching for a higher meaning.

# 48

• • •

## Harness the power of particularity.

I have never before this moment noticed the words *part* and *particle* at the root of the word *particular*. A particle is a tiny part of a part, a small but authentic representation of something much bigger. Language can be general or particular, and the reader or writer must be versatile enough to travel back and forth between the two. Writers and readers look for the small thing that represents the big thing, whether in the form of a microcosm (a closed auto plant used to exemplify the depressed economy), a telling character detail (a man who wears his grandmother's wedding ring in her honor), the objective correlative of the poet (the object that correlates to an emotion—the red wheelbarrow glazed with rain), or a specific example used to make a point or to teach a lesson.

Story editor Sol Stein expresses his fondness for the particular:

> In his book *On Becoming a Novelist*, John Gardner said, "Detail is the lifeblood of fiction." My only quarrel with that statement is that detail is also the lifeblood of nonfiction. And I want to go a step further. It is not just detail that distinguishes good writing, it is *detail that individualizes*. I call it "particularity." Once

you're used to spotting it—and spotting its absence—you will have one of the best possible means of improving your writing markedly. (from *Stein on Writing*)

I'm sure by now that you are looking for a particular example, and here it is. Former secretary of state Colin Powell once appeared on *Meet the Press* and was asked about the wild rumor that then-candidate Barack Obama was a Muslim and not a Christian, as he had claimed. Here is part of Powell's answer:

> The really right answer is, what if he is? Is there something wrong with being a Muslim in this country? The answer's no, that's not America. Is there something wrong with some 7-year-old Muslim-American kid believing that he or she could be president?

Powell's argument is a broad one: That American civic virtue requires tolerance not just of generally approved groups but of ones that stand on the margins, in this case Muslim Americans. There are two nods toward the particular, the first a reference to a hypothetical young Muslim child, and then to anonymous members of his party with whom he disagrees. But the case for tolerance cries out for a more telling example, and Powell delivers:

> I feel strongly about this particular point because of a picture I saw in a magazine. It was a photo essay about troops who are serving in Iraq and Afghanistan. And one picture at the tail end of this photo essay was of a mother in Arlington Cemetery, and she had her head on the headstone of her son's grave. And as the picture focused in, you could see the writing on the headstone. And it gave his awards—Purple Heart, Bronze Star—showed that he died in Iraq, gave his date of birth, date of death. He was 20 years old. And then, at the very top of the headstone, it didn't have a Christian cross, it didn't have the Star of David, it had a crescent and a star of the Islamic faith. And his name was Kareem Rashad Sultan Khan, and he was an American.

He was born in New Jersey. He was 14 years old at the time of 9/11, and he waited until he can go serve his country, and he gave his life.

I love language that moves: moves from the abstract to the concrete, moves from showing to telling, moves from the general to the particular. Sometimes this movement goes in one direction, sometimes the other, and sometimes back and forth. But move it must. Move, move, move! Go, man, go!

Here's a passage from a book I like very much, *The Arithmetic of Life and Death* by George Shaffner:

> At one time or another, most American children are told that they can be anything they want to be. The message is an American tradition; the traditional messengers are good-hearted parents, grandparents, aunts, and uncles. What they mean is that the United States is a land of great opportunity, which is true. But young children, who have yet to compare American economic, social, racial, and religious obstacles to those that exist in other nations, don't always get the intended message. Instead, what the children may actually hear is that they really can be anything they want to be—which is not true and never has been.

That's one clever paragraph, somehow ballsy and iconoclastic without being disrespectful. Shaffner begins with a generalization—something that most kids in America hear—and then steps on it like a potato chip.

Now think of your reaction to that paragraph as a reader. Perhaps you permitted yourself to be persuaded by his argument, or you recognized something you learned in school or from a parent. Or you're a traditional patriot who bristles at words that tear at your beliefs. Or you despise unreflective flag-waving, so you silently cheer when you reach the point of Shaffner's argument. Whatever your position, what you crave most is evidence to endorse it. Not the general but the particular.

Here's Shaffner's next paragraph:

> Gwendolyn Sharpe, a very fit twenty-year-old at five-foot-two and 105 pounds, is never going to play defensive end for the Green Bay Packers. She's too small. Even though he loves to race, Billy Ray DeNiall, who at age sixteen is already six-foot-three and 190 pounds, is never going to ride a Triple Crown winner. He's too big. Although he loves airplanes, Joe Bob DeNiall... never had a chance to be a Naval fighter ace. He is colorblind and has 20/400 vision.

I love the movement from general argument to particular evidence. To nail down that argument, Shaffner relies on specific examples, each with a name and vital statistics, each with a reference to a particular profession. Three examples provide a sense of the whole. There's a language tool hiding not far beneath the surface: To persuade the reader that your general propositions are true, follow them with specific, particular evidence. In addition to proving your case, it will make your writing move, move, move, daddio.

What makes a great detail in fiction or nonfiction? It depends.

From the first time I heard the radio report, I have been fascinated by the image of Lisa Nowak, the infamous lovesick NASA astronaut, driving nine hundred miles wearing a diaper. The diaper detail stands above the rest, above her wig, above the implements of mayhem that police say she carried: "a compressed air pistol, a steel mallet, a knife, pepper spray, four feet of rubber tubing, latex gloves and garbage bags."

According to John Schwartz in the *New York Times,* "She is charged with the attempted murder of a woman who she believed to be her rival for the affections of a fellow astronaut. Police officials say she drove 900 miles to Florida from Texas, wearing a diaper so she would not have to stop for rest breaks."

Such was her crazed nonstop urgency that Lisa Nowak wore an adult diaper. A diaper. As a reader and a writer, I wonder about that diaper. I imagine such a diaper as heroic armor in the iconography of space travel. In the confinement of space suit, capsule, shuttle, and space station—bodily functions monitored by the nanosecond—the diaper becomes the loincloth of the space gladiator, an emblem of training, self-control, discipline. Of mission. Of mission control.

The troubled space cadet brought a diseased version of that mission to land travel. She got in a car. Wore a wig, not a helmet. Headed east. Drove nine hundred miles. (Did she stop to refuel? Did she have something to drink?) She traveled with weapons. And she wore a diaper. A small step—it appears—from heroism to madness.

What makes the diaper a great detail? I'm struggling to understand. Perhaps it's the diaper's gritty specificity. Or the way it defines character. Or the way it stands as a symbol of the protagonist's tragic flaws. Or the way it marks the orbit of her narrative from the apogee of heavenly exploration to the perigee of piss and shit.

When Olympic figure skater Johnny Weir competed for America in the 2006 Winter Olympics, some controversial reports seemed to out the skater as gay. Critics attacked the press for revealing private information that was not relevant to his athletic prowess. When asked, I expressed the opinion, rather insensitively, that I did not think that the exposure of a gay male figure skater was a surprise—or news.

Then I read a story by Libby Copeland in the *Washington Post* in which the word *outing* or *gay* is never used but is implied in every detail about a Johnny Weir shopping spree:

> "I like to shop," Johnny says.
>
> So far, Weir, 21, who came in fifth in the men's figure skating competition for the U.S. team last week (but first in matters of beauty and brashness), has bought the following items here: five pairs of shoes, a pair of rabbit fur hand warmers, a Dolce & Gabbana hoodie he says reads "Sex trainer: Best to practice seven days a week," and a sable scarf that was supposed to be $715 but was instead $415 because he spoke French to the saleslady.

Ah, the fabulousness that is Johnny Weir! The fur collars! The special deals! His absolute favorite item of clothing is a Roberto Cavalli beaver-and-python coat. He is also proud that the "Louie" in Boston "pre-sold me a bag before it was allowed to be released," he says. "I'm the first person in the entire world to have this bag."

There is much more showing here than telling, a lesson that readers and writers must learn over and over again: show me your best evidence so that I, too, can reach a conclusion. That is the power of the particular.

The search for the particular can lead the writer and reader down some crooked pathways. Which brings me to one of my favorite stories of all time. It appeared in my hometown newspaper and told the tale of a woman saved from a serious bullet injury by her seat-belt strap and her bra.

"A lucky combination of her van's windshield, seat belt and her thick bra straps helped deflect a shot fired at [Robin] Key and her husband, Donald, as they sat in traffic Monday in Riverview," reported Abbie VanSickle. "The bullet grazed her shoulder, but Key, 44, wasn't seriously injured. Deputies later accused two men of the apparently random shooting."

The first part of this story lacked some crucial information: What kind of bra was Ms. Key wearing? If a bra can stop a bullet, I want my wife wearing one. But what brand, reporter, what brand?

"On Wednesday Maidenform called the [*St. Petersburg*] *Times*. The bra company had heard Key's story. A spokeswoman offered free bras and lingerie." Oh, so this wonderbra came from Maidenform? Not so fast.

Key told the reporter, "I'm a Playtex girl." That company was ecstatic, eager to send their warrior-princess new bras. But what model? The Secrets bra? The Thank Goodness It Fits bra?

VanSickle reports that Key giggled: "It was an 18 Hour bra," said Key. "It has these cushy straps I just love." Out of healthy curiosity, I did a Google search on the 18 Hour bra. No wonder that bra helped deflect a bullet. It looks stronger than the body armor we send our soldiers in Iraq.

My interest in this example of particularity is now, happily, exhausted, thanks to a reporter whose enterprise should remind all writers to get the name of the dog, the brand of the beer, the color and make of the sports car, and now, who would have guessed, the brand and model of the bra. Such are the joys of living inside the English language.

## KEEPSAKES

- The particular separates the character from the crowd.
- Good writing moves: from concrete to abstract, from particular to general, from showing to telling. It can move from top to bottom, from bottom to top, or back and forth, up and down.
- Particular details provide persuasive evidence in an argument but can leave room for the reader to draw conclusions.
- Get the name of the dog and the brand and model of the bra.

# 49

### • • •

## Have fun with initials and acronyms, but avoid "capital" offenses.

There are days when I feel like I'm drowning in a sea of capital letters (make that SCL for short). From government documents to text messages, from technical manuals to 140-character Tweets, from company brands to love notes, abbreviations rule the day. Even some classic abbreviations, such as F.D.R. (for Franklin Delano Roosevelt), have been abbreviated by the strategic dumping of the three periods. I may have grown up in the Age of Aquarius, but I'm growing old in the Age of the Acronym.

Strictly speaking, an acronym is a type of abbreviation in which the first letters in the words of a phrase combine to form a neologism, that is, a new word you can pronounce. For example, the words *scuba, radar,* and *laser* are acronyms, even though most of us do not know the phrases from which they are derived:

- "Self-contained underwater breathing apparatus" gave us *scuba.*
- "Radio detecting and ranging" gave us *radar.*
- "Light amplification by stimulated emission of radiation" gave us *laser,* for which we offer thanks.

While those remain traditional examples of acronyms, I believe that the meaning of the word *acronym* has expanded to include abbreviations that technically fall under the clumsy rubric *initialisms*. According to this distinction, the NAACP (National Association for the Advancement of Colored People) is an initialism because we say the letters individually; but CORE (the Congress of Racial Equality) is an acronym because we pronounce it as a word, like the core of an apple.

If common usage is to serve as any guide, however, the more restrictive definition of *acronym* has fallen out of favor. I call to the witness stand none other than R. W. Burchfield, former editor of the Oxford English dictionaries and a reviser of *Fowler's Modern English Usage.* In that revision, Burchfield acknowledges the traditional definition of *acronym:* "The test of a true acronym is often assumed to be that it should be pronounceable as a word within the normal patterns of English." By that standard, he argues, BBC is not an acronym but an abbreviation. Among proper acronyms he lists AIDS (acquired immunodeficiency syndrome) but not HIV.

Here is where Burchfield jumps aboard my bandwagon: "The limitations of the term not widely known to the general public, *acronym* is also often applied to abbreviations that are familiar but are not pronounceable as words." He cites FBI and VCR as examples. I am a member of an organization called the American Society of News Editors, for which the written abbreviation is ASNE. Some of the members refer to it by the individual letters A-S-N-E, but others turn it into a two-syllable word that sounds like "az-nee." So is it an acronym or an initialism, and, really, what difference does it make?

This expansion of the meaning of *acronym* takes into account the abbreviations created for text messages and other forms of online communication. By now, even us geezers can interpret messages such as ROTF from TMI: "rolling on the floor" from "too much information." When used in text messages, these abbreviations can become a kind of tribal code that bonds friends but excludes teachers, parents, and other authority figures. Some common abbreviations have ooched their way into common usage: your BFF is a "best friend forever"; BTW means "by the way"; IMHO stands for "in my humble opinion"; LOL means you are "laughing out loud."

But there are snarkier expressions designed to stick it to "the Man": PLOS sends a warning that "parents looking over shoulder"; KMA invites the reader to "kiss my ass," to which the reader may respond STFU, that is, "shut the fuck up."

Curiously, such language has prospered not only in the emoticonic coding of Twitter and IM (instant messaging) but also in the world of technocratic communication and conversation. It's impossible in the Internet Age to think of verbal or written communication without the prolific—perhaps profligate—use of mysterious abbreviations. In her book *Wired Style,* Constance Hale includes these terms in her glossary: CD, CDA, CDMA, CD-ROM, CGI, CORE, CPM. And those are just under the letter *c.* Add the other twenty-five letters in the alphabet, and it's easy to see why any Luddite might feel as if entry into this world requires learning a secret code.

Many acronyms and other similar abbreviations have developed bad reputations as blood clots in the flow of technical or bureaucratic information, as in this real draft of a company brochure:

> The CompIQ eBill process will allow for provider bills to be reviewed and paid electronically by facilitating the submission of bills to payers in the state required ANSI 837 format. We supply payers the ability to return Electronic Remittance Advice, ERAs, to medical providers in the required ANSI 835.

It should come as no surprise that such jargon includes language gadgets (ANSI, ERA) that are technical in nature, which become not building blocks but stumbling blocks to common understanding. On the flip side, acronyms can also serve a subversive function, as when soldiers in World War II created *fubar* to express their frustration that military matters and strategies always seemed "fucked up beyond all recognition."

According to British lexicographer Jesse Sheidlower, "Acronyms are extremely rare before the 1930s." In his astonishing compilation *The F-Word,* Sheidlower debunks the notion that the F-bomb is an ancient acronym derived from some legalistic term, such as "for unlawful carnal knowledge." It must be said that in the past fifty years, acronyms and other forms of abbreviations have become more important and much more common in many types of expression.

Initialisms are a more formal expression of the abbreviated imagination. While the *New York Times* still uses periods between the letters of words such as I.B.M. and G.O.P., those dots disappear in most other publications, giving us JFK, LBJ, NBA, NFL, and in the case of a recent president, a single middle initial, W. (Thank goodness there has been no movement to shorten the current president's identity to BO.) I confess to loving my own initials when I see them, even on someone else's license plate. Imagine then my special joy when a friend, Dave Angelotti, baked me an apple pie and daintily carved RPC into the crust. For that alone he became my BFF.

Finally, consider the way novelist Ian Fleming used acronyms in the adventures of his hero, superspy James Bond. With the help of the CIA, British secret agent 007 fought against evil organizations such as SPECTRE (Special Executive for Counterintelligence, Terrorism, Revenge, and Extortion) and SMERSH (Russian for "death to spies"). And who can forget Mr. Bond's introduction to laser technology? Remember the scene in which Goldfinger points that laser between Bond's legs?

"Do you expect me to talk, Goldfinger?"
"No, Mr. Bond, I expect you to die."

## KEEPSAKES

• There are few ancient surviving examples of the acronym, but business picked up after 1930 with the growth of technology and bureaucracy.

• Some groups use acronyms and initials as simple short-hand, others to exclude outsiders. For example, bureaucrats and technocrats use acronyms as a form of professional jargon; young people use them as codes to exclude adults.

• Examples of acronyms once included only those initial letters that could be pronounced as a word. Common usage has expanded the definition of *acronym* to include other abbreviations.

• When an acronym is absorbed into the language, it can lose its identity as an acronym. Such is the situation with words like *snafu,* meaning "situation normal, all fucked up."

• Play with acronyms. Create your own. When writing about technology, business, government, and the military, be careful not to use acronyms or initials that may hinder the understanding of your readers.

# 50

• • •

## Master the grammar of new forms of writing.

When it comes to technological innovation, I remain a curious student but also a "late adopter." Just about the time I get a Facebook account, that social network will be sliding out of style. I've long been skeptical of the efficacy of all those PowerPoint presentations and for workshops prefer a simple paper hand-out. My favorite technology is still the book, although my new iPhone (with all its crazy apps) is catching up fast. I admit it: I still write the occasional essay longhand, especially on airplanes.

But something nifty (an old-school word) happened to me when my friends at the Poynter website, poynter.org, uploaded the podcasts for my book *Writing Tools* on iTunesU. Before you could say "Steve Jobs," those little audio essays were number one with a bullet, with close to a million downloads. O Brave New World...

Filled with confidence—and with the help of my much younger colleagues—I set off on my first Twitter experience. It did not take long to learn the basics, and I soon attracted hundreds of "followers" (I'd prefer "acolytes") and tried to post one brief message each day. My primary motivation was not to grow an audience or to keep up with the latest gizmo but to pursue my interest—as a writer and a scholar—in short forms of writing.

Twitter was made to order. With its limit of 140 characters, it encourages a long sentence or a couple of short ones or a string of fragments, with the appropriate abbreviations and liturgies for linking. Let it be said that Twitter does not offer itself primarily as a writing vehicle. But one person's abbreviated message is another person's genre. And genres, all English majors know, have certain requirements and certain unimagined potentials. So off I went on a search for what I mischievously called "The Grammar of Twitter."

Not everyone gets Twitter. *Newsweek*'s Daniel Lyons writes that "Twitter has become a playground for imbeciles, skeevy marketers, D-list celebrity half-wits, and pathetic attention seekers." One sports radio talk-show host predicted that Twitter, a favorite of athletes, would soon flame out as a fad, going the way of the pet rock. He looked forward to that day, he said, because sites like Twitter "have set back the English language 100 years." He condemned the "lazy" shortcuts required to pare a message down to 140 characters, the limit for a so-called Tweet. By shortcuts, he meant the way that a message such as "Before you hate why not be great!" could become "B4 U h8 Y not be gr8!" On another occasion, the same host ridiculed the self-indulgent sharing of the humdrum details of daily life enabled by Twitter: "I'm sitting on the couch. Pillow lumpy. Life sucks."

No doubt, the language of the license plate and the navel gaze has influenced the abbreviated messages required for some forms of online communication. But rather than hate such forms or imagine that they somehow set back the language—as if anything could—why not explore the potential of new forms of expression and communication, aided and abetted by new technologies? After all, writing was once a new technology, as was the printing press, two enduring advances that have allowed me to write this book, another once-new technology.

Are there, then, certain strategies of language—a grammar of intent—that can be applied to short forms of communication of the kind now ubiquitous on the Internet and on mobile technologies?

I met a university professor who reported that his daughter had sent thirteen thousand text messages to her friends in a single month. If each message took, say, fifteen seconds to key in, the father calculated that the daughter spent hours a day *texting*, a word my spell-checker does not yet recognize. Sending text messages—and cell-phone use in general—is obviously an addictive and compulsive behavior. My wife and I once drove past a young man riding no hands on a bicycle. In one hand he was thumbing a text message. In the other he held what looked like a three- or four-month-old baby.

In spite of all that sending and receiving of messages, research has demonstrated that young people do not think of these acts as reading or writing at all. It must seem more like telegraphy than a literary act, which only reminds me that some telegraph messages were more important than others, a result of both their content and language. The book *Telegram!* by Linda Rosenkrantz and an article in the *New York Times* by Sam Roberts contain a sample of some of the most famous and curious:

- Samuel F. B. Morse, inventor of the telegraph, sending his first formal message, 1844: WHAT HATH GOD WROUGHT?
- April 15, 1912: SOS SOS CQD CQD TITANIC. WE ARE SINKING FAST. PASSENGERS ARE BEING PUT INTO BOATS. TITANIC.
- Mark Twain from London in 1897: THE REPORTS OF MY DEATH ARE GREATLY EXAGGERATED.
- Edward Teller on the first H-bomb detonation: IT'S A BOY.
- Reporter to a famous actor, inquiring about his age: HOW OLD CARY GRANT? Famous actor to reporter: OLD CARY GRANT FINE. HOW YOU?
- And perhaps the most economical exchange of messages in history, between author and publisher about sales of a new novel:
  Author: ?
  Publisher: !

In our time the publisher might have responded with a smiley-face emoticon, but I hope not. The longest of these telegrams, the one from the *Titanic,* is about eighty characters, proving that by some standards a Twitter message might be considered down-right windy or discursive.

In my own early experiments with Twitter, I've published a haiku: "Captured on the shore / a chorus line of horseshoe crabs / unlucky in love." Another original poem: "The kid's bike / a Schwinn, a beauty / waits in the rain / kickstand sturdy / reflectors ready / to catch light that never comes." And perhaps the most famous short poem in the history of American literature, by William Carlos Williams: "So much depends / upon / a red wheel / barrow / glazed with rain / water / beside the white / chickens." All easily fit within the 140-character limit.

The moral is that the brevity of an e-mail message, a blog post, a text message, even a Tweet is no obstacle to powerful information, a persuasive argument, a literary moment, a zinger, a joke. These new forms need not be word dumps, any more than were the short forms that preceded them by decades and centuries.

I asked my "followers" on Twitter to nominate the writers who consistently provided the most creative and compelling Tweets. Among the most interesting was a Manhattan writer, "formerlyCwalken," who looks and sounds a lot like actor Christopher Walken, but whose best messages include short bits about neighbors:

- "There's a dead squirrel in the driveway. Mrs. Liebowitz is worried that the death might be gang-related. She's checking FOX News to be sure."
- "I am now invited to a dog wedding. I don't have the words to make that stupider than it already sounds. They're registered at Whiskers."
- "A neighborhood kid shows up from time to time dressed as Superman. I think it's him anyway. Very difficult to say for sure without the glasses."

Most provocative were the cryptic, poetic, postcard-style messages from Dawn Danby of San Francisco, who writes on-line as "altissima":

- "claimed: fog-belt community garden plot in a former sand dune. Semi feral. Neglected chard flowering into giant squid. Embryonic onions."
- "untangling nina simone progressions, voice raspy after a late campfire night in Sonoma. Passing ships play chords into the bay."
- "On the ferry a Korean economist plies me with pop mp3s of his favourite songs. Hands me an earbud, sings along to Queen."

Reporters and photographers rushed to Haiti in 2010 after an earthquake devastated the island, destroying many buildings, killing more than 230,000 people, and injuring many more. The narratives they produced from the rubble told a story of hardship that inspired a great outpouring of support for the Haitian people from across the globe. Of all those reports, I was especially taken with the series of short vignettes created on Twitter by Joanna Smith, a reporter for the *Toronto Star*. I found it remarkable how much she could convey in scenes or snapshots of 140 characters:

- "Was in b-room getting dressed when heard my name. Tremor. Ran outside through sliding door. All still now. Safe. Roosters crowing."
- "Fugitive from prison caught looting, taken from police, beaten, dragged thru street, died slowly and set on fire in pile of garbage."
- "Woman shrieking, piercing screams, 'Maman! Papa! Jesus!' as dressing on her wounded heel is changed outside clinic. No painkillers."

Smith made sure to capture the occasional moments of light:

- "Little boys playing with neat little cars constructed from juice bottles, caps. Fill with rocks and pull with string. Fun!"

What stands out for me in these examples, and countless others, is the variety of voice, rhetoric, even genre, everything from reports to anecdotes to narratives to descriptions to editorials. The voice of each writer comes across as authentic and distinctive, directed to a specific audience of followers, defined as a miniature discourse community (in some cases, more like a discourse platoon or posse). Some write in complete sentences. Some in creative fragments.

No doubt, there is infinite room for formal language in the expansive polluted ocean that is the Internet (formerly known as the information superhighway). For example, I just downloaded an application that allows me to store the texts for every Shakespeare play on my iPhone. Before I die, I'll probably have the Library of Congress at my fingertips. But that is not what online communication is famous for. The fame comes from its acronymic, telegraphic (sometimes telepathic), and emoticonic informality. What too many online writers fail to realize is that there are formal requirements for the most effective, most economical informal style.

I first read of those strategies in the book *Wired Style* by Constance Hale:

> Look to the Web not for embroidered prose, but for the sudden narrative, the dramatic story told in 150 words. Text must be complemented by clever interface design and clear graphics. Think brilliant copy, not long-form literature. Think pert, breezy pieces almost too ephemeral for print. Think turned-up volume—cut lines that are looser, grabbier, more tabloidy. Think distinctive voice or attitude.

Most writers I know strive for that "distinctive voice," the sum of all strategies used to create the illusion that the writer is talking directly to the reader from the page—and now from the screen.

## KEEPSAKES

• Writing for the Internet has become identified with short forms: the e-mail message, the text message, the blog post, the short blast on a social-networking site. That said, the virtually limitless space available online increasingly allows the publication of long forms, even books, old and new: Orwell's diary turned into a blog.

• Writing effectively online requires the mastery of an informal conversational style. To create the illusion of a conversational voice, the writer must put into practice certain formal strategies. These include:

   ✓ questions and answers
   ✓ shorter words and sentence fragments
   ✓ punctuation (like the exclamation point) that can substitute for discursive descriptions of emotion
   ✓ familiar and innovative acronyms and abbreviations
   ✓ the strategic omission of functional words, the absence of which can be compensated for by context
   ✓ particular words, details, images that stand out from the text
   ✓ the discipline of a sharp, transparent focus

• Many new forms will draw on older forms—such as the log, diary, journal, and telegram—for their strategic uses of language.

• The Internet need not be a dumping ground for jargon, geek speak, or cluttered language. A bit more time for revision creates a message with sharp focus, wit, and polish.

...

# Live a life of language.

Thank you and congratulations. If you've read to this point, you've completed a curriculum of sorts, fifty short lessons on the magic and mystery of practical English. Consider this final bonus lesson a commencement address.

So how can something magical or mysterious—a deep knowledge of the English language—also be practical? In my mind, I see a scene from the movie *Mary Poppins* in which the magical nanny snaps her fingers and slides up the banister of a long staircase. You might wish that you could produce a brilliant piece of writing with a snap of the fingers, but then what fun would that be?

My hope is that you will no longer consider yourself one of those people who associate reading, writing, and learning the elements of language with drudgery and frustration. My wish for you is that the knowledge you've gained from these pages gives your work with the English language more fluency—and more joy.

The practical magic in this book has been designed to take some of the mystery out of the process of understanding grammar and its cousins. When we see a great magician in action, we can be struck with awe and delight at the illusion. But even the naive know that the trick *is* an illusion, that turning a fierce tiger into a beautiful lady is the product of a set of strategic steps, the marriage of art and engineering. But before those steps can take effect, they must work in the service of the magician's imagination.

Each of the grammar "tricks" you've encountered here can help you create an effect that may seem magical to a reader or a listener. Living inside the language gives you the power to read, write, and speak in a new way. And think of the journey you've taken from simple letters and words to using language for a powerful purpose. Even tiny babies use their babbling language for a purpose, to get attention, or to voice a complaint, or to get access to mother's nurturing bosom.

Language is a gift, a treasure of evolution but also a spark of the divine. The ancient Hebrew word *dabar* describes the power of a personal God to speak directly to men and women. In the Gospel of Saint John, Jesus is *Logos*, the Greek form of *Word*. The word *spirit* comes from the word meaning "to breathe," and breath gives us life and something more, the ability to turn air into language. The book of Genesis tells the story of the Tower of Babel, about how arrogant humans tried to build a structure high enough to reach God and that God's justice scattered mankind to the corners of the earth in a confusion of languages—babble. Another story in John tells of how the timid apostles of Jesus secluded themselves in a tiny upper room after his death, fearful of persecution. And suddenly the Spirit of God came to them, filling them with both courage and language, so that the crowds gathered from many lands could understand them in their own language—a reversal of the curse of Babel.

The truths embedded in those stories can be practiced every day in our lives as students, teachers, workers, children, parents, and citizens. It is the power of the written and spoken word within us, a power so great it can feel—when used for a good purpose—like magic. The grammar has glamour after all. In the end, *The Glamour of Grammar* may not be about dictionaries, parts of speech, syntax, or the forty-seven other tools and strategies of language it covers. I have come to think that this book is about freedom and power and life in a democracy. For what good is freedom of expression if you lack the means to express yourself?

...

# Words I have misspelled

When I came into journalism in 1977, I was commissioned by the American Society of Newspaper Editors to create a spelling test for reporters and editors. That idea seemed lame, I thought, until the day I stood next to a news editor, Mary McKey, who had misspelled the word *dilemma* in a huge headline. When she saw she had added an extra *l*, she began to cry. Now a Presbyterian minister, Mary confessed to me that she still regrets the mistake—thirty years later. OK, I get it. Spelling counts.

So I set out to create a list of twenty-five commonly misspelled words. My criterion was simple: They had to be words that I might find misspelled in any given newspaper on any given day. If they were words I had misspelled, all the better. Exotic and foreign words were not the problem. Any goofball can Google *schadenfreude* or *eleemosynary*. The problem was a word like *dilemma*. How many *l*'s, how many *m*'s?

After I compiled my list, I took the test myself and got five wrong out of twenty-five. (Yes, I compiled the test and still got five wrong.) I've learned over the years that anyone who gets fewer than five wrong turns out to be a pretty good speller, and is usually an avid reader. Some working journalists get as many as fifteen wrong.

When I first gave the test to a group of professionals, the most experienced journalist scored the lowest, missing nineteen. "I'm a terrible speller," moaned Wilbur Landry, who had covered the world as a foreign correspondent and now lives in that hellmouth for bad spellers: France. (It turns out, though, that Wilbur can spell and order red wine in several languages.) But Wilbur's editor once assured me, "He never misses a word. He knows he's a bad speller, so if he's unsure he looks it up."

You need not be a spelling-bee nerd to learn how to spell a word. It's not magic. Look it up. Better yet, keep a list of the tough words handy. When you misspell a word, memorize the correct spelling and vow that you'll never get that one wrong again.

The universe of commonly misspelled words is finite, not vast. You'll go a long way by mastering this list of sixty-three. Build on it by including your own problem children, then review it often.

*acknowledgment:* The *AHD* also permits *acknowledgement* but prefers to drop that extra *e,* and so do I.

*acquiesce:* The *-sce* ending always gives me problems, as in *reminisce.*

*aphrodisiac:* Derived from Aphrodite, Greek goddess of love. Would that make an *afrodisiac* something that gives you a desire to listen to Earth, Wind and Fire?

*appropriate:* Most words beginning with *ap-* are followed by another *p,* so if you have to guess, go with *app.*

*camaraderie:* I don't understand how we get from *comrade* to this vowelly abstraction, but I learned how to spell it by following a simple consonant-vowel-consonant-vowel pattern.

*carcass:* I can now spell any word that ends with *-ass.*

*Caribbean:* You'll have to look up exotic place names, except for Lake Titicaca, of course. But commit to memory the ones you are likely to use most often: Mediterranean, Schenectady, Mississippi, Albuquerque.

*cemetery:* Just remember "three *e*'s."

*colonel:* A homophone with *kernel.* Just remember "the colonial colonel."

*commitment:* If the suffix begins with a consonant, as -*ment,* you do not double the previous letter. I remember how to spell this because of *The Commitments,* Roddy Doyle's novel about an Irish soul band.

*committed:* A reliable rule is that when you add -*ed* to a verb ending in a consonant, you double the consonant: *referred.*

*congratulate:* Sounds like that first *t* should be a *d.* You can see part of the word *gratis* in the middle, derived from the Latin for "gift."

*conscience:* While homophones—words that sound the same but have different meanings—are always a problem, so are words that sound alike but not exactly alike, which is why we confuse *conscience* with *conscious,* even though one is a noun and the other an adjective.

*definitely:* It helps me to see the word *finite* in the middle.

*diaphragm:* The *g* is silent in words such as *phlegm* but can be heard in *phlegmatic.*

*dilemma:* After seeing the weeping news editor who became a Presbyterian minister, I can never misspell this one.

*dumbbell:* A bit old-fashioned when describing exercise weights or dumb jocks, but it retains an enduring if politically incorrect charm.

*embarrass:* Two *r*'s and two *s*'s.

*flier:* My high-school team name was the Flyers, so I object to the use of *flier* to denote both the aviator and the leaflet.

*forty:* What happened to the *u*?

*gauge:* A tough one to remember, as is *gouge.*

*genuine:* Just take out your wallet, which probably claims to be "genuine leather."

*handkerchief:* When I was a kid, I was blown away by this spelling, until I realized it denoted a small kerchief, one you held in your hand.

*hemorrhage:* If you can spell this, you can spell *hemorrhoid.* Cheers.

*hors d'oeuvres:* Damn the French, except for the food, of course—and Brigitte Bardot. Looks like it could mean the work of horses or the work of whores, but it literally means "outside the main work." Yummy.

*inoculate:* Most people want to add another *n.* I remember the phrase "in the eye" because *oculus* is Latin for "eye."

*judgment:* Now that I remember to leave out the *e* in the middle, the *AHD* gives its blessing, but not its preference, to *judgement.*

*liaison:* Three vowels in a row are bound to screw you up.

*lieutenant:* Now that I've learned the origin, I'll never misspell it again. It comes from the French word *lieu* or "place," as in "in lieu of flowers." A lieutenant is a placeholder.

*limousine:* Did I say something nasty about the French?

*millennium:* Misspelled a thousand times. It literally means "a thousand years." The Latin word for year is *annum,* as in *per annum* or *anniversary,* which gives us the double *n.*

*minuscule:* I misspelled this until I remembered the word begins with "minus."

*misspell:* It's always fun to get this one wrong.

*neighbor:* I learned this in fourth grade: *i* before *e,* except after *c,* and when pronounced like *-ay,* as in *neighbor* and *weigh.*

*occurrence:* See rule under *committed.*

*paramour:* You say to your sweetheart, "Oh, you!" or *o-u.*

*pastime:* Baseball fans usually get this one.

*perseverance:* A good severance package helps you persevere.

*playwright:* Playwrite is the understandable mistake, until you learn that wright means "maker," as in cartwright or wheelwright or wainwright or boatwright.

*pneumonia:* Not sure why that initial *p* before a consonant likes to keep its mouth shut. It's Greek to me.

*premiere:* This refers to an event held for the first time, as in the premiere of a movie, but if you mean a head of state or the first among many, lop off that final *e.*

*ptomaine:* Old, bad joke: if you get ptomaine poisoning, we may have to call a toe truck and then cut off your main toe.

*questionnaire:* See rule under *committed.*

*receive:* Classic *i* before *e* except after *c.*

*reconnaissance:* My editor alerted me to the fact that I misspelled this word in my first draft of this list.

*reconnoiter:* Military slang shortens this to *recon.*

*relieve:* My mom taught me to remember certain *ie* words this way: You be*lieve* a *lie.*

*renaissance:* Some words mark a specific historical period but can be used in a broader sense, without the initial capital letter, in this case to mean "rebirth."

*rendezvous:* Sometimes it helps to remember a foreign word by giving it a conventional English pronunciation, just for fun: "Sweetheart, let's have a romantic ron-dez-voos."

*rhythm:* Often paired with *rhyme.*

*sabotage:* I now know that a *sabot* is a wooden shoe that could be taken off and banged on a table to subvert work.

*seize:* I remember *seize* and *siege* as a pair. If I say "seize the day," I know the other one is an *ie* word.

*separate:* People want to write *seperate,* but to a golfer like me, it would be below "par."

*sergeant:* It appears as though care is needed with words of military rank.

*siege:* The other half of the *seize/siege* problem.

*suede:* From the French word for *Swede.*

*supersede:* I never get this right. Grrr. Perhaps I will remember that the secret of success lives in the first letter.

*thoroughfare:* Folks who learn English as a second language find the *-ough* spellings and pronunciations a huge problem.

*threshold:* The way I pronounce it, sounds like it should have another *h.*

*traveling:* *AHD* allows both a single *l* and a double *l* version.

*vacuum:* *Vacume* would be too easy and not as visually arresting as that double *u.*

*vignette:* The French word for "vine" is *vigne.* A vignette is a little vine, a metaphor for a little story.

*weird:* It seems to me that it should be *ie,* but then the word is, after all, weird.

APPENDIX B

• • •

# Words I have confused

Many common expressions are misused because their origins are lost or forgotten. George Orwell noticed that people wrote "It's time to *tow* the line," meaning "to face the challenge," when the proper spelling was "*toe* the line." So it's not about someone grabbing a rope and pulling; the phrase refers to the early days of boxing, when an injured fighter proved he could continue by putting his toe on a line drawn in the middle of the ring.

There are endless examples. People write "soft peddle," meaning to sell it softly, instead of the correct "soft pedal," refer-ring to the pedal on the piano that tones the music down. "A tough *row* to hoe" became "a tough *road* to hoe," especially for writers who never had the experience of working a hoe through a row of crops.

A handy guide through such confusion is Paul Brians's *Common Errors in English Usage*. The book is 246 pages long and could easily be twice its length. Here are a few examples of con-fused words and phrases, chosen because they lead to common mistakes I have made or observed in the work of others:

*allude/elude:* When you *allude* to something, say a line in Shakespeare, you make reference to it. But you *elude* the police who are trying to arrest you. An *allusion* is a reference, but an *illusion* is a trick of vision.

*all right/alright:* Please, just spell this as two words. Avoid *alright,* even in casual usage. My dad used to say something like "All right, already," which may have led to the misspelling *alright* to match *already.* In street slang *all right* can be scrunched to "aite."

*anecdote/antidote:* These words are confused all the time, even by writers with some experience. An anecdote is a short narrative, the kind you may share at a party, a little story often used to make some larger point. We hear of "anecdotal evidence," for example, a story about a bad teacher. *Antidote* is the remedy for a poison.

*anxious/eager:* These words are often used interchangeably, but I prefer their distinctions. I try to use *anxious* in more negative contexts, and *eager* in more positive ones. I'm *eager* to hear Bruce Springsteen's new album, but, because I'm intimidated by crowds, I'm *anxious* about going to a live concert.

*appraise/apprise:* If I *appraise* something, I estimate its value; for example, an appraisal of an antique automobile. If I tell you how much it's worth, I *apprise* you of its value.

*assure/ensure/insure:* The last word, *insure,* I tend to reserve for the context of insurance policies. I need to *insure* my Florida house against rising water. I'll use *ensure* when the context is something other than insurance: how can I *ensure* your cooperation? And *assure* means to offer confidence.

*cement/concrete:* Learn this distinction, and you won't piss off burly construction workers. *Cement* is mixed with water and sand to form *concrete.* So you have a *concrete* driveway, not a *cement* one.

*cite/sight/site:* Very confusing. *Cite* is a verb, *site* is a noun, and *sight* can be either. You can *cite* an expert to make your argument. I can *sight* a pelican zooming above the water, a magnificent *sight*. *Site* refers to a place, either a virtual or terrestrial one: the construction *site*.

*complement/compliment:* If I *compliment* you, I offer you praise. If I *complement* you, I make up for what you lack—but in a good way.

*compose/comprise:* You can find these words confused in the media almost every day, a mistake I made for years. Here's a decent formula: The whole *comprises* the parts. The parts *compose* the whole. A class comprises students; a zoo comprises animals; but many new paintings compose the art exhibit.

*dire straights/dire straits:* Another example of a misplaced etymology. A *strait* is a narrow passage of water, which can be difficult, something dire, to navigate. So it's *dire straits*. If you know the rock band, you're cool in an old-school kind of way.

*disinterested/uninterested:* The first word does *not* mean "not interested." It means neutral or nonpartisan. It means you lack a special interest that may create bias.

*eminent/immanent/imminent:* It will be important for you to distinguish among these words, especially if you write theology or metaphysics. *Eminent* means "well-known," which is why a prince of the Catholic Church may be referred to as "Your Eminence." *Immanent* is most often seen in a religious or philosophical context, as it refers to the continuing presence of God or something inherent, like beauty, in life or in the universe. *Imminent* means that something, usually something important, is about to happen, which is why the word is so often used to modify "threat."

*farther/further:* I've given up trying to figure out this distinction, or remember it. According to Brians, it helps to remember that *farther* refers to distance, and *further* to time or degree.

*flaunt/flout:* Rarely used these days but often confused, *flaunt* is a word I remember from the lyrics of a song in *The Producers,* when the sexy Ula gyrates to "When you got it, flaunt it," that is, show off. If you have contempt for a rule, you *flout* it.

*heroin/heroine:* Mistaking these two will have the reader distracted or laughing. *Heroine* is the female version of *hero,* but only in a narrative sense, that is, as the main character in a story. Chop off that final letter by mistake, and suddenly your story is about a highly addictive drug.

*imply/infer:* As early as the eighth grade, my teachers would school me: "I *imply*. You *infer*." That is, the sender of the message *implies* that women are inferior writers, from which the receiver of the message *infers* that the sender is a fool and a sexist.

*lectern/podium:* I catch myself mistaking these two, especially in speech. The *podium* is where the speaker stands. She reads from a *lectern*.

*media/medium:* If you know Latin plural forms, you recognize that *medium* is singular and *media* is plural. Failure to recognize this difference can lead to mistakes in subject-verb, or pronoun-antecedent agreement. We often talk about "the media" as one big thing: "The media is responsible for the current state of the economy." But such usage leads to crude generalizations. It helps your readers think critically if you remind them that the media comprise many different platforms.

*peak/peek/pique:* That last word means "arouse" and often comes with words like *curiosity* or *interest*. I have written *peak,* which means "high point," when I really meant *peek,* meaning "sneak a glance." It may seem childish, but to keep these straight it helps me if I think of the game peekaboo.

*predominantly/predominately:* Look it up. Every time. Unless you can remember that it should always be *predominantly,* formed from *predominant.*

.   .   .

Finally, there is a special category of confused words that inexperienced writers find hard to master and that experienced writers often mistake through haste or lack of careful proofreading. They are:

*its/it's:* You use the apostrophe when you mean "it is," not to form the possessive.

*their/there/they're: They're* looking for *their* galoshes over *there,* in the corner.

*to/too/two:* The *two* girls skipped *to* their grandmother's house. Their little dog, Toto, *too.*

*your/you're: You're* driving *your* parents crazy.

Hope that your spelling or grammar checker alerts you to these common snake pits of error. The higher the stakes, say, in a state writing test, the greater the need for close proofreading. Don't let anyone punish you for something you already know.

...

# *The Glamour of Grammar* quick list

Use this quick list of language tools as a handy reference. Make multiple copies. Tuck one into your favorite dictionary. Keep one on your writing desk or near your computer. Share the others with friends, colleagues, or fellow students.

## Part One. Words

1. Read dictionaries for fun and learning.
   *Learn where the language has been and where it's headed.*
2. Avoid speed bumps caused by misspellings.
   *Keep track of the words that are hardest for you to spell.*
3. Adopt a favorite letter of the alphabet.
   *Remember that letters are symbols for sounds.*
4. Honor the smallest distinctions—even between *a* and *the*.
   *The closer you look at the language, the more you can learn.*
5. Consult a thesaurus to remind yourself of words you already know.
   *Never use big words to show off. (Well, almost never.)*
6. Take a class on how to cross-dress the parts of speech.
   *Be ready to transform one part of speech into another.*
7. Enjoy, rather than fear, words that sound alike.

*Use sound to link language and ideas.*

8. Learn seven ways to invent words.
   *Doing so will help make you a more discerning reader and a more creative writer.*

9. Become your own lexicographer.
   *Gather words used by particular discourse communities and share them with readers.*

10. Take advantage of the short-word economy of English.
    *Learn how the Norman invasion in 1066 led to two dominant influences on the language.*

11. Learn when and how to enrich your prose with foreign words.
    *A smaller world requires a greater understanding of the languages of others.*

## Part Two. Points

12. Use the period to determine emphasis and space.
    *As the Brits insist, the period is a "full stop."*

13. Advocate use of the serial comma.
    *In a series a final comma before "and" helps the reader keep the elements straight.*

14. Use the semicolon as a "swinging gate."
    *Learn how this mark separates and connects.*

15. Embrace the three amigos: colon, dash, and parentheses.
    *Use the dash with intention, not as a "fallback" punctuation mark.*

16. Let your ear help govern the possessive apostrophe.
    *Be careful with words ending in s.*

17. Take advantage of the versatility of quotation marks.
    *They can highlight language, emphasize words, frame dialogue, even offer editorial opinion.*

18. Use the question mark to generate reader curiosity and narrative energy.
    *Good stories pose a question that the narrative answers for the reader.*

19. Reclaim the exclamation point.
    *Use it to smash emoticons.*
20. Master the elliptical art of leaving things out.
    *Those three dots can help you generate suspense.*
21. Reach into the "upper case" to unleash the power of names.
    *But first you must gather names through your research or reporting.*
22. Vary your use of punctuation to create special effects.
    *It is the cumulative effect of good decisions that influences the reader's experience.*


## Part Three. Standards

23. Learn to *lie* or *lay,* as well as the principles behind the distinction.
    *It will help you understand the differences between transitive and intransitive verbs, as well as regular and irregular verbs.*
24. Avoid the "trap" of subject-verb disagreement.
    *Separating subject and verb is always asking for trouble.*
25. Render gender equality with a smooth style.
    *Fairness need not be at odds with beauty.*
26. Place modifiers where they belong.
    *Keep them close to their partners.*
27. Help the reader learn what is "essential" and "nonessential."
    *If the phrase is not essential, then commas are essential.*
28. Avoid case mistakes and "hypergrammar."
    *Only a prig would say "It is I."*
29. Be certain about the uncertain subjunctive and other "moody" subjects.
    *Use the subjunctive when the ideas expressed in a sentence are contrary to fact.*
30. Identify all sources of ambiguity and confusion.
    *And recognize the difference between a strategic ambiguity and the kind that results from careless language.*
31. Show what is literal and what is figurative.
    *Don't tell me.*

## Part Four. Meaning

32. Join subjects and verbs, or separate them for effect.
    *Togetherness leads to clarity.*
33. Use active and passive verbs in combination—and with a purpose.
    *Ask yourself: is my subject a doer or a receiver?*
34. Befriend the lively verb *to be.*
    *It need not be the weakest link.*
35. Switch tenses, but only for strategic reasons.
    *Rely on that workhorse the historical past.*
36. Politely ignore the language crotchets of others.
    *Split infinitives; end sentences with prepositions; begin sentences with* and *or* but.
37. Learn the five forms of well-crafted sentences.
    *That is, the verbless sentence, the simple sentence, the compound sentence, the complex sentence, and the compound-complex sentence.*
38. Make sentence fragments work for you and the reader.
    *Especially when a short fragment adjoins a long sentence.*
39. Use the complex sentence to connect unequal ideas.
    *Then create an independent clause linked to a subordinate clause.*
40. Learn how expert writers break the rules in run-on sentences.
    *Earn the right to break the rules by first learning the rules.*

## Part Five. Purpose

41. Master the uses of nonstandard English.
    *Be ready to defend such uses in the face of criticism.*
42. Add a pinch of dialect for flavor.
    *Be sure to avoid even a suggestion of language prejudice.*
43. Tame taboo language to suit your purposes.
    *You can always find a way to speak uncomfortable truths.*
44. Unleash your associative imagination.

> *You don't need to be a poet to use metaphors, similes, and analogies.*

45. Play with sounds, natural and literary.
    > *Begin with alliteration and move to words that imitate sounds.*

46. Master the distinction between denotation and connotation.
    > *Many words have associations that you may want—or not want—to unleash.*

47. Measure the distance between concrete and abstract language.
    > *The movement from one to the other gives a work "altitude."*

48. Harness the power of particularity.
    > *A tiny particle of language can offer a sense of the whole.*

49. Have fun with initials and acronyms, but avoid "capital" offenses.
    > *Do not assume that your reader can crack the code of technocratic or bureaucratic jargon.*

50. Master the grammar of new forms of writing.
    > *Learn the formal requirements of an informal style.*

# Acknowledgments

• • •

I begin what could be an endless list with an expression of gratitude to Jane Dystel and Tracy Behar, the two glamorous New York women to whom this book is dedicated. The three of us made a lively and productive team with *Writing Tools: 50 Essential Strategies for Every Writer.* The success of that venture inspired another collaboration, and *The Glamour of Grammar* was born. To write books with an agent like Jane and an editor like Tracy is to be twice blessed.

In writing about language, I do not stand on the shoulders of giants. I dangle from their bootstraps. My sincere hope is that readers of this book might find their way back to those tireless compilers of the *Oxford English Dictionary* and the hard-working members of the Usage Panel of the *American Heritage Dictionary.* On that trip, I hope they bump into the work of H. W. Fowler; Sir Arthur Quiller-Couch; George Orwell; Aldous Huxley; William Empson; William Strunk and his more famous student E. B. White; Wayne C. Booth; Noam

Chomsky; Donald Murray; Donald Hall; Joan Didion; Tom Wolfe; S. I. Hayakawa; Virginia Tufte.

That pantheon is being replaced by a new generation of practical language experts, many of whom influenced the direction of my work. These include Brian A. Garner, Francine Prose, Ben Yagoda, Constance Hale, Patricia T. O'Conner, and Mignon Fogarty, to name a few. Ms. Fogarty, known as "Grammar Girl" to fans of her book and website, reminds me how much I appreciate the efforts of supportive and constructive word workers. I happily add to this list the British (and American) language bullies, including the likes of Lynne Truss, who seem to believe that if the sign on the restroom door is mispunctuated, the only morally correct posture is to hold your water until you can find another toilet with a proper sign. Thanks to Ms. Truss for serving as a convenient target.

They say you should not judge a book by its cover, but I say please ignore that advice. If publishing a book is like giving birth to a baby, then seeing the cover design for the first time is like viewing the sonogram. For both *Writing Tools* and *The Glamour of Grammar,* I've benefited from the talents of cover designer Keith Hayes, one of the best in the business. Under the leadership of publisher Michael Pietsch, the Little, Brown support team included Heather Fain, marketing director; Sabrina Callahan, publicist; Laura Keefe, online publicity manager; and Christina Rodriguez. Thanks to story doctor Tracy Resnik Roe for her diagnostic proofreading. Special thanks go to the eagle-eyed Marie Salter, who cheerfully assumed the responsibility of copyediting a book about language and grammar.

More than fifty folks now work at the Poynter Institute, the school for journalism and democracy that has been my professional home for thirty years. Poynter is the kind of place where everyone helps everyone, so I say with confidence that all my colleagues have contributed in some measure to my efforts. Special gratitude goes to president Karen Dunlap and former dean of the faculty Keith Woods. Julie Moos, Jeff Saffan,

Mallary Tenore, and Ellyn Angelotti provided special attention when I needed it most.

One of my oldest and dearest friends, Don Fry, was the first to read early versions of the manuscript, and provided great advice on what to keep and what to cut. Stuart Adam, Canada's great scholar of journalism, listened carefully in the office, on the phone, and on the golf course, as I thought out loud through my writing process.

Thanks to Kelley Benham French, for taking the author's photo and making him look so darn good.

It was my great fortune to be writing this book while my BFF Tom French was writing his. Mornings of writing led to great lunch conversations at the Banyan, as each of us encouraged the other to keep at it.

I come finally to the Clark family, especially the women in my life who continue to support, encourage, and love me, even when my grammar gets a little shaky. Thanks to my mother and first editor, Shirley Clark, who proves that ninety is the new sixty; to my spunky daughters, Lauren, Emily, and Alison; and to my wife, Karen, the world's most beautiful construction worker. And let me not forget the one whose love is most expressive and unconditional: my dog, Rex. (Thanks for sixteen great years, pup. Let's go get a cookie.)

# INDEX

• • •

# About the Author

. . .

By some accounts, Roy Peter Clark is America's writing coach, a teacher devoted to creating a nation of writers. A PhD in medieval literature, he is widely considered the most influential writing teacher in the rough-and-tumble world of newspaper journalism. With his deep background in traditional media, Clark has illuminated the discussion of writing on the Internet. He has gained fame by teaching writing to children, and has nurtured Pulitzer Prize–winning authors such as Thomas French and Diana Sugg. He is a teacher who writes, and a writer who teaches.

For more than three decades, Clark has taught writing at the Poynter Institute, a school for journalists in St. Petersburg, Florida, considered among the most prominent such teaching institutions in the world. He graduated from Providence College in Rhode Island with a degree in English and earned a PhD from Stony Brook University.

In 1977 he was hired by the *St. Petersburg Times* to become one of America's first writing coaches and worked with the

American Society of Newspaper Editors to improve newspaper writing nationwide. Because of his work with ASNE, Clark was elected as a distinguished service member, a rare honor for a journalist who has never edited a newspaper. He was inducted into the Features Hall of Fame, an honor he shares with the likes of Ann Landers.

Clark has authored or edited fifteen books about writing and journalism, including his most recent, *Writing Tools.* Humorist Dave Barry has said of him: "Roy Peter Clark knows more about writing than anybody I know who is not currently dead."

He lives with his family in St. Petersburg, Florida.